THE GOLD LEAF LADY AND OTHER
PARAPSYCHOLOGICAL INVESTIGATIONS

The Gold Leaf Lady

AND OTHER PARAPSYCHOLOGICAL INVESTIGATIONS

Stephen E. Braude

THE UNIVERSITY OF CHICAGO PRESS

Chicago & London

STEPHEN E. BRAUDE was educated at Oberlin, the University of London, and the University of Massachusetts at Amherst, where he received his PhD in Philosophy in 1972. He has taught since 1971 at the University of Maryland Baltimore County, where he has been professor of philosophy since 1987. He was chair of the department from 1998 to 2005. Braude is the author of sixty journal articles and four previous books, including *The Limits of Influence: Psychokinesis and the Philosophy of Science* (1986) and, most recently, *Immortal Remains: The Evidence for Life After Death* (2003).

The University of Chicago Press, Chicago 60637
The University of Chicago Press, Ltd., London
© 2007 by The University of Chicago
All rights reserved. Published 2007
Printed in the United States of America

16 15 14 13 12 11 10 09 08 07   1 2 3 4 5

ISBN-13: 978-0-226-07152-7 (cloth)
ISBN-10: 0-226-07152-9 (cloth)

Library of Congress Cataloging-in-Publication Data

Braude, Stephen E., 1945–
The gold leaf lady and other parapsychological investigations / Stephen E. Braude.
p. cm.
Includes bibliographical references and index.
ISBN-13: 978-0-226-07152-7 (cloth : alk. paper)
ISBN-10: 0-226-07152-9 (cloth : alk. paper)
1. Parapsychology—Case studies. 2. Parapsychology. 3. Braude, Stephen E., 1945– I. Title.
BF1031.B736 2007
133.8—dc22
2006036517

In memory of John Beloff

CONTENTS

PREFACE

Not long after publishing my first book on philosophy and parapsychology, I began to receive offers to conduct my own paranormal case investigations. That came as quite a surprise, because my book never suggested I had either the competence or desire to dirty my hands with paranormal fieldwork. Granted, the book was all about parapsychological data and their implications, but it dealt primarily with formal experimentation. I had very little to say, and in fact at the time I knew very little about anecdotal reports or field investigations. Nevertheless, word had gotten out, not just locally but even internationally, that there was a new ghostbuster in town, and some apparently thought I'd be interested in checking out spontaneous phenomena for myself.

As it happened, I *was* interested. My research was already leading in that direction, and I had even begun work on my next book, which dealt entirely with large-scale, nonexperimental evidence in parapsychology. Contrary to what you might think, this evolution in my interests was both natural and appropriate, and probably overdue. For one thing, I realized I had at most only a cursory acquaintance with non-laboratory evidence, and I felt that it would have been intellectually irresponsible to draw sweeping conclusions about the significance of parapsychology without giving that material a serious look. And for another, once I began that course of study I came to appreciate how profoundly and inevitably unilluminating parapsychological lab experiments were, and how naive it was to think that one could conduct tests for psychic (or as many prefer to call them, psi) abilities under strict experimental controls. I also discovered that the quality of non-laboratory evidence was far better than even most parapsychologists made it out to be. In fact, I discovered that parapsychologists, like many others, were reflexively and ignorantly perpetuating a widespread myth about parapsychology: that data from outside the lab was—and could only be—vastly inferior to what we could obtain from formal experimentation.[1]

At any rate, I found myself faced with an opportunity for which I had received no preparation: to investigate reports of spontaneous paranormal phenomena. But I was young and stupid enough to think that my inexperience didn't matter. So, fortified by blind confidence and the conviction that I could always learn from my mistakes, I took the plunge. And immediately I was confronted with situations I couldn't handle. Among my first contacts were people who claimed that others were assaulting them telepathically, and these cases completely freaked me out. I had no clue how to deal with the level of personal distress and possible psychopathology they involved.

For example, one of the first people to reach me was an Israeli woman who insisted she was being attacked psychically by one of her mentors, someone who (at the time) was a well-known parapsychological researcher. She was obviously in great mental and physical distress, and very quickly she flooded my office with letters, poems, and diaries documenting her suffering. Several months after our first communication, she fled from Israel to Belgium, hoping to escape from these alleged assaults, but she claimed they continued unabated. And those attacks, she said, focused both on her physical and mental health. Her husband was frantic about the extent of his wife's misery, and at one point he phoned me to complain about her alleged assailant. He said, "I'm a peaceful Jew, Dr. Braude, but I want to kill that man." As far as I know, he never followed through on that impulse, but his remark haunts me to this day. I'm quite sure I provided no help or comfort to this couple. I had no idea even how to begin. Evidently, whatever lame suggestions I made did little good. I continued to receive written material from the woman indicating that her suffering had not diminished and had possibly even escalated. And eventually, nearly two years after our correspondence began, I learned from the husband that his wife had passed away, ostensibly from the stress of this ongoing assault.

Fortunately, most of my early investigations were less traumatic. For example, I sat with several mental mediums and spent many hours recording and then transcribing ostensible postmortem communications. Since all these proved to be nonevidential, I quickly grew impatient with the process. Furthermore, I realized that before I could competently tackle the evidence for postmortem survival, I needed extensive preparation in several related areas of study. It was clear to me that this project would need to be postponed until much later.[2] So before long I had decided to limit myself only to investigations of apparently spontaneous and observable psychokinesis (or PK).

Initially, those investigations all concerned alleged haunting or poltergeist disturbances, and although some of them were tantalizing, the best were no more than frustratingly inconclusive. I recognized two things very quickly. First, even though these cases could be as inconclusive and time-consuming as my studies of mental mediums, I had a preference for the drama and immediacy of seemingly paranormal physical phenomena. In part, that's because I believed that PK phenomena were at least potentially easier to document than various forms of ESP. Second, I concluded that if I was going to investigate observable (or macro) PK, I needed to use my time and financial resources wisely. After all, I was a full-time professor of philosophy, and I was also working actively as a musician. That left little time for ghostbusting, especially for cases where the probability of observing something interesting was very low.

Unfortunately, that meant that I could devote little time or energy to poltergeist or haunting cases. Because the phenomena are typically sporadic and unpredictable, investigators usually spend a great deal of time waiting for something to happen. And all too often, either nothing happens or else phenomena occur at inappropriate times—for example, when the recording equipment is turned off, or when cameras are pointed in another direction. So these sorts of investigations are viable only for researchers with considerable patience and relatively open schedules. Moreover, it's often expensive to sit around and wait for something to occur, especially if the case requires travel or the rental of equipment. That was certainly an issue for me. Like most philosophers, my salary was modest, and (not surprisingly) there were no provisions in my university's philosophy department budget for paranormal case investigations. As a result, I started limiting my investigations to those in which the phenomena seemed to occur with some regularity. Occasionally I financed the excursions myself; sometimes I received monetary support; and a few times I rode on the media's coattails.

That's where this book comes in. Except for a few opinionated (and occasionally truculent) prefaces, I wrote my other books on parapsychology from the emotional distance considered appropriate to scholarly works. Now, although much of this present work is still philosophical and scholarly, it's largely autobiographical, and often it's extremely personal. This book describes my most memorable—and sometimes frustrating—encounters with the ostensibly paranormal. And apart from its first-person perspective, it picks up where my earlier books on parapsychology left off. The empirical portions of those previous books were devoted primarily to defending the quality of the evidence (experimental or otherwise). In this work, too, I'll make a case for the reality of some paranormal phenomena—mostly psychokinetic. But overall, my goal here is different from that of my earlier books. The principal theme of this work is the appearance—and sometimes *only* the appearance—of psychic or paranormal events in everyday life. And it's as much about the frailties and foibles of ordinary folk as it is about some of the exotic things we can do.

Five chapters discuss individual case investigations and the theoretical issues related to them. In chapter 1 I present the case of the "gold leaf lady," a Florida woman whose body would break out spontaneously and at close range in a golden foil that turned out to be brass. I describe the careful conditions under which that phenomenon has been observed, as well as a noted magician's inability to replicate it, and also a botched attempt by the TV show *Unsolved Mysteries* to study and document its occurrence. I also consider why the phenomenon took the peculiar form of brass leaf, and whether (if genuine) it should be regarded as a materialization or an apport (i.e., the paranormal movement of an object from one location to another).

Chapter 3 concerns my exasperating attempts in New York to study the alleged psychokinetic superstar, Joe Nuzum. I describe Nuzum's efforts to circumvent previously agreed-upon controls and how I apparently caught him cheating. I also describe how Nuzum was—sometimes innocently— aided in his evasions by his enthusiastic but uncritical supporters. To some extent this chapter is a cautionary tale. It indicates the sorts of things that can go wrong when a subject is given too much control of test conditions. It also details what at least appears to be both incompetence and treachery on the part of Nuzum's principal sponsor.

Chapter 4 is a kind of sequel to the Nuzum case: it's the story of a subject from California who seemed able in informal settings to produce impressive observable psychokinetic effects. But when he was brought to New York for careful testing, his previously confident attitude was thoroughly undermined by his sponsor—the same person who had funded my experiments with Joe Nuzum, and who apparently wanted to retaliate against me for having claimed I caught Nuzum cheating. This, too, is a cautionary tale, concerning the psychological delicacy of even the most promising subjects, and the need for extreme care and sensitivity in dealing with them and in designing experimental protocols.

Chapter 5 describes a peculiar encounter I had with a policeman who believed he could transfer images from photographs onto other objects (including his own body), simply by placing the photos on those objects. Although nothing of the sort actually happened, the policeman, remarkably, continued to insist that the phenomenon was real and obvious. I consider this yet another cautionary tale, about how even presumably trained observers can be blinded by their own credulousness.

Chapter 6 concerns paranormal photography. It's a postscript to the famous case of Ted Serios, the subject of one of the most fascinating, and undoubtedly one of the strongest, investigations of observable PK. In the 1960s, Serios produced a variety of images and other effects on "instant" Polaroid film under well-controlled conditions—for example, while separated at a considerable distance from the camera and while wearing clothes provided by the experimenters. Moreover, because Serios never handled the film and because the pictures developed immediately upon removal from the camera, the results couldn't be explained away as darkroom tricks. This chapter brings the case up to date and describes my own encounters with Serios, years after the major investigation of him had concluded.

To lend perspective to these case reports, in chapter 2 I survey the dramatic and fascinating history of physical mediumship connected with the heyday of the Spiritualist movement (roughly 1850 to 1930). The best cases from that era make it very clear why concerns about possible fraud are both legitimate and sometimes overrated. Moreover, they supply a yardstick by which we can measure the significance of contemporary cases. I give special attention to the careers of D. D. Home and Eusapia Palladino, explaining why their best-documented phenomena can't be dismissed as fraudulent, and why effects of the magnitude found in these cases seem no longer to occur.

With chapter 7 we get a bit more abstract, although the chapter begins with a personal matter. I start by describing one of my more curious apparent encounters with the paranormal—a very strange and seemingly meaningful coincidence. Inevitably, this raises a recurring hot topic originally introduced by Carl Jung—namely, synchronicity (acausal meaningful coincidence). However, because this concept is especially confused and widely abused, I take the opportunity to clarify it. As a result, I theorize at somewhat greater length than in the previous chapters. In the process, I make several crucial and related points. Perhaps most important, I show that it's incorrect—in fact, incoherent—to claim (as many do) that synchronicity is a principle in nature that organizes events into meaningful clusters. Ultimately, I argue for a controversial—but I believe unavoidable—position: namely, that if genuinely nonrandom meaningful coincidences occur, this would be best explained in terms of a refined, extensive, and potentially very intimidating form of large-scale psychokinesis.

In chapter 8, I go out on a limb and also literally bring my discussion home, to describe some of the intriguing activities of my wife Gina, an academic and clinical psychologist who also happens to be a virtuoso astrologer. Gina has successfully used her astrological skills to help several European and Asian professional soccer teams rise to the top of their respective leagues, and her startlingly detailed and accurate predictions were also highly valued within the Serbian mafia (yes, that's right). This chapter presents some of the episodes from Gina's history and from our life together that have forced me—to my great discomfort—to confront my own prejudices against astrology. Finally, I bring this chapter and the book to a close with some speculations about the place of psychic abilities in the general scheme of things.

I believe that the various adventures I recount in this book are interesting in themselves, quite apart from their relevance to empirical and methodological issues in science generally and parapsychology in particular. Nevertheless, in their own distinctive ways all the reported cases are empirically significant. Some provide provocative evidence for the reality of psychokinesis; others document only human duplicity and delusion. Some offer object lessons about how *not* to investigate the paranormal. Some illustrate the fragility and context-sensitivity of the phenomena, as well as the need to probe beneath the psychological surface to understand their psychogenesis. Some show how evidence can be suppressed or compromised by the zealousness of both believers and nonbelievers. Moreover, the case of the gold leaf lady illustrates how the collection of evidence can be undermined by the interest and funding of the media.

Now, to the really cathartic portion of the program. Beginning with my second book, I learned that prefaces offer valuable and satisfying opportunities to get things off one's chest. So, without further ado, here's my rant du jour.

I began looking carefully at parapsychological research in 1976, five years into my career as a professional philosopher. In the three decades since then, I've lost my innocence about academic freedom, and I've learned a good bit about human nature. And I can tell you, it's been a real eye-opener to see how my colleagues treated me once I started down this path.

Initially, my philosophical research was at the intersection of the philosophy of language, the philosophy of time, and logic. I published a number of respectable technical articles in several of the most prestigious professional journals (easily enough to get me tenure), and I'd begun to form alliances and friendships with some of the major figures working in my areas of philosophy. But once I declared my interest in investigating the issues and data of parapsychology, my professional status and relationships underwent a rapid and profound transformation. It didn't matter that I had no ax to grind (one way or the other) about the outcome of my investigation. Several years earlier I had witnessed an impressive and apparently paranormal occurrence,[3] and I felt professionally and morally obligated, with the freedom allegedly provided by tenure, to confront the matter and try to understand what had happened. Moreover, I knew that some thoughtful and very important philosophers (most notably, William James, Charles S. Peirce, Henry Sidgwick, C. J. Ducasse, C. D. Broad, H. H. Price) had found parapsychological research an area worth examining. And I thought it would be not simply interesting but important to see what the fuss was all about, and to consider whether the material merited even deeper study. For some this turned out to be enough to brand me as a crackpot, and it became even worse when I decided that, in fact, there was something here worth sinking my philosophical teeth into.

I certainly don't regret having chosen to pursue this line of research, and I'm actually grateful for what I've learned about my academic colleagues. The situation I confronted is a bit like what happens in divorces (another matter in which I've had some experience). Because divorces are stressful for many besides the couple in question, they provide opportunities to discover previously hidden aspects of a person's character, and as a result, you quickly gain a fresh perspective about friends and acquaintances. The insights may be painful, but it's usually better to be clear about such things. Here, too, I had quite a few revelations. Some philosophers I expected to be open-minded and intellectually honest instead behaved with surprising rigidity and cowardice. I clearly knew the evidence and issues much better than they did, but they condescendingly pretended to know this material well enough to ridicule my interest in it. And suddenly I found that I was no longer welcome in certain professional conversations, as if these philosophers' former confidence in my intellectual ability had been a complete mistake. My surprise over this treatment shows just how naïve I was. I had really thought that as philosophers—as people presumably devoted to the pursuit of wisdom and truth—my colleagues would actually be willing to admit their ignorance and be curious to learn more. I genuinely believed they'd be excited to discover that certain relevant bits of received wisdom might be mistaken.

Fortunately, at least some revelations were more encouraging. Several philosophers whom I thought would be inflexible or disinterested surprised me with their honesty, courage, and open-mindedness. And some reactions I've never fully understood. One famous philosopher (I won't say who) said to me, "Well if someone has to do this I'm glad it's you." I think that was meant as a compliment, but it's obviously open to multiple interpretations.

This all started thirty years ago, and since then I've become somewhat marginalized for pursuing my interest in the paranormal. I'm sure that wouldn't have happened if I had assumed the role of steadfast debunker. History has shown that's a very safe activity, professionally; in fact, it's something academics can easily exploit in order to gain prominence in their field, and for which they needn't even do their homework. (It also enabled one formerly and deservedly obscure, but now notorious, magician to achieve a remarkably unwarranted degree of fame and respect.) And although I believe I understand how intellectual cowardice and dishonesty can take root, it still amazes me that when I so much as raise the subject of parapsychology to my academic colleagues, I often find nothing but stiff body language, sarcasm, and (perhaps most surprising of all) sometimes even *outrage*. Not exactly the way you'd expect truth-seekers to respond to serious and thoughtful empirical and philosophical investigation. In fact, it seems plainly to be a fear response.

And perhaps that's why it's so often dishonest. As I've noted elsewhere, when academics and scientists don't want to look carefully and fearlessly at the data of parapsychology, they often lapse quickly into various disgraceful behaviors. For example, some try to dismiss all the evidence by generalizing from the obviously weakest cases, a ploy they'd be quick to detect and condemn if it had been used against them. In fact, philosophers educate and warn students about that disreputable strategy in virtually every class in logic or critical thinking.

Moreover, some promote their skepticism about parapsychology with a confidence that's wildly disproportionate to their command of the data. That's what I find so striking about the sarcasm I frequently encounter. Arguably, sarcasm is not an admirable personality trait, and perhaps it's seldom an appropriate conversational response. In any case, when it's used to dismiss a person's informed interest in parapsychology, it could only be *warranted* if its user had the knowledge to back it up. In that situation, sarcasm is always employed with a presumption of authority. But in fact, those who sarcastically dismiss parapsychology typically know little, if anything, about the field. They haven't carefully studied the data or issues for themselves. Even more remarkably, they *know* they lack this knowledge. They know their opinions, no matter how strongly held, have no authority behind them.

That's why, when people passionately and arrogantly tell me how weak the parapsychological evidence is (especially the non-laboratory evidence), it's very easy to make them look foolish by demanding that they demonstrate their command of the data. Simply insist that they describe *in detail* the cases that matter—not the ones easiest to dismiss; insist that they explain why those cases are thought to be so good, and then insist that they explain *exactly* why that opinion is wrong. This is a very effective way to study the varieties of human discomfort.

It's not that I expect others to agree with my views simply because I've done the research and considered the issues, and they haven't. I'd be satisfied with a little curiosity and honest humility. When my interlocutors are aware that they haven't studied the evidence, a more admirable response would be something like, "I was under the impression that this evidence was flawed, because . . . Do you disagree? If so, why?" Tellingly, I'm most likely to encounter that sort of modest response from other philosophers only when I interview candidates for faculty openings in our department. Those people are in no position to engage in the posturing and dishonest bluffing they'll likely lapse into once they're comfortably ensconced in a job.

Of course, not everyone in the academy fits this gloomy picture. A few others have also done serious research into the paranormal, but they're the exceptions that prove the rule. And (like me) some of them chose to break ranks only after getting tenure. Others have simply refrained from open condemnation, while privately admitting to me their interest in what I'm doing. Some of those have even confided their own apparent encounters with the paranormal, and they've made those admissions while conceding that their experiences seem to be paranormal and that they're at a loss to explain them away. I've actually had quite a few conversations of that sort, and for some reason, most of the reported experiences are of apparitions. I think it's significant and revealing that these scientists and scholars will admit their experiences to me, but not to their other colleagues. I believe it shows just how cutthroat the academic community can be. Even senior and prominent members of that community recognize that their reputations hang tenuously on remaining conspicuously within the mainstream. They realize they'd be treated with the same ignorant and cowardly disdain and dishonesty I've faced for the past several decades.

I've had similar experiences with mental health professionals, including MAs, PhDs, and MDs. I've come to know quite a few members of that community since writing my book on multiple personality.[4] Once it became known that I'd done extensive and open-minded research in parapsychology, many started confiding to me apparent psychic episodes involving their patients. They also made it very clear that these conversations needed to remain confidential. And that wasn't because they were protecting therapist/patient confidentiality. (In fact, nothing they said to me revealed the identity of their patients.) Rather, they were simply unwilling to risk possible ridicule and ostracism by revealing their experiences to their colleagues. As far as I'm concerned, that's a great shame. These researchers are missing a potentially valuable opportunity to compare notes and possibly discover illuminating patterns in the data. I suppose to some extent I can do that for them, based on the information they've provided. But this is a job that should be undertaken by a mental health professional, someone who understands more deeply than I the subtleties and dynamics of clinical encounters.

Predictably, faculty and researchers aren't the only ones targeted for what should be seen as a laudable expression of intellectual curiosity. Students also pay a price. I hear this frequently from young audience members at invited talks and in unsolicited letters and e-mails. In fact, many of my students have told me that their mentors (usually in the psychology department) threatened them with reprisals, or at least lavished on them the sort of ridicule I've often encountered, simply because they declared their intention to take my seminar in philosophy and parapsychology. However, most of those students merely wanted the opportunity to study the material and make up their own minds about it. I know this; I taught them and saw how critical and curious they could be, and how most didn't enter the class with their minds made up one way or the other about what was going on.

Perhaps it will be helpful to consider how the type of intellectual dishonesty I've been discussing plays out in detail, in a real case. In February 1985 I was invited to give a talk and appear on a television program at the State University of New York (SUNY) at Brockport. Both my talk and the subject of the program were titled "Taking Mediumship Seriously," and both focused on the issues I raised in *The Limits of Influence*, which I was then in the process of completing, and which was published the following year.[5] That book, and my presentations in Brockport, dealt with the evidence for the dramatic forms of physical mediumship that flourished during the late nineteenth and early twentieth centuries. Even more generally, I wanted to defend the search for parapsychological evidence outside the lab and also explode the myths concerning the relative merits of strictly experimental work. So I wanted to show not only that eyewitness testimony is much better than it's typically made out to be, but that some older cases from the heyday of spiritualism are (contrary to the received wisdom) spectacularly good and important. (Some of these cases, and the relevant issues, are discussed here in chapter 2.)

So my hosts at SUNY Brockport were offering me two opportunities to present my opinions on these topics, and I was told that on the TV program I'd be asked to defend those views against challenges from a skeptic. That was fine with me. I was accustomed to fielding questions from (sometimes hostile) audience members during talks on the subject. I was confident about the positions I was taking, and after more than five years of immersion in the material and issues, I felt I knew the subject probably as well as anybody on the planet. However, I naïvely expected that my critic and I would engage in a relatively high-level dialogue, of the sort that I'd had already with several of my friends in the parapsychological community. In fact, I'd been told that the matters under discussion were among my critic's special interests. At the very least, I expected him to be well-informed.

I appeared on the television program with two members of the SUNY Brockport philosophy department. One served mainly as host, and evidently he had no views on the matter he was eager to promote. In fact, throughout my visit he displayed a commendably careful and inquisitive open mind. The other participant turned out to be the department's self-styled debunker, who was there ready to discount everything he apparently felt I stood for. There's no need to mention this person's name (we can call him M. G.). The important thing is that he provided a classic, and not even remotely sophisticated, example of the sort of resistance and dishonesty I've encountered many times since. The show was videotaped, and I've often played the tape for my students. I'm pleased to say they've usually been appalled by this philosopher's attempts not only to evade the issues, but to dismiss the mediumistic evidence with an authority I demonstrated he clearly lacked, and which he must have known that he lacked. In fact, by the time my students viewed the tape, they knew the evidence better than my critic did, and they understood easily how M. G. tried to conceal his ignorance, and how he intentionally and repeatedly reverted to disreputable straw man arguments: generalizing from irrelevant or weak cases, and ignoring precisely those reports to which the usual skeptical objections don't apply. (Reproducing our dialogue verbatim would undoubtedly be instructive, but it would also take us too far afield. For now, a paraphrase will have to do.)

It was really a remarkable, and embarrassingly transparent, performance. M. G. began by repeating a familiar skeptical refrain: that mediumistic evidence was all collected under poor conditions of observation, with the phenomena under complete control of the medium, and reported by credulous observers with no expertise in legerdemain. I quickly cited a case (Crookes's accordion-in-a-cage test, described in chapter 2) to which those concerns didn't apply, and shortly thereafter I was able to add a few others (also described in chapter 2). Oddly, however, M. G. kept reiterating his initial criticism regarding the quality of the evidence. And he tried dismissing all the evidence at once by saying the reports were nothing but hearsay. I realized immediately that he didn't know how much of the best evidence was first-person testimony written immediately after séances or (in some Palladino investigations, see chapter 2) dictated to a nearby stenographer as phenomena happened. I assumed M. G. wouldn't have been so foolish as to think (or claim) that first-person testimony counted as hearsay, because then *all* testimony would have counted as unacceptable from his point of view. I never found the opportunity to see if M. G. held a double standard, by asking him whether his reservations about testimony applied equally to skeptical reports that the phenomena in question *didn't* happen. But I did ask him if he'd ever read the source material for the cases I had cited, and he admitted he hadn't and that his information about the mediums in question had been taken entirely from the literature attempting to debunk the evidence. So M. G. admitted, and certainly demonstrated, that he had no clue why anyone would have doubted the accounts as presented in the debunking literature.

But since it was clear that M. G. couldn't then challenge me authoritatively on the best documented and most scrupulously investigated cases, the ones I had argued mattered and were most difficult to explain away, over and over he tried to shift attention away from those cases. Repeatedly, he mentioned examples of mediums who'd been caught cheating, or to particular investigations of the better mediums which had been poorly controlled or which were otherwise unimpressive. In response, I conceded again and again that many hundreds of fraudulent mediums had been exposed and that many séances had been conducted for convinced spiritualists with no attempt made to control for fraud. Furthermore, I insisted that this was why, in order to decide whether mediumistic PK was genuine, it was important to look at the strongest cases, precisely those in which fraud or malobservation are least likely. Naturally, these would be studies conducted under good controls and conditions of observation, with critical and experienced observers, and with reported phenomena of a magnitude that couldn't be accounted for either in terms of existing technology or sleight of hand. But M. G. ignored this, and in addition to once again citing weak and irrelevant cases, he also retreated to marginally relevant generalities about the age of the material and the impossibility of ever being certain how a mediumistic trick might have been performed. In response to that last gambit, I tried to keep M. G. on track. I kept trying to force him to demonstrate how his concerns applied to any of the obviously strongest cases. But since he didn't know the specifics of any good cases, M. G. returned to his original skeptical mantra: that mediumistic evidence was all gathered under poor conditions, etc. Of course, that was a position whose inadequacies we had already discussed.

I remember vividly what passed through my mind as I sat, with uncharacteristic patience, listening to M. G. as he reintroduced the same feeble and irrelevant objections whose flaws I had already exposed. M. G. had trouble looking at me as he spoke; he was stumbling over his words and clearly grasping for something substantial to say. It became clear to me that he had already exhausted the skeptical weapons in his arsenal and that he was unprepared for a knowledgeable debate. So as the program progressed and M. G. kept repeating his handful of stock objections, I felt that he only disgraced himself further. M. G. was digging himself into an increasingly deep hole by allowing me to remind viewers—over and over—how little he knew about the material. Ironically, his attempts to appear authoritative were having precisely the opposite effect.

What amazes me most about this exchange is that my critic was ready to appear in a public forum, knowing that his performance would be recorded for posterity. Although M. G. must have known he had only a cursory and one-sided acquaintance with the evidence, he was ready to flaunt his ignorance on television and go head-to-head with someone who very likely knew much more about the subject than he did. To me, it was a remarkable display of hubris and stupidity, and I have to think it was motivated largely by M. G.'s firmly held belief, or deep fear, that my views represented or entailed a worldview that was dangerously irrational, signaling a reversion to a primitive and magical form of thinking that needed to be resisted at all costs. If I'm right about this, then M. G. was at least correct about the implications of my position. As I see it, there *is* something fundamentally correct about allegedly magical thinking and reputedly outmoded animistic conceptions of the world (for more on this see chapter 7, and also *The Limits of Influence*). But my critic's response to me was anything but scholarly or admirable. Ironically, in fact, it exemplified a form of irrationalism and dishonesty that's at least as repugnant as anything he was trying to combat.

But enough ranting. Time, instead, for acknowledgments. First, in light of my critical remarks above concerning my professional colleagues, I want to express my great respect and appreciation to some prominent philosophers for their unwavering support and encouragement of my parapsychological investigations over the years. My thanks especially to Bruce Aune, Joseph Margolis, and Richard Gale, and also to the late Wilfrid Sellars, Roderick Chisholm, and Hector Castañeda. Unlike many who simply profess their intellectual integrity, these philosophers have reliably demonstrated the open mind of genuine wisdom.

I'm grateful also to those who've helped me as I've worked on this project. My thanks to Dean Radin, Bert Schwarz, Karl Petry, and Rick Eisenbud for their assistance in keeping my recollections accurate, and to Tom Beck, chief curator of Special Collections at UMBC's Albin O. Kuhn Library and Gallery, for managing in the midst of great distractions to supply me with the Serios images I needed for chapter 6 (and in general, for his care in preserving and respecting the Eisenbud/Serios documents donated to the library). Thanks, also, to the Parapsychology Foundation, without whose support and generous assistance I'd probably have been unable to conduct much of the research described in this book. I'm especially grateful to my wife and resident psychologist, Gina, for her helpful discussions about Jung, her thoughtful and critical comments on my manuscript, her patience with my distractions as I wrote the book, and more generally for expanding my horizons in ways I never expected. And finally, I want to thank the BIAL Foundation in Porto, Portugal, for their continuing support of my work, and in particular for the very generous research grant that enabled me to extend my recent sabbatical and write this book.

July 2006

Katie, the Gold Leaf Lady

1. Preliminaries

I was seated across a table from a woman, no more than three feet away. And while we were talking, a small piece of gold-colored foil appeared suddenly on her face. I knew that her hands were nowhere near her face when this happened. In fact, I was certain they were in full view on the table the entire time. I knew also that if her husband, seated next to her, had placed the material on her face, I would have seen it clearly. But nobody's hands had been anywhere near her face. So I knew that the material hadn't been placed there; it *appeared* there, evidently without normal assistance.

This was one of several similar incidents that occurred during my most fascinating paranormal investigation: the case of a woman much of whose body—not just parts of her face—would break out in what looked like gold leaf. But first, some background. We need to be clear about just how unusual and potentially important this case is.

Parapsychologists study several interesting phenomena, but they focus primarily on the evidence for extrasensory perception (ESP), psychokinesis (PK), and survival of bodily death. Of course, many consider all of these incredible and unworthy of serious attention. Others agree that they're extraordinary, but believe they're both possible and worth studying. And still others consider at least some of the phenomena to be natural and part of everyday life. In fact, many would say ESP is merely a form of intuition and leave the matter there.

At any rate, everyone has a "boggle threshold," even those who embrace the paranormal without batting an eye. Typically, believers in the paranormal draw the line at accepting conspicuous and large-scale PK, because those phenomena seem simply too weird to be true. Moreover, many find them threatening, hinting (uncomfortably) that we live in a world where our thoughts can remotely harm others. But we find boggle thresholds even among those who accept the reality of PK on observable objects (so-called macro-PK). For example, although some believe that PK can influence pencils, compass needles, and other small objects, they refuse to grant that PK could occur in larger-scale or more exotic forms.[1]

In a way, this is hardly surprising. After all, some truly spectacular and apparently incredible phenomena have been reported throughout the history of parapsychology. Of those, perhaps the most intriguing are *materializations* and *apports*. Materializations (assuming they really occur) are cases where objects seem to be produced out of nothing. Apportations (sometimes called "teleportations"), on the other hand, would be cases where already existing objects disappear from one location and reappear (usually suddenly) in another location.

Many confuse these two phenomena, and it's easy to see why. For one thing, depending on how we explain the process of apportation, it might be thought to involve materialization. According to one theory, an agent (living or dead) performs a feat similar to a *Star Trek* transporter, disintegrating an object into micro-level components and then reassembling the object at another location. That last stage, of course, might count as a kind of materialization (or rematerialization) of the object. Another reason some confuse materializations and apports is that objects show up unexpectedly in both, without the usual transitions or intermediate stages we perceive when things move from one place to another.

But despite these similarities, materializations and apports still differ in important respects. For example, although objects appear unexpectedly in both and seem to come from nowhere, only in the case of apports do objects actually change location. By contrast, materialized objects seem to be produced *de novo*; they are evidently *created*, not moved. According to reports, these new objects take many different forms, including full human figures, parts of human figures (e.g., hands that end at the wrist), nondescript knobby objects, and flat, two-dimensional pictures. They also include extensive and flexible projections or pseudopods emanating from a person's mouth, navel, or vagina. Observers claim these projections travel away from the person, sometimes to move nearby objects and sometimes to transform themselves into familiar shapes (e.g., a human hand). Sometimes these novel objects appear fully formed, and other times witnesses observe them in the process of formation. In fact, sometimes the newly formed objects emerge so slowly and gradually that observers have been able to describe their evolution in considerable detail. But at other times the objects seem to appear nearly instantaneously.

Moreover, although materialized and apported objects may be either animate or inanimate, it's rare to find reports of *metallic* objects materializing. One possible contemporary exception to this rule concerns the Indian guru Sai Baba, who reportedly materialized newly formed articles of jewelry and other metallic objects, some of them valuable.[2] Unfortunately, however, his manifestations have been loosely controlled at best. Apart from that, the only examples come from cases usually classified as visual apparitions. Now that might seem surprising, because most visual apparitions are of persons or other creatures, living or dead. But apparitional figures sometimes include metallic accessories, such as belt buckles or jewelry. So if some animate apparitional figures are materializations,[3] then presumably their metallic components would also count as materialized objects. But again, all these cases are rare. In apports, however, metal plays a more prominent role. It's relatively common to find accounts of stones or metals passing through barriers, or at least leaving one location and arriving at another. And curiously, in many of those cases, the newly arrived objects are too hot to touch. Perhaps significantly, that thermal phenomenon seems to be common only when the apported objects are of large or moderate size.

Another important difference between materializations and apports is that the former exist only for a short time. Eventually (usually pretty quickly), materialized objects dematerialize, as if their solidity is inherently unstable. In fact, in many cases observers report that the objects formed or coalesced out of a cloudy or wispy mass, and then later returned to that diffuse state and disappeared entirely.[4] Similarly, observers sometimes claim that the initially cloudy shapes emerge from, and then later seem to be reabsorbed by, a part of the subject's body.[5] By contrast, apports only move from one place to another; they don't entirely vanish or dissolve and disperse. Some alleged apports *have* been described in the process of taking shape at their new location. But I can think of no case in which a new—not transported—object was *observed to materialize and take solid form*, and then didn't reportedly dematerialize later.

Once again, the alleged materializations of Sai Baba might count as an exception. The jewelry and powdery ash, or vibuti, he ostensibly produces are permanent objects. But I believe that those phenomena, even if genuine, may not fall into this category. Witnesses report seeing the objects already formed, not in the process of coming to be.

Now it might be that these issues are relatively unimportant and have little, if anything, to do with the nature of the phenomena themselves. It might simply be a sociocultural artifact that materialized objects eventually dematerialize, or that they dematerialize sooner rather than later. The largest body of evidence for materializations comes from the heyday of the Spiritualist movement—roughly 1850 to 1930. Those reported phenomena occurred within a powerful system of belief and expectation that might have profoundly influenced the manner in which they occurred. Sai Baba's alleged materializations occur within a very different social and cultural milieu. So perhaps it's not surprising that they differ dramatically from spiritualist materializations. Perhaps eventual or hastened dematerialization is—as Aristotle would have said—an accidental rather than an essential feature of materialization phenomena.[6]

At any rate, I was understandably intrigued when, in the winter of 1987, I learned of a case in which large quantities of metal were allegedly produced paranormally. According to the reports, the metal was gold in color, it did not later disappear, and sometimes it seemed to take shape and grow while witnesses looked on. I realized immediately that the case was potentially a great opportunity and a considerable puzzle. It was an opportunity because the substance didn't disappear, and so investigators could examine it carefully. And it was a mystery because, if the anomalous metal was genuinely paranormal, it was unclear how to classify it. Should we consider it an apport or a materialization? It seemed to be created *de novo* and develop like materialized objects, but unlike those objects it didn't later disappear. However, unlike apports, the material didn't seem to come from anywhere.

2. Introduction to Katie

The subject of this case is a Florida housewife named Katie, now in her mid-50s. She was born to a poor family in the mountains of Tennessee, the tenth of twelve children. When Katie was in the second grade, one of her older sisters unexpectedly left home, taking her baby with her. That event apparently caused Katie's mother (who had been raising the baby) to develop serious psychogenic paralysis.[7] As a result, Katie dropped out of school so that she could administer physical therapy to her mother, attend to her mother's other needs, and take care of most chores around the house. And because Katie never resumed her formal education, she has remained functionally illiterate. She knows how to write her name, she knows the letters of the alphabet, and she knows numbers. But Katie can't synthesize letters into words, and she can barely do simple arithmetic. She's earned a living primarily doing housework.

My impression of Katie, both as a person and as a psychic subject, is very positive. She strikes me as intelligent and honest, and she's always been fully cooperative with investigators. Moreover, unlike many who find themselves the center of academic scrutiny and media attention, she's refreshingly modest and non-opportunistic. Significantly, Katie is not a professional psychic and has never demonstrated an interest in becoming one. The only money she receives in her capacity as a psychic is compensation for time away from work, and occasionally a modest honorarium for the indignity of submitting to intimate physical examinations as investigators search for concealed foil or other objects. So I think it's fair to say that Katie neither reaps nor seeks financial reward for her psychic activities. Furthermore, unlike some who are or at least fancy themselves to be highly psychic, Katie has no ax to grind for any particular philosophical or religious point of view. Refreshingly, she has no pretensions about her understanding of the role of psi in the grand scheme of things. In fact, although I understand that Katie attends church, as far as I'm aware she's not particularly religious.

In addition to being gratifyingly cooperative, Katie is an unusually versatile psychic subject. The apparent gold foil on her body is only one of the interesting phenomena swirling around her. For example, Katie frequently seems to receive apported objects; seeds reportedly germinate rapidly in her cupped hands; and observers have also claimed to see Katie bend metal. Katie is also reported to be both a healer and a medium (or channel). And in that latter capacity she has been observed and videotaped writing quatrains in medieval French, ostensibly from Nostradamus, and similar in both style and content to Nostradamus's actual quatrains.

Katie has also worked successfully with police and other authorities in the investigation of crimes. One of the more spectacular of those efforts took place near Vero Beach, Florida on John's Island, the location of many luxurious homes. My information on this case came from an interview I conducted in January 1988 with the island's director of security, Jerry Burr.

Burr and his associates were having trouble solving a burglary from one of the island's homes, and although he said he was skeptical at first, he had heard about Katie's abilities and figured it couldn't hurt to ask for her assistance. All he told Katie initially was that a valuable ring had been stolen from a house. He didn't tell her in which house the burglary occurred, and he gave her no other information about the case. He said he wanted to see what Katie could do with a minimum of information.

Burr then took Katie for a drive around John's Island. They were accompanied in the car by two other security officers and Burr's assistant, but only one other passenger besides Burr knew where the burglary had occurred. Moreover, they didn't drive directly to the house. They simply drove around the island, waiting to see if Katie could identify the house in question as they drove near it. Burr told me he would often take his foot off the gas pedal and coast along the streets, to avoid slowing down suggestively near any particular house, and he did this as well when they reached the street where the burglary had occurred. Burr said he also looked straight ahead as they neared the house, not wanting to give Katie any additional clues.

As they coasted past the burgled home, Katie identified it. She correctly claimed that the room from which the ring was taken was blue and decorated in a Japanese motif. She also described the box from which the ring was taken, and she accurately described the maid as a short, heavy-set blonde. Moreover, although Burr eventually told Katie there were two suspects, Katie claimed that there were three, all of them friends of the family. One she described carefully; another she described more sketchily, and Katie claimed that a third person was driving the getaway car. Burr told me that Katie was so detailed and accurate in her descriptions that at first he thought he should regard her as a suspect. He said he didn't realize initially just how good Katie was. In any event, Burr claimed that Katie's information allowed him to solve the crime and recover much of $185,000 worth of stolen jewelry.

As they drove away from the house, they were traveling near the ocean, and suddenly Katie asked Burr to stop the car and pull into a nearby driveway. This was at 1:15 p.m. Katie claimed she could hear helicopters and smell marijuana very strongly. She said the smell of pot made her very ill, and she asked the other passengers if they were having similar perceptions. But no one else heard the helicopters or smelled the pot. Katie then claimed that in two weeks marijuana would be washed up on shore near where they were parked. Burr took note of the time of Katie's prediction, but he said he didn't think anything more about it until two weeks later, at noon, twenty-five bales of pot washed ashore near where they had parked, and the area was swarming with police helicopters. Of course, drug traffickers do a lot business near the Florida coast, and it's hardly unprecedented for pot to be discovered and seized in this way. But it's also not an everyday event or (arguably) even a common occurrence, and it's certainly intriguing that Katie's prediction was accurate almost to the hour.

Of course, I was interested in the full range of Katie's apparent psychic gifts, and since I was writing a book about dissociation and multiple personality when I first learned about the case, I was especially intrigued by Katie's automatic Nostradamus scripts. But the most unusual aspect of the case was the mysterious foil that appeared on Katie's body. More than anything else, it was the prospect of both observing the foil appear and collecting it for analysis that brought me to Florida.

3. All That Glitters

I learned about Katie from her principal investigator, psychiatrist and parapsychologist Berthold E. Schwarz, who happened to live in Vero Beach, not far from Katie.[8] Bert alerted me to what he had been observing and encouraged me to check it out for myself. So in January 1988, during a break between semesters, my wife and I traveled to Vero Beach.

Bert generously gave me a detailed introduction to the facts of the case prior to my first meeting with Katie. I learned that the golden foil appears on various regions of Katie's body—primarily on her face, arms, hands, and torso, but occasionally on her legs as well. It sometimes manifests in layers (i.e., foil appears on top of other patches of foil), and eruptions sometimes cover relatively large areas—for example, four-by-five-inch patches or larger. Unlike some of Katie's other unusual capacities, manifesting the foil is beyond her control. It can happen at any time, and (not surprisingly) Katie regards it as an affliction. For one thing, it's often uncomfortable, accompanied by a burning or itching feeling and sometimes leaving behind reddened skin when it's removed. And for another, it's frequently embarrassing. After all, the foil may appear suddenly while Katie is shopping or dining out. Of course, Katie never knows what to say when that happens, and she'd rather not deal with such situations at all. Sometimes, months may pass without any appearance of the foil, but then it starts again and it may be weeks or months before Katie enjoys another break from the phenomenon.

It's tempting at first to think that the foil is exuded through Katie's skin. And in fact, that's often how it looks to those who've seen it appear and who've noted (for example) how Katie's skin sometimes starts to glisten and develop tiny droplets before thin layers of foil appear. But reportedly the foil appears also on Katie's clothes and on objects in her vicinity (and, I'm told, sometimes at distant locations). I haven't seen these externalized manifestations, but Bert has shown me sealed containers from around his office, with large quantities of foil inside. Since I have no doubt whatever of Bert's honesty and have found no reason to distrust Katie, I accept Bert's claim that the containers were sealed beforehand and not handled by Katie.

In any case, there's another reason to doubt that the foil is exuded through Katie's skin. Several different analyses of many samples reveal that the gold-colored foil is actually brass, roughly 80 percent copper and 20 percent zinc. Considering the quantity of foil removed from Katie's body, for Katie to have "sweated" the foil through the pores of her skin would have required lethal amounts of the metals in her system. Besides, blood work on Katie has never turned up the abnormalities one would expect if Katie had been "manufacturing" the brass from substances already inside her.[9]

I've had Katie's foil analyzed at several labs, and none have found anything obviously remarkable about it. We looked at it under scanning electron microscopes at two University of Maryland campuses, and analytical chemists on my campus also began work on a careful study. I've also had the foil scrutinized at Denver University, Johns Hopkins University (JHU), and the U.S. National Institute of Standards and Technology (NIST). My experience with the Johns Hopkins Department of Materials Science and Engineering is especially noteworthy.

At first, department chair Bob Green and his colleagues were intrigued when I introduced them to the details of the case, including the strong reasons for thinking that the foil manifestations were not fraudulent. They graciously agreed to see whether anything in the foil's underlying structure distinguished it from commercially available samples of brass leaf, usually called "Dutch metal" or "composition leaf." Their analysis determined that Katie's foil had the same granular structure as ordinary pressed or rolled leaf, like that of the commercial samples.

That was an important piece of information, because it ruled out one skeptical hypothesis as to how Katie might have fraudulently caused the foil to appear as witnesses looked on at close range. According to that hypothesis, Katie could have dissolved brass in a solution which she applied to her skin prior to test sessions. Then, the solution would evaporate, apparently miraculously leaving behind areas of brass. But as the JHU scientists pointed out, any brass evaporated out of a liquid applied to Katie's body would have a *crystalline* structure, not a pressed or rolled structure.

Regrettably (but not really inscrutably), the JHU team lost interest in Katie at this point. They apparently made the tacit, but unwarranted, assumption that if the foil had been produced paranormally, its structure would be unusual in some flagrant way. But of course, that's a non sequitur. As far as we know, paranormally produced substances might mimic the structure of normal substances. Similarly, anomalously structured foil would not establish the paranormal origin of the material; it might simply indicate an unusual mode of production. Still, I can understand why the JHU scientists found Katie's foil less intriguing after their analysis. After all, they're *materials* scientists, and they found that there was nothing special about Katie's foil, considered simply as a sample of brass. And, I suppose, there was little (if anything) more they could have added to my research at that point.

I figured that the next analyses should be conducted by analytical chemists. I thought this might shed light on the material's origin and classification within parapsychology. My first collaborator was Mike Epstein, a senior chemist with NIST. I provided Mike with thirty different samples of Katie's foil, taken on thirty different occasions from various parts of Katie's body. I suggested we look first for similarities or differences between the samples, to see what (if anything) they suggested. I also provided Mike with several control samples taken from Maryland and Pennsylvania art supply stores. I thought we should see whether they differed significantly from the samples of Katie's foil. And eventually, I thought it might be helpful to analyze control samples purchased in Florida. Conceivably, they might help resolve the issue of where Katie's samples came from in case she was apporting the material (or, less likely, purchasing it) from a remote location. For example, if Katie's foil was chemically similar only to Florida samples produced by a certain manufacturer, that would be worth knowing, even if it still left open the question of how Katie's foil found its way onto her body.

Of course, my proposed course of analysis was a fairly long-term project, and Mike could only work on it in his spare time, both at NIST and with his students at St. Mary's University in Maryland. The job remains unfinished, and it's clearly too soon to draw any sweeping conclusions, but the results so far can be studied in appendix 1. More recently, chemist William LaCourse at UMBC and some of his graduate students began their own follow-up analysis, which was interrupted by the tragic events of 9/11/2001 when analytical chemists had more urgent forensic matters to attend to. The preliminary results of the UMBC study can be found in appendix 2, and that's where the detailed analysis of Katie's foil stands at the moment.

4. Observing the Foil

I and others have tried following Katie around with video recorders, hoping to document one of the foil's unpredictable spontaneous occurrences. Usually, that proved difficult and annoying to all concerned, and the recorders never seemed pointed at Katie (or the right spot on Katie) at the right time. As a result, it became obvious that a somewhat more formal arrangement would be necessary.

The usual strategy developed for observing Katie was as follows. Katie would be ushered into a back room in Bert Schwarz's office. A chair awaited her in the center of the room, and one or more video cameras would be ready to go, usually mounted on tripods. Since Bert is a physician and Katie's confidant, he would search her for hidden foil in a way that would be inappropriate for other observers. So he would first examine Katie's body and hair carefully, and he would ask Katie to remove her false teeth so that he could examine them and look carefully in Katie's mouth. Then the other observers would carefully check Katie's hands and arms, which (since Katie always wore a short-sleeve T-shirt for these sessions) was easy enough to do. They would also ask Katie to lift her shirt to just below her breasts, so that they could determine that no foil was present on her torso or on the underside of her shirt.

Of course, this scrutiny can never lead to fully relaxed interactions, especially when it's followed by the unremitting observation (staring, actually) of several people along with video recording. Nevertheless, Bert and the others would engage Katie in a somewhat forced casual conversation, hoping that something would appear on the exposed regions of her body, or at least manifest under her shirt. Foil appeared in plain view only once in my sessions with Katie (more on that below). But whether or not it manifested before everyone's eyes, observers would eventually ask Katie to lift her shirt, to see whether there had been some undercover activity during their conversation. Bert and others report that on many occasions large quantities of foil would at that point be spread over Katie's abdomen. It was clear that if that amount of foil had been hidden under Katie's shirt, it would not have escaped detection by any moderately attentive person.

Regrettably, I didn't observe any foil on the several occasions when Katie lifted her shirt. But I did observe stigmata-like raised and reddish patches on her skin that had not been there before, in the shapes of a cross and of a butterfly. I also observed several instances of automatic writing in medieval French, some other displays of ostensible mediumship, and also a peculiar incident with a video lamp bulb (which I'll describe shortly).

Apparently, Bert had never succeeded in capturing the emergence of foil on video. Every time I asked him to show me some evidential footage, he always produced a sample in which the foil had already appeared. Moreover, I don't believe Bert has unbroken footage beginning with the initial search of Katie and continuing through the eventual appearance of the foil when she lifted her shirt. But I also don't believe Bert cares particularly whether he managed to obtain video evidence of the sort I hoped for. He was already certain the foil manifestations were genuine, and he was more interested in documenting Katie the subject, probing the psychogenesis, meaning, and variations of the phenomenon. I actually respect Bert's perspective and share it to a great extent. I also share his impatience with the continued emphasis in parapsychology on proof-oriented research. However, I believe Katie's phenomena are so important and unusual that they merit the fullest possible documentation.

Fortunately, I managed to videotape the appearance of foil at fairly close range. But even that piece of evidence is problematical. Here's what happened. Only one tripod-mounted video recorder was available on this occasion, and I operated the camera. As usual, I examined Katie's face, hands, arms, torso, and the underside of her T-shirt after Bert conducted his more intimate inspection. During the ensuing artificially casual discussion between Bert, Katie, and me, Katie apparently began experiencing an irritation in the outer corner of her right eye. Evidently, it was of the sort that often foreshadowed the appearance of golden foil. As Katie began to rub that part of her eye, I zoomed in on her face, hoping to catch something worthwhile at close range. At that point, the tape shows that no foil was near Katie's eye. Repeatedly, Katie wiped the corner of her eye with her finger and then looked at the finger to see if any foil had been deposited on it. On one of those occasions, a very tiny speck of golden material was visible near Katie's eye when she removed her finger. And the next time Katie wiped her eye and removed her finger, the spot had grown to about a quarter-inch square.

Now, Bert and I had examined Katie carefully beforehand, inspecting her face and hands. Without doubt, no foil was present in those areas at that time. Also, it was obvious that Katie had no access to foil during our conversation and taping. She was in full view, her arms exposed in a short-sleeve shirt, and there was no place in her vicinity into which she could have reached to put foil on her finger and thereafter transfer the foil to her eye. But you have to accept my and Bert's word on this; there's no way to tell from the videotape. I was recording Katie with only one camera, in a tight headshot. So when Katie looked at her finger to see if something had been near her eye, she took her hand out of camera range. Viewers of the video have no way of telling, from the video alone, that Katie didn't dip her finger into some golden foil and then transfer it to her eye.

However, if you can accept my word and trust the minimal observational prowess required to determine that Katie had no foil hidden on her hands or face beforehand, the brief video footage is an important piece of evidence. It documents an instance of what many have observed, often in more florid form. And it may be the only record of the foil in the process of formation.

I suppose skeptics can glibly insist that Katie somehow managed to hide a small piece of foil and surreptitiously place a speck of it, and then a larger piece, near her eye. But as a highly skilled magician later confirmed (see below), and as any person who handles the foil can easily determine, the foil is clingy and very difficult to manipulate. So no one should be satisfied with the confident-sounding pronouncements of magicians that the phenomenon is easy to fake. Confidence is easier to feign than the appearance of Katie's foil under watchful eyes and after a close bodily inspection. Magicians need to *demonstrate* that they can do what they claim is easy to do. The proper response to skeptical critics is to demand that they put up or shut up. Significantly, the only thing close to an attempt by skeptics to replicate the phenomenon was laughably inadequate, arguably dishonest, and (in fact) quite irrelevant. I'll discuss this later in the chapter.

Incidentally, this was not the only occasion on which I was present for both the appearance and enlargement of some foil on Katie's face. But the other incident was more informal, and more typical of the difficult-to-videotape real-life situations in which the foil would manifest. Shortly before a scheduled formal session during our 1988 visit to Vero Beach, my wife and I met up with Katie outside Bert's office. When Katie arrived, she walked up to my wife and they embraced. At that time, no foil was on Katie's face, and during the embrace her hands were nowhere near her face. Katie's left hand remained at her side, holding her purse, and her right hand was on my wife's shoulder. But when they stepped back from the embrace, a small piece of foil, perhaps an eighth-inch square, was on Katie's left cheek. Of course, my wife observed this at close range, and I observed it at a distance of four or five feet. It was clear that no foil was on Katie's face before she embraced my wife, and it was equally clear that Katie's hands were in no position during the embrace to place any foil on her cheek.

Immediately thereafter, we walked inside to Bert's back room for the planned videotaped session. My wife walked next to Katie on her right and I walked behind them. From the time we entered Bert's office to the time we entered the back room, Katie's arms and hands were in clear view at her side, with her left hand still holding her purse. So Katie had no opportunity to touch her face without being observed, and she clearly made no effort to touch her face. But when we arrived in the back room, the piece of foil on Katie's cheek had doubled in size.

5. Why Golden Foil?

All of Katie's psychic functioning began after she married her current and second husband, Tom. Evidently, this is a difficult and psychologically abusive relationship. Bert Schwarz knows many of the details, but of course they were revealed to him in confidence. At any rate, it appears that Katie's case falls within one of the more (actually, one of the few) established regularities discovered in parapsychology.

Probably many readers are familiar with the standard profile of poltergeist cases. With very few exceptions, poltergeist disturbances center around a person, dubbed the poltergeist *agent*. Usually, this person is a troubled teenager or adolescent—in any case, someone suffering from emotional turmoil that apparently can't be resolved through conventional means. So it seems that poltergeist agents unconsciously and somewhat spasmodically manage to discharge their intense pent-up feelings. In a kind of brute psychic flailing about, they cause objects to move, break, burst into flame, etc.

Naturally, teenagers aren't the only people experiencing emotional turmoil. As I can personally attest (though I suppose my testimony isn't necessary), marriages can also be a fertile ground for deep emotional distress. And in fact, Katie's isn't the only case I've seen where paranormal physical phenomena occur in the context of a troubled marriage. This merits a brief digression.

Several years after meeting Katie, I investigated the case of a Maryland woman whose photographs showed anomalies of a sort familiar to many psi researchers. Some contained white clouded areas (where none existed in the original scene), and others were marred by white, squiggly, noodle-like streaks (needless to say, those were also not part of the scenes she photographed). This woman, let's call her S. S., was married to a man diagnosed with bipolar disorder (formerly called "manic depression"). From what

I could gather, he was a cruel and domineering husband, and S. S. may have experienced physical as well as psychological abuse. One photo S. S. showed me is particularly interesting. It's a portrait of her husband in which he's staring into the camera in anything but a friendly manner, and to the right of his face are some squiggly lines that seem to spell *HELP*. The last three letters are quite clear; the *H* is somewhat more indefinite and is tilted to the left. Of course, there's no way to be certain, but the photo looks very much like a psychically mediated unconscious cry for help; probably from S. S., but possibly from her husband instead. If so, it's a good example of how paranormal physical phenomena may originate from the psychopathology of everyday life.

Now, back to Katie's case, which also seems clearly to reveal potent real-life forces shaping both the emergence and the character of spontaneous PK. The foil first appeared on March 5, 1986, in the midst of an active period of paranormal physical phenomena—usually, poltergeist-type disturbances, including apparent apports and the movement of objects. One of those events was the mysterious appearance of a carving set. But when Katie showed it to her husband Tom, he seemed to dismiss her, remarking, "What good is it if it isn't money?" Two days later, the brass foil appeared for the first time.

This actually makes a lot of sense psychologically. Symbolically, the brass foil satisfies Tom's demand for something valuable. But at the same time Katie needn't run the risk of being the goose that lays the golden egg. After all, the pressure of being a psychic subject is weighty enough as it is. If Katie could really produce material of value, the additional pressure and scrutiny could be crushing.

Furthermore, the strategy of producing brass rather than gold might play an interesting role within Katie's marriage. My take on Katie's situation is that she feels trapped within that relationship. I believe she's deeply dissatisfied with it, yet (despite occasional attempts to establish her own independence and on some occasions actually to leave Tom) she's unable to extricate herself fully from the marriage. And no matter how much residual attachment she may feel toward her husband, I believe Katie harbors considerable anger and resentment toward him as well. If so, the brass foil might be a way of thumbing her nose at Tom, expressing her anger or contempt, or retaliating against him. Brass is not what he wanted; in fact, it's a kind of "fool's gold."

Although Katie clearly shows no interest in making a name for herself as a psychic, even the reasonably suspicious might still wonder about possible, and perhaps less obvious, secondary gains. Perhaps there are other reasons why Katie might want to manufacture evidence of golden leaf appearing on her body. After all, even if Katie seems disinterested in fame and fortune, it would be foolish to claim that she gets no psychological benefit from her apparent psychic abilities. For one thing, Katie gets a lot of respectful attention from people who ordinarily would never have come into contact with her, including scientists and other academics. And it's likely that Katie holds the somewhat naive view that these people are distinguished and deserving of admiration, simply because they're members of the scholarly community. (Those who are actually members of that community seldom make this mistake.) Furthermore, Katie's psychic achievements might also help shift the balance of power in her marriage in ways she finds advantageous, although my impression is that Tom wavers between liking the attention he receives in Katie's wake and resenting the fact that Katie is the real person of interest. In any case, these secondary gains strike me as fragile, relatively minor, and as insufficient to motivate fraud—at least in Katie, though perhaps not in someone less modest and more driven to seek the spotlight. Besides, fraud seems out of the question, for the reasons already mentioned and discussed further below.

6. The Light Bulb Incident

My second visit to Katie was in April 1989. As a foil-hunting expedition, it was unsuccessful, but I did view some automatic writing (including ostensible scripts from Nostradamus) and some apparent apports which were interesting but not observed under sufficiently careful conditions. This trip also enabled me to get to know Katie better, for which I was grateful, and which turned out to be helpful in my next visit to Florida (discussed below).

As far as apparent PK is concerned, the most notable event took place during one of the sessions in which we were videotaping Katie, hoping to see foil appear. This time three people (two investigators from Boston and me) operated tripod-mounted cameras. We were doing our usual bit of taping Katie while conducting an innocuous conversation with her, and at one point one of the professional video lamps we were using blew out. The heat from the mini-explosion apparently melted and expanded part of the lamp bulb into a new and irregularly bulging shape. The video technician from Boston who had brought his equipment with him assured me that, although lamps have failed him before, his bulbs had never exploded and bloated in this way. Naturally, we were all curious to take a look at the peculiarly swollen bulb.

So we waited for about five minutes for the bulb to cool, and then we started passing it around. The videographer first showed it to Bert, then Bert passed it back to the two Bostonians, then it went to me, and finally I passed it on to Katie. So before the bulb ever reached Katie, four of us had handled it over a period of several minutes, and that was already several minutes after the bulb had blown. We four saw plainly that, apart from the bulb's novel shape, there was nothing else noteworthy about it. We could see clearly inside the bulb, except for a small part of the glass that had been darkened by the explosion inside.

Shortly after I passed the bulb to Katie, we noticed that smoke was rising from it. It began as a very thin and barely visible stream and then increased markedly in volume. Katie noticed the smoke at about the same time, and two of us who were operating cameras immediately zoomed in on the event. The tapes plainly show a steady stream of smoke rising from the bulb. Katie held it, looked at it with some amazement, and turned it slightly with her hand so that we could get different angles on it. This smoke event lasted for a couple of minutes, and then it was over.

But where did the smoke come from? If had been trapped inside the bulb and then leaked out (through a crack we never discovered), presumably we would have seen it when we handled the bulb earlier and passed it around. And why did the smoke occur only when Katie held it, and not during the seven or eight minutes before that? If something inside the bulb had required handling in order to produce the smoke, one would think the smoke would have appeared before the bulb ever reached Katie. And that still leaves unexplained how the smoke would have escaped from inside the bulb. If there had been a crack in the bulb or in its base big enough to allow the copious amount of observed smoke to escape, I think one of us five would have spotted it. I should add that we can't suppose that Katie somehow had secret access to a smoke-producing substance, sitting there before us in a short-sleeve shirt with nothing around her, and after the usual careful body checks before the session began.

Now I don't want to make too much of this event. I don't consider it strong evidence of PK. But it's certainly suggestive, especially considering Katie's track record of anomalous physical phenomena. And it's continuous with the sort of anomaly many investigators report during their examinations of ostensibly psychic subjects: with apparently unusual (but admittedly hard to quantify) frequency, electronic equipment fails or hiccups, even when the gear is ordinarily very reliable.

7. The Perils of Showbiz

For my next visit to Katie, in 1990, I joined the crew from *Unsolved Mysteries*. The popular television show was preparing a segment on Katie, and they seemed especially interested in the golden leaf. The producers planned to combine dramatizations of incidents from Katie's life with interviews not just of Katie, but also of eyewitnesses and alleged expert commentators. They also hoped to include footage of Katie "in action"—again, especially the foil manifestations, since they were clearly the most novel and spectacular of her phenomena. And to help gather evidence and lend credibility to the process, they enlisted the services of Los Angeles magician Christopher Chacon and parapsychologist Dean Radin.

Chacon is a skilled conjuror who has helped design illusions for some of the country's most famous magicians. Radin, as many readers will probably know, is an extremely bright, thoughtful, and creative researcher with a solid scientific pedigree and an enviable track record in designing and conducting groundbreaking and successful psi experiments. But neither had met Katie before. Since I was well aware how subject-experimenter relations could either make or break efforts to obtain evidence of spontaneous macro PK, and since I felt Katie and I already had a comfortable, trusting relationship and good rapport, I hoped my presence would help make the atmosphere more relaxed and conducive to the manifestations of the foil. I knew also that Chris and Dean were going into this without a feel for the subject's personality and without much information either on Katie's life or the case's background. So I also hoped to provide whatever guidance might be useful. This was a great opportunity to obtain quality footage of the phenomenon and present the evidence to a huge audience, and I didn't want to see it botched.

I had never met Chris before. He struck me as skeptical in exactly the right way: on the lookout for possible fraud, but still open to the possibility of phenomena that couldn't be explained away as sleight of hand. And of course, he had an extensive knowledge of conjuring. Dean is someone I already knew well, and I was confident he'd quickly size up the situation and devise a way to work within the inherent constraints imposed either by Katie's character or by the needs of the TV crew.

Bert provided Chris with samples of Katie's foil and either I or someone else (I no longer recall) provided him with purchased samples of Dutch metal. Chris determined quickly that the clingy material was very difficult to manipulate. He experimented with methods of moving it around his hands and transferring it surreptitiously from his hands to other parts of his body. But he had great difficulty handling the material even when he wasn't trying to conceal or disguise his movements. It was clear to him that Katie couldn't have inconspicuously placed the leaf on her body under the conditions in which she'd been observed. And he certainly had no counter-explanation to the many reports of the material appearing instantaneously and at close range to the observers.

Dean, Chris, and the crew hoped to capture the golden leaf appearing during their filmed interviews with Katie, but the first days of shooting passed without success. However, some crew members reported brief and minor manifestations of the material when they were relaxing with Katie between periods of filming. So it seemed clear that *Unsolved Mysteries* had not arrived during one of Katie's unpredictable periods of quiescence. As a result, there was considerable anticipation among the crew that they would get some good footage during a six-hour planned experiment. Dean, Chris, and I were at least cautiously optimistic.

As it happened, the experiment was colossal fiasco, demonstrating how the needs (or at least the personalities) of the entertainment industry may conflict with the demands of research. However, the design of the experiment had been sound enough. Bert had managed to secure the use of a conference room at a nearby hospital. The crew removed all the furniture from the room, including a very large and heavy conference table. The hospital administrator was horrified when he learned of this, but the point was to have nothing in the room except what the experimenters and crew brought into it. It also enabled Dean and Chris to examine the room carefully, so that they could state confidently that nothing suspicious—and certainly no hidden foil—was discovered there.

As far as the test was concerned, the plan was for Katie, Chris, and Dean to be in one half of the room during a six-hour period. Three video cameras, a camera operator, and I were to be in the other half of the room. Katie would be dressed in a flimsy garment, like a hospital gown, provided by the crew. That would prevent Katie from using her own clothes to sneak foil into the room. As an additional precaution against Katie furtively bringing foil into the experimental area by hiding it on or in her body, she was to undergo a fluoroscopic examination before entering the room. Once in the room with the cameras rolling, Chris and Dean were to directly supervise whatever Katie did, and I was there to help Katie feel more at ease under what were likely to be somewhat strained, or at least artificial, test conditions with people she had only recently met. For toilet breaks, a female member of the crew was appointed to accompany Katie and certify that she hadn't accessed a hidden stash of foil during that time.

Initially, it looked as if everything was running smoothly. Katie felt encouraged that some foil would appear during the six hours, the cameras were ready to record the event from different angles and different degrees of closeness, and Dean and Chris were ready either to endorse or debunk the phenomena if they occurred.

But problems arose right from the beginning. Katie arrived at the hospital at 9 a.m., in a good mood and ready to go. However, the *Unsolved Mysteries* director had other plans. He wanted to shoot various set-up shots before embarking on our experiment. First, he wanted to shoot Katie entering the hospital. Then he wanted to shoot Katie undergoing the fluoroscopic examination. And finally, he wanted to film Katie walking down the hall to the conference room and entering the room. Of course, preparing each one of these shots is a time-consuming process. The equipment has to be moved to the appropriate location and set up, the lighting and sound have to be just right, and the shooting must proceed to the director's satisfaction (possibly with multiple takes). Dean and I pleaded with the director to shoot these later, since they were required only for dramatic continuity and since Katie was "in the mood." But the director insisted on doing things his way.

As a result, the experiment scheduled to begin at 10 a.m. actually started at about the time we had expected it to end—at 3:30 p.m.! And by that time, Katie's mood had changed completely. Now she was tired and irritated by the delays and by the apparent insensitivity of the production team. And not surprisingly, nothing happened during the experiment. The entire six hours passed very slowly. Chris and Dean tried gamely to relax Katie and chat with her, and I talked to her as well, hoping to introduce an element of familiarity and trust. But it seemed as if the atmosphere had been poisoned. I'm not even sure Katie realized that Chris and Dean had nothing to do with delaying the start of the experiment. Also, it was my impression that Katie was irritated by Chris's glib demeanor; the magician seemed "on stage," slick, and insincere in virtually all of his interactions. In fact, I believe Chris saw this experience with *Unsolved Mysteries* as a kind of breakout opportunity, a chance to make a mark in the rather lucrative magician / ghostbusting / debunking business, and he acted like he knew he was on camera. In any case, the result was something quite different from what had been planned. I'm not sure what Chris was expecting, but Dean and I were anticipating only a mildly artificial test situation led by two people Katie hardly knew and one of whom she seemed to dislike. What we got instead was an ordeal; it was a tedious, often obnoxious, and probably psi-repressive experience for Katie.

I don't consider Katie to be the most delicate of psychic subjects. After all, she had worked successfully with incredulous strangers in law enforcement, and she had produced foil and apparent mediumistic messages for many people she had only recently met. But she's not someone who thrives on the skeptical challenges or tests that seem to inspire, say, Joe McMoneagle.[10] Apart from her apparent psychic gifts (or afflictions), Katie seems perfectly normal. Like virtually everyone else, she can be inspired or discouraged by the situations in which she finds herself, and her abilities can flow freely on some occasions but not on others.

So the planned six-hour test was a flop, and the crew had wasted money and time, and squandered a golden opportunity (pun intended) to study a promising subject under excellent conditions. Nevertheless, the *Unsolved Mysteries* team produced a generally favorable segment on Katie, highlighting her psychic detective work with local authorities, the mysterious foil, and Katie's apports. Someone close to the production told me that the original version of the segment was almost entirely positive, but that the relevant NBC executives felt it needed to be more skeptical. So at the last minute the team filmed interviews with the skeptical philosopher Paul Kurtz, some of his students, and a magician colleague from CSICOP.[11]

8. Sleazy Skepticism

In my view, Kurtz is so passionately concerned to wage a war (really, a religious crusade) against what he sees as the forces of irrationalism, he knowingly adopts disreputable tactics to defeat his opponents. In particular, he uses transparently weak arguments whose flaws he must surely recognize and would be quick to spot if he had been the target of such arguments himself. For example, he generalizes from the weakest pieces of evidence, ignores relevant details, and bases his confident dismissal of classic parapsychological cases on already questionable second-hand accounts.[12]

Kurtz was in typical form for his *Unsolved Mysteries* interview. First, he acted as if he really knew the details of the case, claiming (inelegantly), "I don't think there's any objective, hard evidence that this is exuding from her pores. Most likely, the point is, someone wants other people to believe this, and so they put this metallic paper on them." Now, since Kurtz had only just been introduced to the case and had never met Katie or spoken to anyone involved in evidence-gathering, he had no business making any authoritative pronouncements at all. My guess is that Kurtz knew nothing about the foil except that he'd been shown one or two photos or video clips of Katie with the foil already on her body. I doubt he knew anything about the conditions under which the foil had been observed. But undaunted by his ignorance, Kurtz directed his students to show how the phenomena could be produced by stealth. The students purchased some Dutch metal, and one of them demonstrated for the camera how she had placed the foil on her body, secured it there with hair spray (except for the foil placed on her tongue), and walked around in that condition for several hours. This, she claimed, is what Katie must have done.

Of course, this demonstration was completely irrelevant and showed a flagrant disregard for the details of the case. In fact, Kurtz and his students displayed no interest in even learning those details, which would have been easy enough to do. After all, there were no secrets about who had been studying Katie and examining the evidence. That information was known to the production team of *Unsolved Mysteries*, and Kurtz could have found it out with a simple inquiry. So for example, had Kurtz or his students taken the trouble to contact me, I could have presented them with the evidence that no foreign chemicals (like hair spray) had been found in analyses of Katie's foil. And I could have filled them in on the sorts of conditions under which the foil had been observed.

But this is all too often the dedicated debunker's approach to parapsychology. As I mentioned above, one standard ploy is to focus only on targets that seem easy to demolish, pretend that others don't even exist, and generalize from the weakest cases. (I believe that's why Kurtz's magazine, *Skeptical Inquirer*, has never reviewed one of my books on parapsychology.) That was clearly Kurtz's strategy in Katie's case. His student's demonstration would apply at most to reports of those who've merely observed the foil once it was already on Katie's body. It's irrelevant to cases where the conditions of observation were more critical. It doesn't address the testimony of those claiming to have seen the foil appear on Katie at close range, or who've examined her body and clothing before the foil appeared beneath her clothes.[13] (In the next chapter, we'll take a look at some general issues concerning eyewitness testimony of apparently paranormal phenomena, and we'll see why the usual skeptical concerns are toothless in cases as good as this.)

I'm pleased to say that when I've shown the segment on Katie to my students, most recognize immediately how flimsy Kurtz's response is. But some don't, and I'm sure many have been taken in by it—especially those who share Kurtz's will to disbelieve. Sometimes it's enough just to hear an alleged authority declare confidently that a case is worthless or that the phenomena are fraudulent.

That's what magician James Randi did in 1967 on the *Today* show in connection with the psychic photography of Ted Serios, one of the most significant recent cases in parapsychology. Serios was a Chicago bellhop who could make images appear, at a distance, on carefully controlled Polaroid film.[14] But Randi insisted that the phenomena were fraudulent, and he claimed that he could reproduce them under conditions similar to those in which Serios succeeded. That would have been a neat trick, because those conditions included wearing clothing supplied by the experimenters and being separated from the camera (sometimes in another room, and sometimes in an electrically shielded Faraday cage). Nevertheless, with his usual bluster, Randi accepted a $10,000 challenge (a considerable sum in those days) to duplicate the Serios phenomena and make good on his claim.

Of course, confidence is easy to feign, and Randi does it routinely in his role as magician. He also cleverly takes advantage of the occasional high-profile case he successfully exposes as fraudulent, by publicizing those successes and creating the impression that he's a generally reliable guide when it comes to the paranormal. So Randi's dismissal of the Serios case was all it took for those already disposed to believe that Serios was a fake, and it was probably enough even for those sympathetic to parapsychology but unaware of Randi's dishonesty. Many (possibly most) viewers were left believing that the case was without merit.

What the TV audience never learned was that when the show was over and Randi was pressed to make good on his wager, he simply weaseled out of it. To keep that side of the story under wraps, Randi prohibited publication of his correspondence on the matter. That was undoubtedly a shrewd move, because the letters show clearly how Randi backed down from his empty challenge. However, Randi's original letters now reside in the library at the University of Maryland Baltimore County, and researchers, finally, can easily confirm this for themselves. When Serios's principal investigator, Jule Eisenbud, died, I was assigned the task of going through his papers. I collected all the material relevant to the Serios case and deposited it in the Special Collections section of the UMBC library. (This includes correspondence, the original photos and films, and signed affidavits from witnesses.)

In any case, if Randi had actually been able to do what Serios did, you can be sure he would have done it publicly and with considerable fanfare. He's too much of a publicity hound to pass up such an opportunity. But there's no documentary evidence of Randi having even *attempted* to duplicate the Serios phenomena under anything like the conditions in which Serios succeeded, much less evidence of his having actually pulled it off. Interestingly, this paucity of evidence never prevented the widely read and respected but (under the circumstances) despicably non-authoritative Martin Gardner from claiming that Randi "regularly" duplicates the Serios phenomenon, "and with more skill."[5] (For more on the Serios case, see chapter 6.)

9. Summing Up

But I digress. Let's return to Katie. As things stand now, the study of Katie remains frustratingly incomplete. More could be done—and needs to be done—in the analysis of the foil taken from her body. If nothing else, that might provide a clue as to whether we should classify the substance as an apport or as a materialization. And of course, it would be great if we could obtain better video documentation of Katie's foil in the process of formation or manifestation. Nevertheless, the evidence for the paranormal origin of the golden leaf is compelling, even in its current and still somewhat preliminary state. The anecdotal testimony is too extensive, and the conditions of observation have been too clear and straightforward, for the reports to be attributed to malobservation, fraud, or collusion. Too many honest eyewitnesses have seen the foil appear close up, or have seen it on Katie's body after prior examination and under conditions that clearly prevented her from surreptitiously placing it there. (Remember, the foil is very difficult to manipulate, even in plain view.)

I wish I could report confidently that studies of Katie will continue. But as I write this, the prospects are not encouraging. My academic chemist friends have other pressing obligations, and I'm certain they always have reservations (even when they're free) about tackling a job that many of their colleagues will ignorantly ridicule. So it's unclear when—or if—the foil analyses will resume. I'm also not optimistic about the prospects for conducting more tests with Katie. I would be happy to do so, but Bert Schwarz tells me that Katie's domestic situation makes it unlikely either that she could break free for more testing or that she would be in the appropriate frame of mind. So I'm reluctant to apply right now for external funding.

However, Bert tells me that Katie still occasionally reports outbreaks of foil. So I remain hopeful that eventually her personal life will improve and allow her to cooperate again with investigators. We've still only scratched the surface of Katie's psychic abilities. The foil phenomenon needs to be studied further, and we also need to look more closely at Katie's ESP, healing, and apparent channeling phenomena—especially her ability to produce apparent writings from Nostradamus in medieval French. Subjects this versatile, impressive, and cooperative don't come along every day.

Historical Interlude

1. Introduction

Of course, parapsychological investigations don't occur in a historical vacuum, and Katie's case is no exception. It's part of an extensive, interesting, and very complex history, not only of psychic phenomena generally and paranormal physical phenomena in particular, but also of hypnosis, dissociation, and psychiatry. In this chapter I want to digress a bit and fill in at least some of the relevant parapsychological background. This should provide a useful perspective both on Katie's case and also those described in later chapters. I've discussed much of this history in detail elsewhere;[1] but for now, a brief survey will do.

Katie's case falls within a fascinating tradition that began in the 1850s, with the rise of the Spiritualist movement in the US and then later in Europe. This movement quickly seized the public's imagination and spread like wildfire throughout the West. It was during this period that mediumship made its first significant appearance in industrialized countries, and not simply as a central feature of a new religion. Spiritualism in the West fostered a more secular *spiritism*—the view that personal consciousness persists after bodily death, and that although some people are especially gifted mediumistically, the rest of humanity can also experience a direct connection to "the other side." Consequently, many began holding séances on their own, without the participation or direction of an acknowledged medium, and sometimes merely as a form of entertainment. And as a result, many people seemed to discover their own previously hidden mediumistic abilities. In fact, the second half of the nineteenth century witnessed a kind of mediumistic explosion. Suddenly, mediums seemed to be everywhere, emerging from all corners of society. Some even became international celebrities. Of course, before long scientists also took an interest in mediumship, especially since it had escaped the confines of underdeveloped countries and found its way to middle-class living rooms and Victorian parlors.

Traditionally, the Western form of mediumship comes in two basic varieties. All mediums claim (or appear) to be vessels for communications from departed spirits. But whereas *mental* mediums seem to transmit messages or allow themselves to be possessed by deceased communicators, *physical* mediums appear to channel observable manifestations—beyond their own body—of spirits' continued existence. Typically, spiritualist physical mediums would become entranced, and then objects would move, voices or other sounds would be heard at a distance from the medium, or sometimes objects would apparently materialize from nothing.

Although mediumistic séances were often of great personal relevance to the other participants (usually termed "sitters"), the Spiritualist movement was—not surprisingly—a bonanza for scoundrels who preyed upon gullible believers. Bogus mental mediums had various techniques for delivering empty but satisfying messages from deceased relatives and friends. And as far as physical mediumship was concerned, unscrupulous magicians found they could produce all sorts of marvels when séances were conducted in the dark. Soon (and predictably), the very practice of mediumship became tainted, and in the first decades of the twentieth century interest in spiritualism declined rapidly. Moreover, because their effects were apparently so dramatic, physical mediums in particular were natural and easy targets of suspicion.

However, it would be a mistake to think either that all physical mediums were frauds or that nobody managed to weed out the charlatans among them. First of all, investigators exposed many hundreds of fraudulent mediums during the heyday of spiritualism (roughly, from 1850 to 1930). Some of those investigators were self-styled skeptical debunkers—scientists or laypersons who made reputations for themselves by exposing mediumistic duplicity, and most of whom believed that spiritualistic phenomena couldn't be genuine. But others combined careful and critical research with a sympathetic or at least open-minded attitude toward the paranormal.

One of the reasons this period is so important is that some physical mediums clearly stood out from the crowd. No matter how carefully they were controlled, and no matter how alert, competent, and familiar with conjuring were their investigators, these mediums produced effects that simply couldn't be dismissed as fraudulent or attributed to malobservation. Moreover, some of the phenomena were mind-bogglingly dramatic. For instance, in the case of D. D. Home (discussed below), accordions reportedly played either untouched or held at the end away from the keys; substantial, fleshy, and warm hands—ending at the wrist—moved around the room, carried objects, shook hands with séance participants, and then dissolved in their grasp; and despite the efforts of many to restrain them, heavy tables moved around the room, sometimes with several people sitting on top. And those were just a few of the startling phenomena associated with Home's mediumship.

Although Home may have been the most impressive medium of all time (at least in the northern hemisphere),[2] he wasn't the only medium apparently channeling (or producing) dramatic, large-scale effects. But that raises an important and interesting issue. Many wonder—reasonably—why such dazzling phenomena occurred during this eighty-year period but not thereafter. After all, we no longer see or hear about the sorts of things that apparently happened frequently during the Spiritualist movement. Of course, this doesn't surprise those who think all mediumistic phenomena are fraudulent, and they have two standard skeptical explanations for the disappearance of large-scale effects. First is what we could call the *Argument from Gullibility*: the contention that people simply were more unsophisticated and credulous in former days. Second is what we could call the *Argument from Technology*: the claim that mediums' tricks couldn't keep up with the detection capabilities of developing science. At first glance, these proposals might seem plausible, but they crumble under a moment's reflection and greater familiarity with the case material.

For one thing, it's actually shameful to claim that the early investigators of mediums were more gullible than their successors. That sweeping generalization simply betrays ignorance about the best cases and the credentials of the investigators, and it can only be made by those who *know* they haven't examined the evidence carefully.[3] Granted, many reports from spiritualist séances were provided by hard-core, uncritical believers. But the cases that matter are the ones that can't easily be dismissed. And one reason the best cases are so good is that the investigators who endorsed them were often experienced and skeptical observers, either skilled in conjuring or at least familiar with the tricks of the trade and savvy about methods for preventing them. Moreover, the Argument from Gullibility suggests a shocking blindness to the current state of public gullibility. When you take into account, say, the widespread use of psychic hotlines and our fascination with sloppy and sensationalistic media coverage of psychic happenings, gullibility today arguably surpasses anything that preceded it. Besides, there's no hard data on gullibility levels (much less a gullibility index) to which we can appeal here. But then the Argument from Gullibility seems merely to be a thinly veiled complaint that since mediumistic phenomena are impossible, people *must* have been more credulous in the old days.

Furthermore, it's equally lame to appeal to advancing technology's potential for fraud suppression. For one thing, the Argument from Technology is a double-edged sword. If nineteenth-century technology limited the means for detecting fraud, it also limited the means for producing it. That's especially important to note in connection with the more outstanding phenomena produced under decent conditions, particularly in séances conducted at the spur of the moment and in locations where the medium had never visited before—thus, in locations where the medium had no opportunity to plant a confederate or conceal an apparatus. It's also relevant for cases where the phenomena seem clearly to exceed *any* technology of the period—for example, dissolving or melting materialized hands, or the large quantities of so-called ectoplasm that emerged from the medium's body and either moved objects or took the form of mobile and living human appendages. (Arguably, those phenomena are beyond even today's technology.) Similarly, if current technology—for example, miniaturized, remote-controlled, and automated electronics—enhances our ability to detect various kinds of fraud, it also enhances our ability to produce it. After all, magicians can perform convincing tricks today that simply were not feasible before. In any case, as we can see from some of the examples discussed below (and in more detail elsewhere),[4] the most challenging cases of nineteenth-century physical mediumship boasted phenomena that were clearly beyond the technology of the day. And that includes somewhat less spectacular phenomena than materializations—for example, massive objects levitated in good light with ample opportunity to inspect them before, during, and after the levitation.

Still, it's both true and puzzling that spiritualist séances offered up phenomena of a magnitude we no longer see—at least in industrialized countries. Elsewhere, however, reports of dramatic phenomena continue to surface, often in connection with shamanstic rituals and in countries (such as Brazil) where spiritistic religions continue to thrive. So the question remains: what happened to the dramatic physical phenomena of spiritualism in America and

Europe? Although the Arguments from Gullibility and Technology don't adequately account for this change, it's reasonable to expect *some* explanation.

Fortunately, I think there is a reasonable explanation for the disappearance of dramatic physical mediumship, and it concerns the phenomenon's underlying psychology. In the early days of the Spiritualist movement, all the great mediums were convinced spiritists. Even if they didn't embrace the details of the spiritualist religion, they all sincerely believed that departed souls acted through them to convey messages, influence objects, and so on. So they believed sincerely that they were merely channels for the production of the phenomena, not the underlying cause. But then, as far as they were concerned, they weren't responsible for anything that happened.

In these respects, Katie very much fits the mold of the former spiritualist mediums. For some reason she had become fascinated with Nostradamus and believed that he used her to produce many of her phenomena. And on many occasions she felt that other entities manifested through her. As far as I'm aware, she wasn't sure why her body would erupt in golden foil. But it's quite clear that, like the mediums of old, she felt no responsibility for what happened. As far as she was concerned, the foil was an affliction outside her control, probably linked to external agencies.

But now consider how liberating that belief must have been to traditional spiritualist mediums. It meant that—from the mediums' point of view—they were off the hook no matter what happened during a séance. If no (or only uninteresting) phenomena occurred, they didn't have to feel they had literally failed. Both mediums and sitters could always attribute the results either to an inept communicator or to a weak link with the spirit world. So from that standpoint, there was no need and little temptation to regard the lack of results with suspicion, as a possible sign of fraud. But more important, mediums likewise didn't need to feel responsible when dramatic phenomena occurred during the séance. As far as they were concerned, they were mere facilitators—not causes—of those events. So neither they nor sitters had to fear the extent of mediums' powers either during or after the séance.

The importance of that last point shouldn't be underestimated. The fear of psi is an important theme running through the history of parapsychology, and that fear apparently expresses itself in several crucial ways. First, it seems clearly to influence the intensity of skeptical opposition to psi research, whose passion seems more appropriate to a religious war than to open-minded empirical inquiry. It even seems to have insidiously infected psi research itself. Ever since the founding of the Society for Psychical Research in 1882, investigators have been more comfortable with ESP than with PK. That's one reason why physical mediumship was called the "lower" form of mediumship. (Another was that the phenomena were often too earthy for contemporary—and especially Victorian—sensibilities. I'll say more about this below.) Moreover, the fear of psi—perhaps PK in particular—arguably affects the way psi researchers, apparently inadvertently, undermine their own experiments.[5]

As I suggested above, what's ultimately behind the fear of psi (especially PK) is our discomfort with the idea that we might unconsciously be wreaking havoc on the world at large. After all, it's a very small step conceptually from psychokinetically nudging a matchstick to psychokinetically causing someone to drop dead, or causing a car to crash. If we concede the former ability, we have to try very hard to convince ourselves that we shouldn't allow the others. Of course, in some societies people are more comfortable with the possibility that their wishes (positive or negative) can affect those around them; but that belief generally doesn't go down very well in most industrialized countries.

Granted, many people embrace the possibility that we can psychically influence the lives of others to produce beneficial effects such as healing—but they inconsistently deny or ignore what follows obviously from this. No process can used only for the good. So if we open the door to the salutary (or simply benign) effects of our thoughts on the external world, we must also open it to the destructive influence of our thoughts. And that's precisely what freaks people out. For example, if we have a hostile thought about a person and then that person has an accident, most of us fiercely reject the idea that we might have helped cause the misfortune.[6] In fact, most of us won't even allow ourselves to entertain this possibility. The responsibility—for what Freud called "the omnipotence of thought"—is simply too intimidating. But the great spiritualist mediums easily avoided that concern. From their point of view, they didn't produce the phenomena they seemed to channel. So although that prevented them from taking direct responsibility for salutary effects occurring during or after the séance, it also absolved them of responsibility for anything undesirable that might occur.

But perhaps the final key to the puzzle is this: in the early days of the Spiritualist movement, few people—including parapsychologists—took seriously the possibility that the physical phenomena of mediumship were produced psychokinetically by the living. Of course, many were ready to believe that those phenomena had been produced *fraudulently* by the living. But to the extent the phenomena were considered genuinely paranormal, most believed they were produced by departed spirits. That's one of the reasons séance phenomena gripped the public's imagination so deeply and so widely. But as the nineteenth century drew to a close, an interesting shift in belief had begun. More and more serious researchers turned their attention to mediumistic séances, and a growing number of them began to suspect that mediums produced their physical phenomena by PK. Gradually, that idea crept into the public consciousness as well, and at that point the mediums themselves couldn't ignore it, even if they didn't believe it. But this development affected the entire psychology of mediumship, and I think it did so in a way that was unfavorable to the production of large-scale physical effects.

By the beginning of the twentieth century, the suspicion that mediums psychokinetically caused their impressive physical phenomena was increasingly "in the air," and the mediums were fully aware of it. They knew that many of their sitters, probably all of their investigators, and a good portion of the world outside the hard-core spiritualist community took this belief seriously. And it wouldn't be surprising if this progressively prevalent secular attitude dampened the production of large-scale physical effects. It's unclear whether the reduction in physical phenomena should be attributed mostly to sitters' fears or to the mediums' own fear. But it's indisputable that as more and more people began to take seriously the possibility that mediums psychokinetically produced their physical phenomena, the phenomena dwindled in both magnitude and frequency. In the 1850s through '70s, D. D. Home produced staggeringly impressive physical effects, and the vast majority of Home's sitters and investigators believed or considered seriously that they were dealing with spirit-produced phenomena. However, turn-of-the-century mediums (for example, Eusapia Palladino) produced fewer and somewhat less dramatic phenomena, and almost none of their serious investigators thought they were studying possible manifestations of surviving spirits. This trend continued into the first decades of the twentieth century, by which time we find (for example) the medium Rudi Schneider, who produced small object movements under very careful conditions, but for experimenters who—from the start—believed that the phenomena (genuine or fraudulent) emanated from the subject.

More tellingly still, by the mid-twentieth century spiritualism had fizzled into a fringe movement. Reportedly, physical mediumship persisted minimally and very quietly in spiritualist enclaves. But as far as the general public was concerned, the only people purporting to produce paranormal physical effects were individuals who were not spiritists and who believed that *they* produced the phenomena. So when we look at the so-called PK superstars of the day (for example, Nina Kulagina, Felicia Parise),[7] we find something quite different from the performances of spiritualist mediums. First, the phenomena tend only to be small object movements. And second, the subjects sweat, strain, and generally agonize or exhaust themselves in order to produce their results. Now think about this from these subjects' point of view. They didn't attribute their results to anyone but themselves, and so they couldn't blame spirits for their failures or successes. Thus, they saw themselves as potentially responsible both for whatever they actually produced *and what they might produce* (possibly unconsciously). But then it's certainly convenient psychologically that they could apparently cause only very small effects. Since they had to work so hard to make a matchstick or a pill bottle move a few millimeters, they probably felt that they'd hemorrhage internally before they did anything really impressive. From their point of view, it would have been physically impossible—or at least fatal—to make a table levitate or produce a materialization.

So the heyday of spiritualism was a period where societal conditions in the West temporarily resembled those in cultures where mediumship and shamanism continue to this day. It was a period unusually, but apparently fragilely, conducive to the production of large-scale paranormal physical phenomena. And it may be a state of affairs we can never duplicate. In a sense, we've lost our innocence, and we may have no choice but to accept the fact that—in our culture at least—we may never be able to witness the sort of overt and impressive paranormal phenomena that had previously been so common. Serious researchers may have no choice but to visit other cultures to come even close.

2. Eyewitness Testimony

One of the common myths about physical mediumship is that it's nothing but deception taking place mostly in darkened séance rooms. We've already had a glimpse of why that's false, and I'll offer more details below. Another myth concerns the reliability of human testimony—in particular, that spectators are too liable to make mistakes, either in general, or at least under the conditions prevailing during séances. So one question many ask about séance reports is "Why should we trust what the witnesses tell us?" Well, suppose I were to say, why not? After all, we rely on observation and testimony all the time, often quite successfully. So even if we grant that eyewitness reports are fallible, it doesn't follow that they're unreliable to a very high degree, or simply too unreliable to be trusted in this context. But in that case, what reasonable and specific concerns might a skeptic raise about eyewitness accounts of physical mediumship?

Before answering that, it's important to note that observation reports are never absolutely (or categorically) acceptable. At best, they can only be *conditionally* acceptable. Granted, sometimes the conditions are clearly satisfied, and so some reports can be highly reliable. Nevertheless, several factors influence whether or not (or to what degree) we accept a particular observation claim. Probably the most important are: (a) the capabilities, condition, interests, and integrity of the observer, (b) the nature of the object/s allegedly observed, and (c) the means of observation and the conditions under which the observation occurred. When we evaluate reports of paranormal phenomena, we weight these factors differently in different cases. But in general, it matters: (a) whether the observers are trained, sober, honest, alert, calm, prone to exaggeration, subject to flights of imagination, blessed with good eyesight, and whether they have strong prior interests in observing carefully and accurately; (b) whether the objects are too small to see easily, whether they're easily mistaken for other things, or whether (like fairies, extraterrestrials, and unicorns) they're of a kind whose existence can't be taken for granted; and (c) whether the objects were observed at close range, with or without the aid of instruments, whether they were stationary or moving rapidly, whether the observation occurred under decent light, through a dirty window, amidst various distractions, etc.

Presumably, then, what's at issue here is not the integrity, in general, of observation and testimony; rather, it's whether (or to what extent) the best cases satisfy sensible conditions for reliability. So the specific question before us is: do we have good reasons for discounting or distrusting eyewitness reports in the strongest cases of physical mediumship? That is, do we have good reasons for thinking that the phenomena in these cases didn't occur as reported?

In my view, we don't. That's not to say it's unreasonable ever to question the reliability of human testimony in mediumistic settings. However, it takes only a little reflection and an acquaintance with the evidence to dispel those concerns, at least for the best cases. Of course, the topic of eyewitness testimony is huge, interesting, and multifaceted, and we clearly can't examine all its nooks and crannies here. But for present purposes, a quick review of some major points will suffice.[8]

Perhaps the most familiar skeptical argument in this context is that the reports in question are examples of biased testimony. That is, witnesses of paranormal physical phenomena—mediumistic or otherwise—are predisposed to see either miraculous things generally, or certain paranormal phenomena in particular. But in that case (so the argument goes), they're likely to be guilty either of motivated misperception or outright fabrication.

Initially at least, this *Argument from Human Bias* might seem perfectly reasonable. After all, there's no doubt that some people misperceive or lie, and there's also no doubt that their predispositions might be one reason for these lapses. Nevertheless, this argument turns out on closer inspection to be remarkably flimsy, for several reasons.

First, even if witnesses were biased to experience paranormal physical phenomena, that wouldn't explain why independent reports agree on peculiar details. For example, one of the most fascinating features of the poltergeist literature is that people of dissimilar backgrounds and cultures, in the absence of any easily accessible literature on the subject (and sometimes in the absence of any literature at all), report the same very strange types of poltergeist disturbance.[9] These include the "raining" of stones or excrement inside a house, the slow and gentle movement of transported objects, and the intense heat of apparent apports. There's no reason to think that, of all the poltergeist phenomena observers might have expected or thought to occur, these would be among the first to spring to mind. But to my knowledge, no proponent of the Argument from Human Bias has developed a psychological theory (much less a credible theory) explaining how people could be biased to make these specific reports.

Second, an argument from bias could be used to undermine virtually every scientific report requiring instrument readings and ordinary human observation. After all, it's not just parapsychologists and "plain folk" who have strong beliefs, desires, and predispositions about how the universe works. Presumably, mainstream scientists have at least as much at stake and at least as many reasons for perceptual biases as do witnesses of the paranormal. They might even have more, considering how success in the lab can make or break their careers, especially when their research is novel and potentially groundbreaking.

Third (and even more important), like the Argument from Technology, the Argument from Human Bias is double-edged. Obviously, biases cut two ways, against reports by the credulous *and* the incredulous. So if a bias in favor of psi phenomena might lead people to misperceive or to lie, so might biases against psi phenomena. And those negative biases are arguably at least as prevalent—and certainly sometimes as fanatical—as those in favor of the paranormal. Anyone who thinks otherwise simply hasn't been paying attention. In fact, the history of parapsychology chronicles some remarkable examples of dishonest testimony and other reprehensible behavior on the part of skeptics.[10] These include subsequently discredited reports that certain séance phenomena failed to occur. So, we adopt an indefensible double standard if we distrust only testimony in favor of the paranormal.

Fourth, the only way to make the Argument from Human Bias with a straight face and a clear conscience is from a position of benign (rather than willful) ignorance regarding the data. It's obvious that many who investigate the paranormal are motivated primarily by curiosity and the need to know (whatever the outcome). In fact, in some of the best cases, witnesses of mediumistic phenomena have clearly been biased *against* the reported phenomena. One of the most compelling examples of this comes from the 1908 Naples sittings with Eusapia Palladino, described later in this chapter.[11]

Fifth, although many observers may be *open* to the possibility of psychic phenomena, that's not the same as being biased in their favor. For example, one can be open to the possibility of a phenomenon (say, alien visitations) while thinking that its actual occurrence is highly improbable. In fact, one can be open to the possibility of a phenomenon and also biased against observing it. For instance, poltergeist victims often had the prior belief that although the phenomena were possible, such things would never happen to *them*. That's similar to the way parents can be blinded to drug use among their children. Even when they concede that it's not literally impossible that their children use drugs, they might also feel strongly that it's something that happens only in other families.

Sixth, the possibility of motivated misperception increases as conditions of observation deteriorate. But in the best cases—again, the ones that matter—phenomena were observed collectively, near at hand, in good light, with clear heads, and with ample opportunity to examine them while they occurred. The cases described below obviously fall into this category. It's irrelevant to point out, as critics often do, that witnesses give inaccurate reports concerning small-scale, fleeting phenomena thoroughly under the control of the medium, and from séances conducted in near or total darkness.

But (I hear you cry), we know from so-called staged incident experiments that people can be guilty of outright malobservation. In these studies, subjects are presented with an unexpected and carefully prearranged confrontation or dispute. Later, when questioned about the incident, it turns out they often failed to observe what happened, and sometimes they report things that never occurred. However, these results are irrelevant to the most impressive cases of physical mediumship. For one thing, the magnitude of error demonstrated in staged incidents (while undoubtedly important for determining guilt or innocence in a court of law) is much smaller than what's required to explain away the best evidence from mediumship. But more important, whereas staged incidents encourage malobservation and misreporting, the best mediumistic cases were actually *conducive* to accurate eyewitness testimony. In those latter cases, observers were not taken by surprise; they often knew in advance what to look for (including what sort of deception to look for); lighting was good; and the phenomena often lingered long enough to permit sustained and repeated observation and hands-on inspection.

Similar considerations apply to the skeptical argument that because memory is notoriously unreliable, witnesses are simply liable to forget or misremember. For one thing, much of the best testimony from mediumistic cases was written at the time or soon thereafter. In fact, in the Palladino case observations were sometimes dictated on the spot to a nearby stenographer. Furthermore, much of the scientific evidence for memory loss concerns experiments with boring or very ordinary material (e.g., dull stories or nonsense syllables). For those with no faith in common sense (or those who think the government needs to finance large research grants to confirm what any sensible person already knew), evidence also confirms the commonsense observation that people tend to remember dramatic, interesting, and relevant events, and that those memories change or fade very little over time. Perhaps it's ironic that one of the best-known critics of eyewitness testimony, Elizabeth Loftus, cites experimental confirmation in support of that position and also approvingly cites D. S. Gardner's claim that:

> The extraordinary, colorful, novel, unusual, and interesting scenes attract our attention and hold our interest, both attention and interest being important aids to memory. The opposite of this principle is inversely true—routine, commonplace and insignificant circumstances are rarely remembered as specific incidents.[12]

Loftus also cites experimental support for the commonsense observation that memory reports are more reliable when the perceived events or objects are observed repeatedly or for extended periods.[13]

At this point, critics sometimes make desperate last-ditch appeals to the possibility of collective hypnosis or mass hallucination. (Significantly, however, the smartest and best-informed skeptics usually avoid this line altogether.) Here, too, there are plenty of issues worth discussing, many of which I've examined in more depth elsewhere.[14] For now, I'll just mention a few salient points. First, regarding hypnosis: there simply is no evidence that the appropriate kind of mass hypnosis has ever occurred—that is, inducing people to issue the same or concordant observational reports in conditions widely recognized as being unfavorable to hypnosis, and despite the well-known and great variability in human hypnotic susceptibility. Also, considering the amount of good evidence, *from different mediums*, proponents of this view would have to explain the sheer multiplicity of apparently untrained but prodigiously gifted mesmerists, all of whom were mysteriously able to do what no one has ever explicitly demonstrated—that is, to transcend the variations in human hypnotic susceptibility and induce collective and concordant experiences in unselected subjects, many of whom were taking specific precautions against suggestion. In fact, if a medium could, through suggestion, get different people simultaneously to experience and report the same phenomena, and also do this under conditions unfavorable to suggestion, arguably that ability would be as paranormal as what it's supposed to explain away. In fact, it looks suspiciously like telepathic influence. Moreover, the hypothesis of collective hypnosis is difficult to square with the permanent physical records of the reported phenomena—for example, mechanically recorded measurements, or broken heavy tables shattered from descending too rapidly from previously levitated positions.

The second hypothesis, of collective hallucination, is simply ridiculous. It can't even remotely account for the *continued* success under good conditions, and often for many years, of mediums like Home and Palladino. Since witnesses weren't engaged in something like mushroom rituals, there would have to be a lot of spontaneous hallucinating going on, over many decades, remarkably resulting in people having the same or similar non-veridical experiences. Besides, this hypothesis fails to account for the causal relevance of the medium's presence. If the medium had nothing to do with witnesses' allegedly false observational reports, why were they hallucinating in the first place? But if the medium was responsible, then (since mediums weren't dispensing hallucinogens) it looks like this hypothesis is really just one of collective hypnosis, which we've seen is clearly inadequate to the facts.

3. D. D. Home (1833–1886)

I must emphasize again that, in order to evaluate fairly the spiritualistic evidence for large-scale PK, the cases that count are the ones most difficult to explain away. It's cheap and easy to dismiss the evidence altogether by focusing only on the most poorly documented or obviously fraudulent cases. Unfortunately, critics often do this as a matter of course.[15] Obviously, it's interesting, sometimes illuminating, but ultimately irrelevant that weak and fraudulent cases litter the history of spiritualism. But if we want to know whether spiritualism's heyday provided evidence for genuinely paranormal phenomena, the cases that matter are the best ones—cases for which the testimony is clear and compelling and for which allegations of fraud seem preposterous. And despite what some critics like to suggest, this interesting period contains a decent number of such cases.

Of those cases, Home's is arguably the strongest. In fact, it's so strong that the prominent critics, Trevor Hall and Ruth Brandon, apparently could do no better than use shabby forms of argumentation in order to discount it. For example, they resort to irrelevant innuendos about Home's character (e.g., whether he was homosexual), and they ignore the strongest pieces of evidence (e.g., experiments conducted under good conditions for critical investigators) and attack admittedly weak reports of informal séances conducted for hard-core spiritualists. The tone and substantial bibliographies of these books might deceive the unwary into thinking that they're both honest and thorough. But many won't realize how incomplete the bibliographies really are and how the authors focus exclusively on insignificant detail. In my view, these works are to respectable research what tabloids are to serious journalism.[16]

The case of D. D. Home is very rich and merits much more attention than I can give it here. One reason it's so good is that Home's mediumship lasted almost twenty-five years, and during that time he was never detected in fraud, despite very careful conditions imposed by many of his investigators. Moreover, Home often produced phenomena in séances held at the spur of the moment and in locations he had never before visited. So in those instances it's obvious that Home didn't know beforehand where he would need to produce phenomena, and accordingly it's clear that he had no opportunity to make the sorts of preparations needed to arrange large-scale effects in advance. That makes it especially intriguing and impressive to read, for example, that as Home entered a location for the first time, the large bookcase at the other end of the room started moving toward him. In general, the objects moved during those séances (tables, bookcases, pianos, and personal items belonging to sitters) were not props Home carried from place to place, or things to which he had access prior to the séance.

Of course, some claimed that Home cheated. But all those allegations were second or thirdhand, and none have ever been substantiated. In fact, it seems as if these allegations were simply cries of outrage that the phenomena couldn't possibly have been genuine. Moreover, considering the technological limitations of the period, it's often amusing to read the contrived attempts to explain how Home managed his alleged tricks. For example, Frank Podmore was perhaps Home's most acute and persistent critic, and he could do no better than to suggest that Home used thin and nearly invisible horsehair threads to move massive pieces of furniture at a distance.

Eventually—and reluctantly—Podmore conceded that Home's phenomena couldn't be accounted for as magic tricks. So he fell back on the different, but equally inadequate hypothesis noted earlier—namely, that Home hypnotized all his sitters to experience the same effect.[17] Perhaps we can forgive Podmore for not realizing that people differ markedly in their degree of hypnotizability and that as a result, his proposal was completely incredible. Individual differences in hypnotizability weren't well-documented until many years later.[18]

Another reason the case of Home is so difficult to discount is that he had an enormous repertoire of impressive phenomena. So if skeptics hope to explain the case away, they must account for a wide range of effects, many of which happened in quick succession (and sometimes even simultaneously)—again, often under conditions in which the effects could easily have been detected as tricks. Home's phenomena included knocking sounds (raps), lights, voices, music, and odors detected throughout the séance room, and in the absence of any visible object that might have produced them—remember, this all happened in the 1860s through 1880s. Other, and even more dramatic effects, include:

- The movement and complete levitation of large objects, including tables (sometimes with several people on top) and pianos.
- When tables moved or tilted sharply, objects on the table would remain in place. Sometimes objects would alternately move and remain still in response to sitters' commands.
- On command, objects would become heavier or lighter. William Crookes tested this phenomenon instrumentally. But before that, it was customary for objects (such as tables) to become too heavy to lift or tilt, or simply more difficult to move than before.
- Partially or fully materialized forms would appear in various parts of the room.
- Sitters would feel pulls, pinches, or other sorts of touches, even when the hands of medium and sitters were all visible above the table.
- Earthquake effects. The entire room and its contents would rock or tremble.
- Supple, solid, warm, and mobile materialized hands, of different sizes, shapes, and colors, ending at the wrist, would carry objects, shake hands with the sitters, and then dissolve or melt in their grasp.
- An accordion, guitar, or other musical instrument would play either untouched (sometimes while levitated in good light) or while handled in a

way that would ordinarily prevent a musical performance (e.g., holding the accordion only at the end away from the keys).

• The handling of hot coals and the transfer of incombustibility to other persons and objects.

Home's phenomena were examined extensively in the U.S. and in Europe, and I strongly recommend reading the many clear—and clear-headed—eye-witness accounts. That's undoubtedly the best way to appreciate the evidential weight of this case—in particular, the full range of conditions under which Home's phenomena reportedly occurred, and the length of time during which alleged frauds would have gone undetected, despite careful efforts to expose or prevent them. But for now, a few examples will have to suffice.[19]

A frequently quoted account from early in Home's career comes from sittings held in 1852 at the home of Rufus Elmer in Springfield, Massachusetts. Several distinguished guests attended, including poet William Cullen Bryant and Prof. David A. Wells of Harvard. Eventually, they published the following signed statement.[20]

> The undersigned . . . bear testimony to the occurrence of the following facts, which we severally witnessed at the house of Rufus Elmer, in Springfield . . .
>
> 1. The table was moved in every possible direction, and with great force, when we could not perceive any cause of motion.
> 2. It (the table) was forced against each one of us so powerfully as to move us from our positions—together with the chairs we occupied—in all, several feet.
> 3. Mr. Wells and Mr. Edwards took hold of the table in such a manner as to exert their strength to the best advantage, but found the invisible power, exercised in an opposite direction, to be quite equal to their utmost efforts.[21]
> 4. In two instances, at least, while the hands of all the members of the circle were placed on the top of the table—and while no visible power was employed to raise the table, or otherwise move it from its position—it was seen to rise clear of the floor, and to float in the atmosphere for several seconds, as if sustained by some denser medium than air.
> 5. Mr. Wells seated himself on the table, which was rocked for some time with great violence, and at length, it poised itself on the two legs, and remained in this positions for some thirty seconds, when no other person was in contact with it.

6. Three persons, Messrs. Wells, Bliss and Edwards assumed positions on the table at the same time, and while thus seated, the table was moved in various directions.

7. Occasionally we were made conscious of the occurrence of a powerful shock, which produced a vibratory motion of the floor of the apartment in which we were seated—it seemed like the motion occasioned by distant thunder or the firing of ordnance far away—causing the table, chairs, and other inanimate objects, and all of us to tremble in such a manner that the effects were both seen and felt.

8. In the whole exhibition, which was far more diversified than the foregoing specification would indicate, we were constrained to admit that there was an almost constant manifestation of some intelligence which seemed, at least, to be independent of the circle.

9. In conclusion, we may observe, that Mr. D. D. Home, frequently urged us to hold his hands and feet. During these occurrences the room was well lighted, the lamp was frequently placed on and under the table, and every possible opportunity was afforded us for the closest inspection, and we admit this one emphatic declaration: *We know that we were not imposed upon nor deceived.*

Wm. Bryant
B.K. Bliss
Wm. Edwards
David A. Wells

This is a typical Home report in several crucial respects. The phenomena were produced in decent light; they lingered long enough for witnesses to inspect them *while they occurred*; Home invited sitters to control him and to examine the séance table; and of course, the phenomena involved the movement of large objects under conditions not dictated or controlled by the medium. That last point is perhaps especially significant. Whereas stage magicians can produce impressive effects under circumstances they prescribe and manipulate, Home was frequently a passive spectator, or at the very least he willingly submitted to test conditions specified and verified by his investigators.

Several prime examples of this come from experiments conducted by the renowned physicist, William Crookes.[22] Crookes devised ingenious, fraud-unfriendly methods for testing and mechanically recording Home's ability to alter the weight of objects. He also contrived a clever protocol for examining one of Home's most spectacular phenomena. As I noted above,

Home reportedly made accordions play either untouched (sometimes while levitating) or while held at the end away from the keys. However, Home evidently preferred to make accordions play *under* the séance table. He apparently had his own ideas about how spirits made the phenomena occur, and he claimed the "power" was strongest under the table. Admittedly, this sounds suspicious, at least at first glance. But Crookes realized that he could still test the phenomenon while respecting Home's avowed belief system.

First, Crookes purchased a new accordion for the occasion, and Home saw it for the first time when the experiment began. Clearly, the test instrument wasn't a prop prepared in advance by Home. Next, Crookes went to Home's apartment and watched him change clothes. That enabled him to determine that Home hadn't concealed some device that would allow him to manipulate the accordion surreptitiously (although it's unclear what sort of hidden—or even overt—contraption in 1871 would have been able to produce the relevant effects). Crookes then brought Home to his house, where he had prepared a wooden cage, wound with insulated copper wire and netted together with string. The cage fit under Crookes's dining table, and the accordion was placed inside it. There was enough space between the cage and the table for Home to reach in and hold the accordion at the end away from the keys. But there wasn't enough space for Home to reach in further and touch or manipulate the keys. Furthermore, Home couldn't operate the accordion with his feet, because the cage rested on the floor. Besides, Home had boots on, and nine observers were keeping an eye on him, one of them eventually located under the table with a lamp. So it would have been obvious if Home had removed his boots and attempted to move or play the accordion with his feet. Home sat beside the table, holding the accordion at the end away from the keys with the thumb and middle finger of one hand. His other hand rested on top of the table.

Crookes describes what then happened.

> ... the cage being drawn from under the table so as just to allow the accordion to be pushed in with its keys downwards, it was pushed back as close as Mr. Home's arm would permit, but without hiding his hand from those next to him. Very soon the accordion was seen by those on each side to be waving about in a somewhat curious manner; then sounds came from it, and finally several notes were played in succession. While this was going on, my assistant went under the table, and reported that the accordion was expanding and contracting; at the same

FIGURE 2.1

time it was seen that the hand of Mr. Home by which it was held was quite still, his other hand resting on the table.[23]

Then, while Home's feet were

being held by those next him, and his other hand resting on the table, we heard distinct and separate notes sounded in succession, and then a simple air was played. As such a result could only have been produced by the various keys of the instrument being acted upon in harmonious succession, this was considered by those present to be a crucial experiment. But the sequel was still more striking, for Mr. Home then removed his hand altogether from the accordion, taking it quite out of the cage, and placed it in the hand of the person next to him. The instrument then continued to play, no person touching it and no hand being near it.[24]

Next, Crookes ran an electric current to the insulated copper wire around the cage. Then,

The accordion was now again taken without any visible touch from Mr. Home's hand, which he removed from it entirely and placed upon the table, where it was taken by the person next to him, and seen, as now

FIGURE 2.2

were both his hands, by all present. I and two of the others present saw the accordion distinctly floating about inside the cage with no visible support. This was repeated a second time, after a short interval. Mr. Home presently re-inserted his hand in the cage and again took hold of the accordion. It then commenced to play, at first, chords and runs, and afterwards a well-known sweet and plaintive melody, which it executed perfectly in a very beautiful manner. Whilst this tune was being played, I grasped Mr. Home's arm, below the elbow, and gently slid my hand down it until I touched the top of the accordion. He was not moving a muscle. His other hand was on the table, visible to all, and his feet were under the feet of those next to him.[25]

I consider Crookes's accordion-in-the-cage test to be one of the most spectacular and significant in the history of parapsychology. First, Crookes recognized that working with human subjects is like working with delicate equipment that can easily fall out of adjustment. Even under careful experimental conditions, his relationship with Home was supportive and not adversarial. Moreover, Crookes understood the importance of devising experimental controls that respected Home's distinctive psychology and minimized his discomfort. Home apparently felt strongly that the accordion phenomenon was most pronounced under the séance table, and so Crookes didn't force Home to produce the effect elsewhere. Second, given the technological limitations of the early 1870s, the accordion phenomenon would have been difficult enough to fake under conditions dictated by Home. But under those imposed by Crookes, it seems impossible. In fact, under those conditions, it's hard to see how it could be faked even today.

And incidentally, if a magician or self-styled skeptic claims this *can* be done, with an accordion never before seen and under conditions similar to those imposed by Crookes, don't simply take that person's word for it. Confidence in these matters is easier to feign than the actual phenomena. In cases as strong as this, the burden of proof is on the skeptic. So if a magician or someone else claims to be able to replicate Home's accordion phenomenon under conditions similar to those described above, the proper response is: put up or shut up. Not surprisingly, no skeptic has even tried to meet this challenge. In fact, several Victorian magicians claimed to be able to replicate Home's most puzzling manifestations, but they never made good on their boasts.

Interestingly, a recent book on Home by parapsychologist, magician, and historian Peter Lamont demonstrates another regrettable skeptical maneuver.[26] Lamont has for years refused to accept any of Home's phenomena as genuine instances of PK, usually citing the sorts of concerns we'd expect from a magician. But until recently, his remarks were confined to public lectures and relatively short published papers. However, Lamont's recent book on Home purports to provide a lengthy and detailed examination of Home's career and the evidence for his phenomena. In this work, Lamont takes an apparently more agnostic stand, but still cites an earlier paper as containing his reasons for not being convinced by any of the evidence. So it's worth asking: how does Lamont deal with Crookes's accordion test? How does he avoid presenting it as a compelling and pivotal piece of evidence, in the face of which skepticism and even agnosticism look like mere intellectual rigidity? The answer is that he describes it only very cursorily, leaving out some relevant details[27] and getting others wrong,[28] and then he barely discusses the experiment thereafter.

I find it especially interesting that Lamont omits and misrepresents some details of this experiment and its setup, especially since he purports to write with an historian's obsessive care and respect for details. These might appear to be relatively innocent oversights or bits of carelessness— but why would they occur in connection with what is obviously one of the most important experiments in Home's career (arguably *the* most important experiment)? To me, it gives the appearance of avoidance behavior, of not wanting to look squarely at the material that matters most. Perhaps, in fact, it's a not-too-subtle example of the easily avoidable errors and misjudgments that often indicate resistance to and fear of psi.[29] Significantly, as in other (and more overtly tawdry) criticisms of Home, Lamont spends a disproportionate amount of time discussing poorly documented reports, such as Home's alleged levitation out the window of Ashley House.[30] This is not the first time an historian's treatment of parapsychology reminds me of Herodotus's comment: "Very few things happen at the right time, and the rest do not happen at all. A conscientious historian will correct these defects."

4. Eusapia Palladino (1854–1918)

The case of Eusapia Palladino is probably at least as important as that of Home, and I'd say it's equally evidential. But ironically, one of the reasons it's so good is that Eusapia had been caught cheating. She even admitted she'd occasionally cheat if given the chance. Ultimately, however, this resulted in Eusapia's being tested successfully under conditions of unprecedented rigor.

In many respects, Eusapia's case differs strikingly from Home's. Home was a cultured gentleman who could hobnob with European royalty; Eusapia was a coarse and illiterate Italian peasant. Home's phenomena were extremely dramatic, richly varied, and (when appropriate, as in the case of performances on musical instruments) refined; Eusapia's phenomena were less dramatic than those of other mediums of the period and also comparatively crude (for example, nothing more than mere sounds ever issued from musical instruments). Home reportedly produced materialized hands in such great and lifelike detail (including characteristic deformities) that séance participants would identify the hands' former owners; Eusapia's materialized hands were considerably more nondescript, often merely knobby or stalk-like objects. Home would give séances anywhere, at the drop of a hat, and he usually invited sitters to confirm that he wasn't cheating; Eusapia frequently insisted on séance conditions that were at least superficially suspicious (for example, the use of a "cabinet"—or drawn curtain—behind her, and also dim light and poor control of hands and feet), and sometimes she cheated.

Naturally, critics made a great deal of noise about Eusapia's suspicious behavior and outright cheating, arguing that all the evidence from her case was therefore worthless. The British Society for Psychical Research (SPR) even generalized that response into a kind of unofficial policy: to ignore all the phenomena of any medium ever caught cheating. However, in my view, that's a foolish overreaction. The crucial issue is not whether there are instances in which the medium cheated, but whether there are instances in which the evidence is strong that no cheating occurred. And in that respect, Eusapia's case is exceptionally good.

Granted, Eusapia's case isn't uniformly good, and to some extent it's perfectly appropriate to regard it with suspicion. But it's a serious mistake to dismiss it altogether, and critics easily made that mistake by ignoring several crucial facts about Eusapia's mediumship. First, Eusapia's tricks were simplistic and clumsy; they were easily detectable and controllable by competent observers. That's precisely why she was caught cheating. Also, Eusapia clearly tended to cheat when she disliked her investigators and when controls were relaxed. Both happened fairly often. Many investigators treated Eusapia either disrespectfully, condescendingly, or simply with no sense of how to interact with someone they perceived as so common and vulgar. Some even intentionally loosened conditions hoping to lure Eusapia into cheating. However, Eusapia apparently understood the dynamics of these encounters. She may have been uneducated, but she wasn't stupid, and so (understandably) she often held her investigators in contempt. A vital fact to remember about Eusapia's case is that under the tightest experimental conditions imposed by her most seasoned, competent, and respectful investigators, Eusapia was never detected in cheating. In fact, under those conditions, her phenomena were often stronger than they were under looser test conditions.

Eusapia's career, like Home's, is extremely interesting and complex. But readers will have to look elsewhere for the many fascinating and often grubby details.[31] We need to focus here on what is undoubtedly the climax of the case—the 1908 series of sittings in Naples. Those séances led to the publication of a massive, graphically detailed account of eleven sessions with Eusapia, conducted by three very experienced researchers.[32] That report describes, play by play, what happened during the séances, and perhaps most important, it documents how the investigators were all reluctantly converted to a belief in the genuineness of Eusapia's phenomena.

But let's back up for a moment. The events leading to these sessions are a crucial part of the story; in a nutshell, this is what happened. Since the earliest days of the British SPR, many of its influential members had been reluctant to deal seriously with the physical phenomena of spiritualism. For one thing, Victorian sensibilities were generally bruised by the sensual and tactile immediacy of many physical phenomena, especially the spectacle of gooey ectoplasm flowing from a medium's nose, mouth, or vagina. In fact, proper investigation of some mediums seemed to require full cavity searches, but those were best left to the less squeamish investigators on the Continent. And for another, many continued to believe that mental medium-ship was simply a higher—that is, more spiritual and less carnal—form of psychic functioning. Moreover, the SPR stuck firmly to its unofficial policy of refusing to take seriously any medium who had ever been caught cheat-ing. Of course, Eusapia played right into these prejudices. Besides, many SPR members were simply uncomfortable with Eusapia as a person, irrespective of her phenomena and concerns about fraud. She was unattractive, vulgar, flagrantly and crassly sexual and seductive (often flinging herself into male sitters' laps), and as Alan Gauld wryly observed, "during the séance sitters' purses and other valuables were rather too liable to dematerialise."[33]

In response to enthusiastic reports throughout Europe of séances with Eusapia, the SPR arranged for their own series of sittings in Cambridge in 1895. The occasion was a disaster. Eusapia's investigators clearly didn't know how to relate to their subject and make her feel welcome and com-fortable. And Richard Hodgson, one of her principal investigators, even re-laxed test conditions to encourage her to cheat. Eusapia obliged, of course, and so the SPR was able to dismiss her mediumship and turn its attention back to more cultivated characters and lofty phenomena.

In the meantime, researchers on the Continent were outraged by the Cambridge fiasco. They refused to accept the Society's blanket condemna-tion of Eusapia, and in fact they continued to conduct successful experi-ments with her. The European investigators were convinced that Eusapia had been uncomfortable and unhappy in Cambridge, disliking the investi-gators, the climate, and the food. And they certainly objected to Hodgson's intentional relaxation of experimental controls. Eric Dingwall, a generally skeptical commentator on psychic investigations, agreed that the situation in Cambridge was unlikely to have yielded positive results. He wrote:

> it was inevitable that [Eusapia's] hosts and their intimates must have felt an antipathy towards her, however veiled it might have been by an icy politeness and attempts at friendliness.
>
> According to Mr. Myers and Mrs. Sidgwick, Eusapia seemed quite happy and at ease at Cambridge, although it seems to me that such is so unlikely to have been the case that any assertion to the contrary should be regarded with some suspicion.[34]

Eventually, the SPR felt pressured to respond, and so they assembled a team of their most experienced, highly skilled, and skeptical investigators to study Eusapia one more time, apparently with the aim of justifying the

Society's negative assessment of the medium. Indeed, it seems that the SPR officers and investigators all expected to find nothing but fraud when they tested Eusapia. The members of this team were the Hon. Everard Feilding, Hereward Carrington, and W. W. Baggally. Feilding had already detected numerous fraudulent mediums and claimed to be a complete skeptic. Carrington was an amateur magician who had recently published a book, three-fourths of which was devoted to the analysis of fraudulent mediumship.[35] And Baggally was a skilled conjuror who "claimed to have investigated almost every medium in Britain since Home without finding one who was genuine."[36]

Dingwall knew the members of this Fraud Squad (as Brian Inglis called it) very well, and he offered his enthusiastic endorsement of them.[37] In fact, it's hard to imagine how this trio of investigators could have been better qualified or better prepared for their tests of Eusapia. They knew in advance what her repertoire of phenomena was; they knew the standard methods by which magicians might try to produce similar effects; they knew how Eusapia had been caught cheating in the past and the methods by which she attempted to deceive her investigators; and they knew how to control the medium to prevent her from committing fraud. So they booked three adjoining hotel rooms in Naples and held their séances in the middle room, which they carefully inspected. That room was illuminated by several electric lights hanging from the ceiling, switchable to any of four preset levels of intensity. The investigators also recognized (as had Crookes) the value of respecting the medium's worldview as much as possible. So, since Eusapia seemed to believe strongly that she needed a "cabinet" in order to produce her phenomena, they prepared one by drawing a curtain across one corner of the room, near where Eusapia would sit. Naturally, they supplied their own table and objects to go inside the cabinet.

To avoid having to rely on their memory of what occurred, the investigators hired a stenographer to record their reported moment by moment controls, as well as whatever phenomena they witnessed. So when a phenomenon occurred, an experimenter would report it, and then each investigator would describe his control at the time. That enabled the Fraud Squad to produce an almost cinematically detailed account of the séances. Consider, for example, this brief excerpt from the ninth séance, held on December 13, 1908.

Medium's feet tied to rungs of chairs of controllers on each side of her, length of rope on left being 20 ins., on right 21½ ins. Hands tied to one another—distance apart 22 ins., also left hand tied to B.'s right, distance being 16½ ins.; medium's right hand tied to C.'s left, distance 18 ins.

10.12 p.m. Séance begins.

Light I [brightest light]

Tilts begin almost immediately.

F. Table tilts on the legs away from her.

10.13 p.m. Complete levitation of the table.

C. Her right hand resting on the table touching mine, my wrist being between hers and the edge of the table. Her right foot in contact with my right foot. I saw a clear space of about eight inches between her dress and the leg of the table.

B. Complete levitation of the table for a second time [during dictation of B.'s control. Dec. 14/08].

B. My right hand on both her knees. Her left foot touching my right foot.

10.14 p.m. Complete levitation for a third time.

B. Another complete levitation.

F. Both medium's hands completely on the top of the table touching C.'s and B.'s.

C. I can see a clear space of about 8 inches between her dress and the table leg all the way down.

B. My right hand on her two knees. My right foot against her left foot, and I can see between her left leg and the table leg.

10.16 p.m. Another complete levitation.

F. Her right hand off the table altogether, left hand on B.'s, pulling it upward and the table appeared to stick to it.

10.17 p.m. Another complete levitation of the table.

F. First of all a partial levitation, which lasted about ten seconds, then a complete levitation, off all four legs.

F. Her right hand touching the table, left hand on B.'s—She raised her right hand from the table and the table slid sideways in the air under B.'s hand.

B. My right hand across both her knees. My right knee against her left knee and my right foot against her left foot, and I see a clear space between her leg and the table leg.

C. Her right hand clenched (at first) on the table within three inches of my eyes. My left hand across her knees. Her right foot on my left foot. I can clearly see a space of at least six inches between her dress and the table leg, all the way down.

[*The light was sufficient to read small print by with comfort, at the further end of the room, the hands were always plainly visible and always situated so that it was clear that the table was not lifted by them. The extreme rapidity of the*

levitations made complete descriptions almost impossible, and it was decided
to confine the description of the control to the feet, the control of the hands be-
ing obvious to all and description rendered unnecessary. . . . F., Dec. 14/08][38]

Despite the rigid controls and good light, many impressive phenomena
occurred during the eleven séances. In fact, the table levitated completely so
many times that the experimenters eventually tired of that effect and asked
Eusapia to produce something else. Moreover, many impressive things happened even while experimenters virtually draped themselves all over Eusapia. Objects moved without being touched, a guitar was strummed in the
cabinet behind Eusapia, a table "walked" from the cabinet into the room,
and the experimenters felt various touches and other tactile phenomena.
Moreover, Eusapia willingly (probably enthusiastically) stripped for the investigators, so that they could confirm that she concealed no devices in her
clothing. After the séances had ended, Baggally itemized and counted all
the phenomena reported. He concluded, "Eusapia was not detected in fraud
in any one of the 470 phenomena that took place at the eleven seances."[39]

After a while, reading the moment by moment detailed descriptions of
those séances becomes fairly tedious, even though they're obviously important and even interesting. Far more riveting, however, are the reflections of
the investigators written after each session with Eusapia. They document,
with great candor, the intellectual struggle each investigator experienced
as he reluctantly came to believe that Eusapia's phenomena were genuine.
Skeptical accusations of favorable experimenter bias in this case would be
outrageous. The Fraud Squad came to Naples expecting to close the case on
Eusapia and demonstrate that previous investigators had been duped. But
unlike many of Eusapia's skeptical investigators, they knew how to commu-
nicate with the medium and they treated her with respect and genuine cor-
diality. So Eusapia felt no need to respond defensively or contemptuously.
She cooperated with the Fraud Squad and made it easy for them to obtain
clear and compelling evidence of macro-PK.

Interestingly, the conversion experiences of the investigators occurred
on two different schedules. Feilding and Carrington were the first to arrive
in Naples, and they conducted four séances before Baggally joined them.
By that time, Feilding and Carrington were well along on their psychological odyssey. They had already obtained excellent results with Eusapia and
had begun their gradual and grudging shift to a belief in the reality of PK.
So when Baggally arrived, Feilding and Carrington were already struggling
with, and apparently deeply shaken by, their inability to explain away the

phenomena they had witnessed. Baggally's participation in the fifth séance marked the beginning of the same struggle for him, and his comments after each of the final seven séances describe it vividly. In fact, the reader can study not simply a third and delayed version of the psychological drama of worldview change, but also the reactions to it of Feilding and Carrington. The Naples report, then, is a fascinating account both of paranormal phenomena and also the psychodynamics of cognitive dissonance and profound conceptual change. It's a document of great importance, integrity, and intellectual courage, and I strongly urge readers to check it out for themselves.[40]

5. Final Thoughts

One reason the above cases are important is that they provide a kind of gold standard for macro-PK investigations. At their best, they illustrate how much can be accomplished with a combination of experimental ingenuity and common sense. One of the standard questions facing psi researchers is: to what extent should we comply with the subject's wishes regarding test conditions? Ideally, investigators would prefer test conditions to be as bulletproof as possible, by eliminating every reasonable ground for suspicion and by guarding against every conceivable opportunity for fraud. The problem, though, is that if experimental controls are too rigid, test situations might diverge radically from those in which the subject feels comfortable and familiar. And in that case, they might strangulate or entirely snuff out the phenomena. On the other hand, experimenters can't allow subjects simply to dictate conditions, because that might increase opportunities for fraud to an intolerable degree. Apparently, the common wisdom is that the latter danger is the more serious of the two, and maybe that's one reason why so few today accept the challenge of macro-PK investigations. They feel that the only cases in which PK can be investigated with any rigor are standard laboratory quantitative tests with random generators.

But it seems to me that when you're dealing with subjects of the caliber of Home and Palladino, this cautious approach merely reveals the limitations of the experimenters. For example, Crookes and the members of the Fraud Squad (among others) demonstrated how it's possible to obtain compelling evidence when investigators are both resourceful and sensitive to the needs and idiosyncrasies of their subjects. Crookes knew that Home preferred to have his accordions move under the séance table, and his strategies for working around that preference were both very clever and very "clean." It's no surprise that magicians have never duplicated the phenomenon under the same conditions imposed by Crookes. Similarly, Fielding and his team struck an ideal balance with Eusapia. Regarding her preference for a cabinet and the occasional need to touch it, Fielding wrote:

> . . . I cannot explain why she wished to do these things, any more than I can explain many other items in her procedure, such as why she should wish to have a table, or why she should require a curtain at all. I find, in talking with friends, that when I mention the curtain, they inevitably say, "Ah, a curtain! Why a curtain? What a suspicious fact!" I agree that it may be suspicious, but it is not necessarily so. It is suspicious when used by a materializing medium who goes behind it, and, when a "spirit" comes out, refuses to allow spectators to ascertain whether he is himself still there. But in Eusapia's case, where she sits outside it, I cannot see that, given certain obvious precautions, it is necessarily suspicious. She says it helps to "concentrate the force." Perhaps it does. I do not know what the "force" is, nor what it requires to "concentrate" it. Nor does anyone else. To a person ignorant of photography it is possible that the use by the photographer of a black cloth over his head would be suspicious. In dealing with an unknown force one can only judge empirically of the utility of certain conditions. That the curtain does have some bearing on the phenomena is clear. Eusapia appears to be *en rapport* with something within. And she constantly seems to experience the necessity of establishing this *rapport* by momentary contact with the curtain or by enveloping the table or part of herself in its folds. We never perceived, however, that the phenomena which followed this action had any normal relation to it whatever.[41]

The moral of these successful investigations seems clear enough: respect the subject's preferences, beliefs, and personality quirks as much as possible without compromising experimental caution. Usually, there's some sensitive and imaginative way of doing this. Besides, it may be the only method for learning something useful about the dynamics and perhaps even the practical limits of PK. In fact, it seems obviously to parallel the optimal strategies for studying other forms of human behavior or performance. We can't expect to evaluate a person's ability to play tennis under circumstances less challenging than real game conditions, or by forcing players to use a racquet or shoes of a kind they dislike. It would be counterproductive to study flirtatiousness, optimism, or diplomatic skills in anything but the kind of setting in which those characteristics or skills are actually manifested. Similarly, it seems counterproductive to require a PK subject to depart radically from standard operating procedures. In fact, history seems repeatedly to bear this out, and the heyday of physical mediumship provides a wealth of examples from a variety of cases.

Naturally, the cases of D. D. Home and Eusapia Palladino are just the tip of the iceberg. The careers of other mediums of the period also deserve attention. They add substantially to the body of decent-to-excellent evidence for PK, and they help dispel many of the lingering myths about mediumistic investigations. We can see clearly from the best cases that observers were not blinded by credulity, that they were often methodologically quite sophisticated and imaginative, that conditions of observations were frequently excellent and not conducive to malobservation, and (given the technological limitations of the period) that the most dramatic phenomena are especially difficult to explain away as due to fraud. The good cases also highlight a number of important theoretical and methodological issues—for example, whether we can specify any limits at all to the scope and refinement of PK, and the extent to which the investigators' belief systems can influence the form of mediumistic phenomena.

But for now, this brief survey will do. It provides a standard by which we can measure the significance of current cases, and it provides valuable clues about how the range of PK effects can be shaped by prevailing social and cultural norms or trends.

So we can return now to my own case investigations, and in the next chapter we'll consider an alleged PK superstar some have compared favorably to Home. We'll see very quickly that this comparison is questionable on several counts.

Joe Nuzum: Subject from Hell

1. Introduction

We've probably all heard the expression "have my people call your people." Usually, we associate that phrase with show business big shots. But some alleged psychic superstars also have their "people." In many cases they play the role of promoters or agents, and all too often they interfere with responsible research. Although they claim (plausibly) to represent and protect their client's interests, often enough they perpetuate an atmosphere of distrust and establish an adversarial relationship between investigators and their subjects. In fact, they may prevent investigators from having any useful direct contact with their subjects. Of course, that only fuels the suspicion that what the "psychic" does is nothing but an act. In other cases, however, an alleged psychic's people are merely passionate advocates (or groupies), individuals who are deeply impressed by what they believe are genuine and dramatic phenomena, and who sometimes want little more than to bask in the psychic's greatness. That might seem innocuous enough, but depending on how tenaciously advocates cling to the psychic, their enthusiasm and loyalty can also interfere with serious research.

Joe Nuzum had, and apparently continues to have, his people: primarily advocates (but at least one promoter) who staunchly insist Joe is a fantastic psychic. I learned of Joe and was introduced to him through his people. And because I was unable to pry those people away from Joe, the story I have to tell about him is equally a story about his entourage—and one person in particular, Alexander Imich.

In many ways Imich is a remarkable man. He was born in Poland at the dawn of the twentieth century, and the account he provides of his life[1] is a saga of frustrations, horrors, and surmounting great obstacles. According to Alex, although he hoped initially for a career as a sea captain, religious intolerance against Jews forced him to leave the maritime school in which he had enrolled. So he obtained a university degree in zoology, but anti-Semitism prevented him from securing an academic position. Alex then switched his field again, received his PhD in chemistry, and finally began earning a living as a chemist. His parents died in a World War II concentration camp, and eventually he emigrated to the US and settled in New York. Alex was in his 90s when I met him, and he had more energy and vitality than most people one-third his age. As I write this, Alex is 101 and still active.

Throughout his life Alex had been fascinated by psychic phenomena. Before moving to the US, he investigated apparently exceptional subjects and published a number of parapsychological research papers in European journals. Throughout his very active retirement in the US, he has continued to support psi research by means of direct funding for case investigations and also by sponsoring an annual prize for research essays.

I first met Alex when in 1994 he invited me to New York City to observe the phenomena of Ronnie Marcus, an Israeli PK claimant hoping, apparently, to replace Uri Geller as that nation's preeminent psychic. But as far as I was able to determine, Ronnie could produce absolutely nothing of interest when he was closely observed. In fact, during one videotaped session, he seemed clearly frustrated by having me and a few others watch him while he was in the vicinity of the test objects. This was consistent with the unfavorable reports (including allegations of documented cheating) I later received about Ronnie from investigators I trusted in Nevada and California.

However, what struck me most about that New York visit was the behavior of Alex Imich. Alex had been enthusiastic about Ronnie's PK abilities, and he wanted passionately to find a case of macro-PK that would convince even the most hardened skeptic. In fact, he was committed to pursuing the lofty—but I believe completely unrealistic—goal of carrying out a *conclusive demonstration* of PK, one that would convince the entire scientific community that PK was real. So he invited me as an observer to lend credibility to the proceedings and to help authenticate the phenomena. Alex knew I believed in the reality of PK—including macro-PK. He knew that I had observed it myself,[2] but that I was careful and critical and had written a tough-minded and sober book in defense of my position.[3] I was happy to help out, eager to see some more good phenomena, and ready to believe that Alex's enthusiasm was justified.

I spoke with Alex several times before making the trip, to make sure we agreed about what needed to be done. It seemed to me that Alex and I both realized the importance of careful documentation. After all, without it, Alex knew that he'd never attain his goal of convincing skeptics that PK exists. So I arrived in New York feeling that nothing more was required of me than keen observation. But what I saw, apart from Ronnie's inability to get results under merely sympathetic and casual—but continued—scrutiny, was how Alex failed repeatedly to watch Ronnie at just those times when his vigilance was most essential. Over and over, as Ronnie approached the test objects on the table before him, Alex would turn his head away and start talking to one of his invited guests.

I was shocked by this, and I naturally wondered whether Alex had been similarly careless on the occasions when Ronnie had impressed him. After this session was over, I couldn't contain myself. I said to Alex, "You know, you don't seem to be a very careful observer." I was ready for—and expecting—a fight. But to my surprise, Alex conceded, somewhat sheepishly, "I know." Unfortunately, however—as this chapter and chapter 4 will reveal—that insight was short-lived.

At any rate, when Alex later told me about the next alleged PK superstar he found promising, Joe (Joey) Nuzum, I couldn't help but harbor some doubts. I was especially wary because Alex was making extravagant claims about Joey's psychic skills. He maintained that Nuzum was as great as the best physical mediums from the heyday of spiritualism. If true, that *would* be something, since (as we considered briefly in the previous chapter) the best mediums of that era produced large-scale phenomena under very well-controlled conditions.[4] Still, I knew also that Nuzum had impressed Bert Schwarz, and it was Bert who had brought Katie to my attention. I was certain Katie was the real deal, and so I was ready to believe that Joey might be as well.

2. Warning Signs

As I soon discovered, however, there were plenty of reasons to wonder why even Bert was so enthusiastic about Joey. First, Bert knew that Nuzum was a professional magician. In his earliest published account of his work with

Joey, he wrote: "[Nuzum] is . . . highly skilled in escapes, illusions, and sleight of hand."[5] Second, despite some intriguing apparent ESP and small object movements, Bert's initial report on Joey offered little (arguably no) evidence that Joey was able to produce anything that couldn't be explained as close-up magic aided by misdirection. Many of the reported effects took place away from where the experimenters had been looking, and Bert's account offered no specific assurance that conditions of observation in these cases were especially tight. The effects in all cases were quite small, and certainly they were not of the sort that would support Alex Imich's extreme claims. And most of the time, Nuzum failed to produce phenomena under conditions dictated by Bert. Bert explained Joey's repeated failures as the result of Nuzum's fragile psyche. But even if there is some truth to that claim, the fact remains that if Bert hoped to establish the reality of Joey's PK, his report is underwhelming at best.

Bert's second detailed report of work with Joey is arguably more tantalizing than its predecessor, but it's still far from convincing. It presented the results of attempts by Nuzum to link various sorts of objects—for example, rubber bands, and Bert's father's engraved fraternity ring with a brass nut. Admittedly, some of what Bert reported suggested that Joey deserved a closer look. But Bert also acknowledged that Nuzum produced his results under "apparent, although limited control."[6]

Bert's third report on Joey offered much less in the way of promising evidence. The article deals with Nuzum's alleged ability to ignite substances by "spontaneous combustion." But most of what Bert reported can't be regarded as even remotely evidential. He relied primarily on descriptions over the phone from Joey and others about what Joey had allegedly accomplished. The few reported effects that Bert personally observed were, again, produced either outside his field of vision or under conditions of no control whatsoever. For example, Bert noted that after he took Joey and his wife to the airport, he discovered some charred tissues in a box of Kleenex back in his office. In fact, looking at the totality of Bert's reports on Joey, it's completely clear that many more phenomena seemed to occur in Bert's absence than in his presence.

In the meantime, Bert sent me videotapes of Nuzum producing various effects. These tapes were all made by Nuzum, and to me they offered additional grounds for concern and suspicion. Dean Radin had also seen tapes of Joey, and we both agreed that what he was doing looked like magic. Considering Joey's history and ongoing activity as a performing magician, that reaction still strikes me as completely warranted. Dean was especially concerned about some suspicious hand movements and what appeared to him to be "misdirection behavior (i.e., trying to influence something at point A, and then suddenly 'noticing' that something at point B is moving)."[7] I had observed this as well in the tapes provided by Bert. I noticed also that when Joey ostensibly made a spoon break in half and then fused the parts back together, he never showed a full view of both parts of the spoon. One hand could easily have hidden a half spoon, and Joey never actually demonstrated clearly that the original spoon had been broken and then restored.

Nevertheless, I realized it was possible that Nuzum might have genuine PK ability even if many of his effects were conjuring tricks. He wouldn't have been the first PK claimant to supplement genuine phenomena with magic tricks—or to fall back on legerdemain when his "powers" failed him. And some of Joey's reported effects remained intriguing, even if the evidence in his favor was generally quite weak. So I remained open to investigating Joey for myself, and I was still cautiously hopeful that he might have real PK ability. I wrote to Dean that "after the Ronnie show, I'm hardly confident about Imich's assurances that Joey is the real thing. Still, just in case he is as good as some claim, I'd hate to miss out on it."

One other preliminary item needs to be mentioned. In November 1994 I learned that another parapsychologist friend, Stephan Schwartz, had arranged for Joey to come to his house and give a demonstration.[8] Stephan insisted he'd do this only if Joey allowed for reasonable conditions of observation. Joey and his wife arrived the afternoon prior to the scheduled filming of the session, and Stephan explained what his requirements would be. Joey claimed to be able to make a dollar bill rotate on a nail head. Stephan wanted to see the effect produced in a fish tank turned upside down and sealed to the table top with duct tape. Moreover, Joey wouldn't be able to enter the room with the fish tank until filming began, and he wouldn't be permitted to get within four feet of the tank. Stephan also requested to examine Joey's clothes and to watch him dress. But an hour after Joey left Stephan's house, Stephan received a phone call from his producer saying that Joey objected to having his clothes examined and to being watched while he dressed. The planned experiment was canceled.

Stephan realized that Joey's fundamentalist and conservative background might explain his apparent shyness over being observed in the nude. But Stephan also suspected that there was more to the story. After all, even if Joey's resistance to being observed in the nude is somewhat reasonable, using that excuse to cancel the experiment allowed him to avoid having his clothes examined. And as we'll soon see, there appear to be good reasons why Joey might have wanted to avoid that inspection—at least for the spinning dollar bill effect.

3. First Encounter

In November 1995 I traveled to New York to test Nuzum for myself. Alex and I had discussed what needed to be done, and with financial support both from Alex and the Parapsychology Foundation, I assembled a team to assist me. Alex and I had discussed the need for ensuring decent controls, especially in light of Alex's expressed desire to obtain indisputable proof of macro-PK. Alex was clear about wanting to document Joey's abilities in a way that would silence all skepticism. Moreover, he assured me that Joey also understood the importance of this and that he was more than ready to work under reasonable conditions of control, at least so long as his investigators were friendly and not merely debunkers. So it seemed to me initially that Alex, Joey, and I were all on the same page. I believed we all understood the importance of obtaining clean and controlled demonstrations of Joey's PK abilities, and I was under the impression that both Alex and Joey realized that investigators could be sympathetic, supportive, and careful, all at the same time.

The plan was to test Joey over two days, November 17 and 18. The first tests were held in the auditorium of the Blessed Sacrament School on West 70th Street. Three camcorder operators and I arrived there around 7 p.m. to inspect the room and set up the equipment. The auditorium is a large room with a small stage, and we set up our gear in the main part of the room. Alex arrived an hour later with Joey and Joey's wife, Sandra. Three other observers were also on hand, including Joanne McMahon, director of the library at the Parapsychology Foundation, and Michaeleen ("Mikki") Maher, parapsychologist and member of the psychology faculty at the New School for Social Research.[9]

Joey arrived with his own collapsible wooden table and a small aquarium tank purchased earlier that day by Alex. He told us immediately that he found the room uncomfortably bright. Sandra added that Joey is generally light sensitive and that he prefers dim lighting at home as well. So the video operators turned off the video lamps and shielded other lights with tape. There was still ample light to operate the cameras and to see what was going on.

I inspected the aquarium tank and then turned it upside down on Joey's table. Because Joey had proposed levitating paper currency under the inverted tank, Alex placed several five dollar bills underneath and I contributed four twenty dollar bills. And because Joey required certain music to put him in a PK-conducive mood, Alex had purchased a cassette boom box for the occasion. It took Joey a while to choose the tape he wanted, but finally he settled on some New Age music that Mikki appropriately described as ethereal. We then waited another five or ten minutes while Joey established the necessary level of concentration or trance. Finally, Joey approached the table and moved his hands slowly over the inverted fish tank.

But nothing seemed to happen to the money under the tank. So after several uneventful minutes, Joey stepped back and expressed his disappointment over the lack of PK activity. Then without explanation, he retrieved a small, ornate, sheathed Tibetan dagger. When I tried to examine it, Joey refused to let me touch it. He then suggested we try a different musical selection. After changing the tape in the boom box and once again preparing himself mentally, Joey approached the fish tank and held the sheathed dagger over it, pointing downward toward the money. Again, we could see no movement in the currency under the tank, and after several minutes Joey ended his effort and stepped back from the tank.

Despite the absence of any visible effect on the money inside the aquarium, Joey said he thought a change of some kind had nevertheless occurred. At his prompting, Alex and I examined the bills we had placed under the tank, but we found nothing unusual. Joey then suggested that deflected PK might have affected money elsewhere in the room. So we all looked inside our wallets, but nobody detected signs of anomalous changes in their money. After an extended break, Joey said that the room didn't feel right to him and that he didn't want to waste any more of our time. We decided instead to continue our tests the following day in what we hoped would be a more hospitable environment. Joey suggested that his hotel room would probably be PK-friendly.

Now I have to admit, that proposal set off my personal crap detector. I realized that this would almost certainly compromise the next round of tests, because it would prevent us from inspecting the room beforehand to certify that the location was "clean." Obviously, that precaution was especially important in light of Joey's activity as a performing magician. Even reasonable skeptics would want to be assured that the site hadn't been somehow rigged in advance. Furthermore, it's been clear since the early days of the Spiritualist movement that the evidence is strongest when it's gathered from locations controlled by the investigators.[10] But I saw no point in throwing in the towel and wasting the money spent to bring Joey and me to New York. I hoped we'd find some way to salvage the situation once we arrived at the hotel, and after all, I wanted Joey to feel comfortable. So I agreed to Joey's proposal, though I wasn't happy about it.

On the evening of November 18 I arrived at the Hotel Esplanade on West End Ave., along with videographer Karl Petry, Joanne McMahon, and Mikki Maher. And right away, I saw that we had a problem. One reason I had consented to this location the night before was that Joey had described his lodgings as his "room." Consequently, I was under the impression that the hotel site was a single room. But it turned out to be a two bedroom suite. That posed a problem because all the tests took place in the living room, and Joey wouldn't let us enter his bedroom, where he frequently retreated—to meditate, he said—before attempting any phenomena. So it was clear, right from the start, that we'd have trouble providing Alex with the conclusive documentation he claimed he wanted. Nevertheless, I still hoped we'd find a way to prevent the occasion from being a complete waste of time and money. I thought we could begin the proceedings informally, just to get the phenomena flowing, and then gradually tighten controls and end up with some good effects documented convincingly.

One main goal for the evening was to observe and record Joey's ability to make a dollar bill rotate both clockwise and counterclockwise on a spindle. Joey had assured us he could do this while the bill and spindle were enclosed in an inverted fish tank. But before we began any of our expected tests, Joey (who has trained in the martial arts) said he wanted to demonstrate a paranormal martial arts effect. He asked our videographer Karl (a tall, strong man) to try to choke him, and he indicated to Karl the martial arts choke hold he wanted him to use. Joey said he would try by paranormal means (presumably PK or telepathic influence) to release himself from the choke hold, and he assured Karl that he wouldn't be injured in any way. Joey then entered his bedroom for about fifteen minutes to meditate and prepare for the demonstration.

When Joey returned to the living room, Karl applied the choke hold as instructed. But Joey seemed unable to break free, and before long he staggered back, his face flushed red, and he slumped against a nearby wardrobe. Karl then released his grip and Joey sank to the floor. Because he seemed to be unconscious, Sandra rushed to his side and expressed her concern over this unexpected result. But shortly thereafter Joey opened his eyes, rose, and told us that although this had never happened before, he found the experience both interesting and pleasurable.

Karl later confided that while he held Joey in the choke hold, Joey struck his chest so strongly that it left a deep bruise. In his view, this would ordinarily have made an assailant release his grip. But Karl decided to hang on. So when Joey stepped backwards after striking Karl, Karl moved with him and maintained the choke hold. In Karl's view, Joey didn't really lose consciousness. He thought Joey pretended to pass out so that Karl would release him, thereby covering up his failure to break free by jabbing covertly at Karl's chest. Furthermore, Karl believed that Joey could easily have avoided this situation. In fact, they had a prearranged plan for ending the demonstration prematurely. Joey had told Karl earlier that if necessary he could signal his submission by touching Karl twice on his arm. But in Karl's view, although Joey had ample opportunity to do this, he was simply unwilling to admit defeat.

After recovering, Joey complained that Karl hadn't applied the choke hold properly, and he offered to try the demonstration once again. So Karl applied another choke hold—presumably correctly. But after a few seconds, Joey tapped on Karl's arm, indicating that he wanted to be released. Joey then apologized for the failure of his martial arts PK demonstration, which he insisted had gone smoothly on other occasions.

After this bizarre and apparently pointless exhibition, Joey said he'd attempt to rotate the dollar bill for us. He produced a large hat pin to use as a spindle, but he refused to let me examine it under the seemingly flimsy pretense that I might hurt myself. The pin was apparently glued inside a plastic crystal, which functioned as a platform that allowed the spindle to be placed upright on Joey's collapsible table. I folded a $10 bill lengthwise and balanced it on top of the spindle. Joey then picked up the bill, handled it for a few moments, and replaced it on the spindle. Although air currents within the room had caused the bill to rotate beforehand, the bill stopped moving once the fish tank was placed over it. Alex and I then secured the tank to the table with masking tape. We also determined that a vigorous waving of hands and paper grocery bags near the aquarium produced no movement in the dollar bill.

Again, Joey retreated to his bedroom to meditate. Sandra then inserted an audio cassette in the boom box, cranked up the volume, and began playing the rhythmic and trancelike music Joey had requested. When Joey finally emerged, he approached the tank and seemed to be in deep concentration as he waved his hands both above the tank and along its sides, several inches from its surface. After about ten minutes, and as the music from the boom box grew in intensity, the bill began slowly to move counterclockwise on the spindle. Joey followed these movements with his hands, and the bill completed several revolutions. Then, apparently with the assistance of Joey's hands, the bill began to move in the opposite (clockwise) direction. It then stopped briefly, continued moving clockwise again, and then it stopped once more. At that point Joey stepped back from the aquarium, indicating that the demonstration had ended.

After another break, Joey gathered up some inexpensive spoons and forks. He handed some of these to the observers and arranged several of the spoons on top of the still inverted fish tank. As he discussed various metal-bending techniques, he picked up one of the spoons and began to handle it. Then he replaced the spoon on the fish tank and went to make adjustments to the boom box. At that point I got up from my position on the sofa, rearranged the spoons on top of the tank, and added a fork to the flatware array. I was curious to see if this would alter Joey's spoon selection when he returned. But Joey noticed what I was doing and seemed troubled. So I asked him if he had a particular spoon he wanted to work with. Joey replied no, but when he returned to the table he picked up the same spoon he had fiddled with before. He then began to wave it rapidly up and down in the air, and with his hand covering most of the spoon's handle, Joey seemed to cause the spoon suddenly to bend. Joanne, Mikki, and I were seated in front of Joey on the living room sofa, and while Joey continued to stand in place holding the spoon, it looked to us as though the visible portion of the spoon just above his hand continued to bend for a few more seconds.

After Joey passed the bent spoon around for us to examine, Mikki lifted the inverted fish tank, removed the dollar bill from the spindle, and balanced the bent spoon atop the spindle. After moving back and forth rapidly for a while, the spoon eventually came to a rest. Joey said he liked the idea of using the bent spoon as a PK target, but he declined to try it.

So we chatted for a while. I assured Joey that his demonstrations had been very intriguing, but I reminded him that Alex was determined to get results under better controlled conditions. I said I hoped we could try again on another occasion, and Joey told me he'd be happy to visit New York again for further sessions. I then reiterated the importance of testing his abilities under careful but sympathetic controls, reminding him of Alex's wish to document his phenomena in a way that would silence all reasonable skepticism. Joey claimed he understood and said he also wanted to achieve this goal. Then after some more amiable conversation, Karl, Joanne, Mikki, and I left.

4. Follow-up

The four of us went to a nearby café to discuss the evening's events and compare notes. We all agreed that there had been inadequate controls of both the environment and the selection of targets. So although the rotating dollar bill had been interesting, we couldn't be certain what actually had gone on. Karl suggested that Joey might have employed some kind of static electricity. We agreed that when Joey went to his bedroom beforehand, ostensibly to meditate, he might have equipped himself with an electrical device of some sort. Moreover, Karl recalled that when Joey emerged from his bedroom, he heard an unusual and persistent electronic noise (or "static") over his headphones, which had been connected to a sensitive PZM microphone used for the taping. If Joey had been employing a concealed device to produce static charges, this is precisely what one would have expected.

Because none of us knew whether any static-producing devices existed that would have allowed Joey to rotate the dollar bill, I started asking around. The answers came quickly. It turns out that there are a number of readily available devices that magicians use to create static charges through their fingers. These can be concealed on one's body and activated surreptitiously (for example, triggered with the toe). They can also be used to make sparks fly from the magician's fingers. Significantly, both the rotating dollar bill and sparks-from-the-fingers are standard effects in Joey's shows for the public.

I obtained a catalog called *Amazing and Fascinating Devices*, on page 9 of which I found an ad for a device called a "Telekinetic Enhancer."[11] I also obtained a photocopy of the instructions for assembling and using this device. The manual claims that the TKE1 "gives the user 'apparent' psychic telekinetic and other strange bizarre powers." It is designed primarily "to cause motion without apparent contact" and (among many other things) "cause visual [sic] and audible sparks to emanate from the body at will." One of the principal effects it describes is making objects rotate on an upright pin or spindle. The TKE1 also allows its user to cause "a gas discharge lamp, fluorescent or preferably neon to ignite." As it happens, Joey reportedly does this as well, although Alex has uncritically cited it as an example of Joey's PK.[12] And as Karl had suspected, the unit can be "strapped to body with insulated wire going to ground via shoe tap."

I promptly informed Alex of these discoveries and sent him a copy of the instructions for building and using the device. Of course, I was now particularly sorry that I hadn't examined Joey's body or clothes before his demonstration. However, I still believed that would have ended the session before it began. As I mentioned earlier, at that point in the proceedings I was hoping to keep things friendly, informally stimulate the production of phenomena, and then gradually tighten controls after Joey was satisfied we were on his side.

As far as the spoon bend was concerned, I took Karl's videotape to video technicians at my university, and we analyzed Joey's performance frame by frame. Joey had been demonstrating the spoon bend primarily for Joanne, Mikki, and me, the three of us seated together in front of him on the living room sofa. But Karl's Super VHS video camera was off to one side, and Karl had a more useful angle on the event. The frame-by-frame analysis showed, first, that while Joey waved the spoon rapidly up and down, his thumb slid down the handle to the bowl of the spoon, at which position the spoon could be bent by force. I confirmed this myself with various spoons and conveyed that information to Alex. Curiously, though, Alex replied and continued afterwards to insist that brute strength couldn't possibly have bent the spoon in that way. As far as I could tell, his only basis for that assertion was that *he*—a man in his mid-90s—couldn't do it. But in my experience, nothing close to brute strength was required; I found that bending each of several different spoons was actually quite easy. Again I mentioned this to Alex, but he (inscrutably) remained incredulous.

Furthermore (and even more damaging), the analysis revealed that as the spoon appeared to continue bending in Joey's hand, Joey simply performed a standard illusion. From Karl's angle of view, it was clear that Joey merely tilted his hand while he held the spoon. The spoon didn't bend further at all. Joey merely tilted his hand in such a way as to make it seem to those of us on the sofa that the spoon handle (and not the hand) was moving.

Of course, if Joey weren't a performing magician, we could easily have dismissed this as an innocent error on his part. But under the circumstances, I felt that we had no choice but to take a more suspicious attitude toward his phenomena generally. It now seemed clear that we couldn't trust Joey in conditions of relatively minimal control.

5. Second Encounter

So there seemed to be a marked discrepancy between Joey's words and his actions. Despite Joey's repeated failure to cooperate fully with reasonable experimental demands, he insisted he understood the need for tighter controls. During my extended conversation with him after our session in his suite, Joey claimed over and over that he appreciated why Alex wanted ironclad proof of his abilities. In fact, Joey appeared to understand when I said it would be better to obtain solid evidence of small-scale phenomena than weak evidence of dramatic phenomena. He seemed to grasp that we didn't need to arrange our tests under the conditions he found most congenial and most conducive to impressive PK feats. It would be enough—in fact, great—if he could do something modest under conditions he regarded as less than ideal. I went over these points with Joey several times, in different ways, to make sure we were communicating clearly about how the next round of tests should proceed. Joey gave no indication that he found any of these issues hard to grasp. And of course, they're not hard to grasp, and Joey's not stupid.

So I agreed with Alex to bring Joey back to New York in March 1996, for another two-day round of tests. I also clearly specified to Alex what I considered to be nonnegotiable guidelines. Somewhat surprisingly, Joey agreed to be tested both nights at the site he had previously found uncongenial: the auditorium in the Blessed Sacrament School. But he said that he preferred to work in front of an audience, because that was a situation he found encouraging and psi-conducive. I told Alex that I would agree to having an audience present, so long as I could arrive an hour beforehand to inspect the surroundings and assure myself (and be able to certify) that neither an apparatus nor a confederate had been concealed there. That would also allow me to optimize camera positions with the three camera operators who agreed to assist me. I wanted all this done in advance so that I could give my full attention to Joey once he arrived. I also mentioned that I still wanted Joey to demonstrate his phenomena in the open area of the auditorium, rather than on the stage, because it was a much larger area and would more easily accommodate three video cameras and tripods. Alex agreed to these stipulations.

So we agreed that my team and I would arrive at the school at 7 p.m., and that Alex would bring Joey there at 8 p.m. on March 15. But when I arrived with Karl and Joanne, I found that Joey had arrived thirty minutes beforehand and had nearly completed his preparations. He had also set up on stage, contrary to the arrangement I had made with Alex. When I asked Joey why he had arrived before me, he said he needed ninety minutes to prepare himself for a show. But this was the first I had heard of this requirement—or of a *show*, for that matter. Joey never explained why he couldn't have taken his ninety minutes *after* my crew and I had inspected the area and set up our own gear. Moreover, Alex could easily have let me know about Joey's need for prep time, and my team could simply have arrived earlier.

Even more surprisingly, Joey claimed that he merely planned to do a magic show the first night and that if something psychic happened along the way, so much the better. He now said that he'd wait until the second night to *really* demonstrate PK. Of course, this was also news to me, and when I questioned Alex about it, he insisted that he'd never made any such arrangement with Joey. Nevertheless, I was furious with Alex. He had been shepherding Joey around all day, and he could easily have taken charge of the situation, making sure that Joey adhered to the conditions we had agreed upon in advance.

Moreover, when I complained to Alex about Joey's early arrival, he replied lamely that he'd had Joe under constant surveillance. But I pointed out to Alex that his claim was clearly false, because when I entered the room I could see that Joey was going about his business while Alex had his back to him. I also reminded Alex of his lapses of observational rigor on other occasions, and Alex conceded again that he's not a careful observer.

So once again, Joey had effectively compromised the process of evidence gathering, and Alex had been his accomplice (despite his avowed commitment to obtaining absolutely convincing proof of Joey's abilities). Nevertheless, I quickly instructed the camera operators to set up on stage and I immediately moved to the table on which Joey had been arranging his props. Of course, for this to have been a serious and careful test of Joey's abilities, he should never have supplied his own props in the first place. So I felt that, at the very least, I'd better take a look at the devices Joey had brought with him.

But when I tried to examine his props, Joey became agitated, accused me of being a skeptic, and said I had destroyed his concentration. He even became physically threatening, lunging toward me and brandishing his ornate dagger. Then he claimed that because I had ostensibly destroyed his mood and concentration, there would be no show and no phenomena that night. Alex had invited about forty luminaries to observe Joey, and I had to tell them that they might as well go home.

For the rest of that evening (and as far as I can tell, for some time afterward), Joey made a point of disseminating two important falsehoods about this occasion. First, he claimed to many of the invited guests that I had interrupted his meditating and thereby undermined his ability to perform. But Joey wasn't meditating when I arrived—at least not in the sense in which, as on previous occasions, he needed to go off by himself to attain the appropriate level of trance. When I arrived, Joey was busily moving about the table with his props, arranging them and talking to the people around him. He wasn't isolating himself to get into his own psychic space; he was actively communicating with others and with his environment. He got bent out of shape, as far as I could tell, simply because I wanted to examine his props and because I was preventing him from giving an unsupervised magic show.

Second, Joey now claimed that he understood, right from the beginning, that he would be performing the sort of magic show he typically gives to schoolchildren and scout troops. But that's clearly nonsense. Alex hadn't spent his money to watch Joey do a magic show, and Joey knew it. Joey knew that Alex had brought him back to New York solely for the purpose of producing phenomena under better conditions than those prevailing in his hotel suite the previous November. He was fully aware that the sole purpose of this second New York visit was to help Alex mount a conclusive demonstration of PK. He also knew that Alex hadn't invited forty distinguished observers to watch him do magic. Joey knew those guests weren't scheduled to be present for the next evening's (and now according to Joey, real PK) session. Clearly, they were there to see him demonstrate PK.

In fact, I've retained a copy of the agreement drafted by Joey's manager, Neil Dryburgh, written on March 6, 1996, and presented to Alex for his signature. Among various things, it specifies the details concerning Joey's honorarium, travel expenses, and lodging. It also states quite clearly that on March 15 and 16 "Joe will participate in psi *experiments*" (emphasis added). It also refers several other times to the *experiments* scheduled for the two evenings. It says nothing whatsoever about a magic show.

I should also mention that Joanne McMahon was watching the fiasco on stage. I had been counting on her to keep an eye on Joey's wife Sandra while I dealt with Joey, and Joanne had the impression that Sandra was encouraging Joey's agitation by saying such things as "You're really upset, aren't you?" In fact, Joanne suspected that Sandra plays a bigger role in Joey's demonstrations than that of merely sitting by supportively.

At any rate, after Joey refused to perform for Alex's invited guests, and after the guests had dispersed, Joey claimed he simply couldn't produce any phenomena in the school auditorium. So Alex spent much of the next day looking for an alternate site. In the meantime, Neil Dryburgh informed me that Joey also now claimed he could produce no phenomena in *my* presence. Alex said he wanted me to attend the second night's session anyway, but I replied that, according to Neil, my absence that night was the best strategy for reestablishing a working relationship with Joey in the future. So because Alex said he'd bring Joey to New York again, and because he said it was critical for me to be there at that later time, Alex and I agreed that I should skip the second evening's session.

Moreover, because I agreed not to be present, at least two other key observers also decided not to attend: Joanne McMahon, whom I was counting on to continue her careful observations of Joey's wife, and Karl Petry, whose keen eye, good instincts, and camera had been so useful during our tests the previous November. Alex later informed me that nothing impressive happened during the four-hour session that night.

6. The Aftermath

Predictably, I left New York feeling less than enthusiastic about Joey. However, I hadn't entirely abandoned the view that he might have genuine psychic ability. Some of the anecdotal reports from Bert Schwarz continued to intrigue me. What was clear, though, was that Joey was a terrible subject, and I wouldn't have blamed anyone for concluding that it's not worth the trouble to test him. Because Joey's a magician and because virtually all of his phenomena are observationally indistinguishable from standard magic tricks, it's obviously crucial that he cooperate with sympathetic experimenters trying to examine him under careful conditions. But as far as my experience with Joey was concerned, his apparent willingness to cooperate appeared to be a sham. In fact, it looked like a convenient and cheap excuse for Joey to claim that investigators are skeptical simply because they try to apply decent controls. At least in my sessions with him, it seemed clear that Joey was merely weaseling out of prior agreements and reasonable experimental demands. But in any case, if he finds it intolerable when he's prohibited from bringing his own props, or when investigators want to examine his props or inspect the room prior to his arrival, and if he dismisses all experimental caution as psi-repressive skepticism, then Joey's simply a worthless subject for any investigator hoping to obtain clean and compelling evidence of his alleged abilities.

In May 1996 I recounted my experiences and conclusions about Joey in a presentation at the annual convention of the Society for Scientific Exploration (SSE). I didn't write a paper for the occasion; I simply gave a talk. But I did write an abstract of my talk, which I ended by saying the following:

> One could reasonably conclude at this point that Joe is a fraud who tries consistently to subvert or circumvent reasonable controls. If Joe is a genuine psychic, as his supporters continue to maintain, he at least seems to be of no value as a subject.

In the meantime, however, Alex's enthusiasm for Joey remained as intense as ever. And I was baffled. After all, Alex had admitted to me that he's not a careful observer; he had to know he's generally ignorant about conjuring; I had sent him the information about the Telekinetic Enhancer; I had told him about the video analysis of Joey's spoon bend and about my successful efforts to bend spoons with my hand positioned like Joey's; and he was fully aware how Joey violated the agreed-upon conditions for the March '96 experiments. Nevertheless, Alex kept demanding that I explain why I was suspicious of Joey. And despite his earlier insistence on the need for ironclad proof of Joey's abilities and the importance of having me secure evidence under careful conditions, he now seemed not to grasp any of the relevant issues. In fact, he now adopted the position that I was simply a skeptic and that I was biased against Joey.

On May 6, more than a week before my SSE talk, I sent Alex an e-mail in which I made my position completely clear. I wrote:

> . . . I remain open to the possibility that Joe is a genuine and outstanding psychic. But I'm also sensitive to the reasons why he strikes [many] as suspicious. . . . I don't doubt that Bert [Schwarz] has never caught him cheating, and I have total faith in Bert's honesty. But I have never seen anything compelling from Joe. His dollar bill movement in the aquarium cannot be regarded as highly evidential. . . . Put that together with the fact that Joe always seems to avoid working under decent controls, and no single piece of evidence I know of is confidence inspiring. Bert's work with Joe cannot be regarded as careful; it can only be regarded as highly suggestive. It is no more evidential than D. D. Home's sittings for convinced spiritualists in poor lighting. If Crookes and others hadn't tested Home under MUCH better conditions, that case would not be worth much today. As of now, Joe's case is at that level of evidentiality.[13]

As far as I'm concerned, Joe has shown himself to be a very poor subject, and he has given no reason to think he merits continued examination (I personally think he squandered your money last time, and that if he had any honor he would not have taken your honorarium). But I truly hope he is as gifted as you and Bert insist, and I honestly and eagerly welcome an opportunity to document his phenomena. But if he can't cooperate better than he has so far, and if he resists examination of his props under the flimsy pretense of experimenter skepticism, then he's simply worthless as a subject who will produce convincing phenomena. In fact, many (justifiably) think it is suspicious that Joe brings his own props. . . . Why (they would ask) should a good psychic need them? The best subjects have never required them.

You need to appreciate the basis for the skepticism that Joe's behavior fuels. Everyone I've told about this case feels that Joe should be dropped like a bad habit, and I've found myself defending Joe against their reactions. But I understand why they react as they do, and if that makes me deeply biased against Joe (so much so that he can't work with me), then again, Joe's a lousy subject. *A psychic who cannot produce phenomena except under conditions of total credulity is a terrible subject, and certainly not someone who will ever produce compelling evidence* [emphasis added].

Inscrutably, Alex wanted to write a favorable report about our sessions with Joe and submit the report for publication in one of the better parapsychology journals. He also wanted to include both me and psychologist Gertrude Schmeidler as coauthors (Gertrude had attended the failed sessions in May '96). But both Gertrude and I requested not to be listed as authors. I made it clear to Alex that because our evaluations of Joe differed profoundly, neither of us would likely be satisfied with a paper acceptable to the other. In fact, I e-mailed Alex on July 11, 1996, urging him not to publish a prematurely favorable report on Joe. I wrote, "I believe you will be asking for ridicule and that any positive conclusions on your part . . . can only damage your credibility, and I would hate to see that."

Alex replied a few days later, accusing me of misrepresenting the facts concerning the March '96 fiasco. According to Alex, the truth was that I had been uninformed about Joey's need for an hour of meditation and concentration prior to any test. So when I approached Joey, asking questions and inspecting his props, my skepticism broke his concentration and upset his psychological equilibrium.

But that's clearly absurd. First of all, if (as Alex now claimed) I approached and talked to Joey because no one had informed me of his need for quiet time, then I was simply acting out of ignorance, not skepticism. But more important, Alex seemed to have forgotten that Joey was attempting to skip all tests and do a magic show the first night, that he had mentioned this in the presence of several witnesses, and that this violated the agreement drafted by Joey's own manager and signed by Alex. Alex also forgot that he could easily have rescheduled my (or Joey's) arrival so that Joey could set up and meditate *after* my crew had arrived and arranged their gear. And Alex conveniently ignored the elementary methodological point that even naive students understand: that for the sort of careful test he claimed he wanted me to conduct of Joey, Joey shouldn't be using his own props at all—and certainly not *uninspected* props. I replied to Alex on July 14,

> . . . it's not a matter (as Joe, I believe disingenuously, tries to argue) of my being so skeptical as to snuff out the phenomena. It's all about not letting the psychic control the test. That's a fundamental element of any decent investigation, and it's the element that has so far been absent in our investigation.

Alex also claimed, astonishingly, that because I had seen Joey bending a fork (I presume he meant spoon) with one hand, and because I had agreed it's not feasible to do this normally, it must have been paranormal. But I reminded Alex that this is not what I had said, and that I had in fact duplicated the spoon bend myself several times. Alex also claimed that if Joey had moved the dollar bill with a hidden static generator, the bill would have moved immediately—not after ten minutes—when he approached the aquarium. But I reminded Alex about the information I had sent him, according to which the device described can be activated *at will* by the toe.

I learned later that in the wake of my SSE speech, John Beloff (editor of the *Journal of the Society for Psychical Research*) declined to publish Alex's favorable account of our November '95 tests with Joey. But I was disappointed to see that account turn up in the journal of the Scientific and Medical Network.[14] And I was especially disappointed to see how Alex neglected to mention a large number of relevant pieces of information, all of which should have been noted in the interest of full disclosure, all of which Alex knew, and (in fact) all of which he and I had discussed on numerous occasions. For example, Alex mentioned that Joanne McMahon, Mikki Maher, and I participated in the tests, but he mentioned none of the reasons we were underwhelmed by the results (e.g., the general laxness of controls, and the specific reasons for suspicion about the dollar bill movement and spoon bend). Alex didn't even mention my own report to him about simulating Joey's spoon bend, much less my frame-by-frame analysis of the video. And he made no mention of the material I provided him about the concealed static device for producing the dollar bill effect. For that matter, Alex neglected to mention the crucial background fact that Joey performs magic shows. As a result, I felt I had to publish a brief reply, outlining my own perspective on the tests and on Joey as a subject.[15]

It would be a considerable understatement to say I was surprised and disappointed by Alex's behavior. When I began working with him, he was explicit about the great importance he placed on gathering carefully controlled evidence for macro-PK. But now he was behaving as if our many discussions on the subject—in fact, his entire justification for bringing me in on the investigations—never happened. And he was acting as if I had never explained why I was suspicious of the November '95 tests, and as if I had never sent him the relevant information about the TKE1 static generator. In fact, in both his *Network* and subsequent JSPR articles,[16] Alex cited as examples of Joey's PK several of the effects listed in the TKE1 instructions.

Under the circumstances, I found it difficult to avoid concluding that Alex knowingly withheld the relevant information about the TKE1 and Joey's background in magic. Similarly, I could see no good excuse for Alex's failure to acknowledge that I was able forcibly to bend spoons with my hand placed as Joey's was. And I saw no excuse for his failure to explain why he believed Joey couldn't bend a spoon with one hand, considering that Joey was young, fit,[17] and (as someone trained in the martial arts) presumably capable of physical maneuvers more impressive than that. In a grumpy, pre-caffeinated morning e-mail to Dean Radin, I complained:

> [Alex's *Network* article isn't] simply selective reporting. When investigators studied Eusapia Palladino, they recognized that she might cheat. The issue was at the forefront of their investigations, and their candid and thorough discussion of the possibility of fraud is part of what makes the case as strong as it is. Alex's failure to do the same, it seems to me, either shows dishonesty in his presentation of the case, or else a massive (and in his case inexcusable) historical blindness or stupidity about what makes good evidence.

To make matters worse, Alex continued for several years afterwards to spread his misinformation. For example, in June 2001 I received some e-mails from psychologist and psychophysiologist Ruth Reinsel, to whom Alex had been complaining about my tests with Joey. Ruth asked if I'd like to reply to Alex's various charges. I gave her a short version of the events related above, and in response to Alex's expressed disappointment over what he called my "hands on" approach to "real psychokinetic phenomena," I wrote back:

> I find this more than a little odd. Alex brought me in precisely because he knew I was sympathetic to—indeed, convinced about—the reality of large-scale PK, and also because he was concerned to get evidence that was so squeaky clean it would convince all but the most stupidly intransigent of skeptics. Joe and Alex agreed, ahead of time, to my suggestions for our second round of tests. These were held precisely for the purpose of getting good evidence. Alex allowed this to be subverted, and Joe didn't stick to his agreement. I concluded simply that Joe is an unreliable subject. There are psychics out there who don't thwart agreed-upon, and perfectly reasonable (i.e., not absurdly constraining) experimental controls and who are ready to cooperate with experimenters. In my experience, Nuzum is not one of them, and Alex, for all his posturing about wanting to arrange a definitive demonstration, is unwilling or unable to help matters along.

I also received a copy of a June 2001 e-mail Alex sent to a Listserv on parapsychology in which he claimed, outrageously (and, I have to believe, completely dishonestly) that Joey "is and has not been involved in the art of magical entertainment." It's important to understand just how detestable Alex's statement was. Joey's·activity as a performing magician has never been a secret—or, for that matter, something that Joey tried to downplay. In fact, it was discussed quite openly. For example, it was a major and overt topic of conversation on the occasion of Joey's aborted magic show on March 15, 1996. With others in earshot of me, Joey made it plain that he was planning to do the kind of magic show he did routinely for children. And in an e-mail to me, Karl Petry recalled, "When Joey was getting his dagger ready to plunge into your chest, his wife and I sat at the foot of the stage where she told me he was a magician back in Pennsylvania."[18]

At least Alex did nothing but spread falsehoods. Joey, who had already threatened me with a dagger, apparently decided that he hadn't gone far enough. After my SSE abstract appeared on several websites, but before I learned about it (and long before my reply to Alex appeared in *Network*), Joey phoned me, yelling at me to stop spreading lies about him. I told him, quite honestly, that I had no idea what he was talking about. He told me to take back what I had said about him, *or else*. In fact, he reminded me he had a gun, that he knew people who had guns, that my life was now in grave danger, and that I should now be looking over my shoulder.

7. Postscript

After my exchange with Alex in *Network*, only Bert Schwarz has continued to pay Joey any attention, at least in print.[19] Unlike Alex, Bert hasn't looked to Joey for conclusive demonstrations of psi. As I noted in chapter 1, Bert is more concerned with unraveling the complex psychological and physical nexus in which psychic events occur—an activity I consider vitally important and thoroughly laudable. So he's studied Joey in the hope of learning something more about the natural history of psi—not as part of an effort to convince the scientific community at large.[20]

Of course, unlike Katie—whom Bert also studied with the same goals in mind—Joey doesn't cooperate fully with researchers, and his phenomena have never been examined under conditions controlled only and carefully by the investigators. I suspect Bert has unwisely accepted too many of Joey's observed—and certainly his reported—feats at face value, assuming they're all legitimate psi phenomena. In fact, he believes that Joey is completely trustworthy.

But Bert doesn't know the story behind my New York investigations of Joey. What he knows was fed to him by Joey and by his good friend Alex, and once that started to happen, Bert's previously friendly (even avuncular) behavior toward me cooled dramatically. In fact, during one attempted conversation with Bert, not long after my second round of tests with Joey, Bert repeated Alex's absurd mantra that I'm too skeptical to work with a gifted subject like Joey. It's only in the past year that I've been able to re-establish cordial communication with Bert. So if reading this chapter and the next doesn't fling me back into Bert's doghouse, I hope we'll be able to collaborate again.

Dennis Lee: Subject in Hell

1. Impressive Beginnings

I met Dennis Lee in November 1996. He had contacted me and several other investigators months earlier, announcing that he was a gifted psychokinetic subject who could move large objects virtually at will, even in the withering presence of skeptical audiences. In a long, articulate letter to me, Dennis described the sorts of phenomena he claimed to produce, and he proposed a reasonable strategy for testing his abilities. He said that for more than ten years he'd been able to demonstrate macro-PK "principally, but not limited to, the movement of suspended objects, e.g., mobiles, hanging plants, etc. The observed effect of my influence on these objects, such as mobiles, is that they begin to spin from a position of rest, including the simultaneous, opposed rotation of mobiles with multiple rings." Dennis proposed testing his ability by placing target objects inside sealed glass containers, and then once the objects were determined to be at rest, he would enter the room and "immediately cause the target object to move discernibly. If the target object is lightweight in nature, it may even 'recoil' (4–6" laterally) upon my initial contact with it."

Dennis assured me he had "no trepidation in regard to 'testing.'" In fact, he described himself as "the perfect 'human guinea pig'" for PK tests. Of course, I'd encountered this sort of claim before. And by that time I had also dealt with Joey Nuzum's attempt (arguably, with concealed electrical assistance) to move an object in a sealed container. So naturally, I accepted Dennis's assurances with more than a grain of salt. But Dennis's letter was intriguing, and since I knew that in November I'd be attending a conference in San Francisco, near his home, I agreed to meet him at my hotel.

Dennis arrived punctually at the Fairmont. He was a stocky, relaxed, and pleasant man, voluble, and clearly very smart. We chatted easily and amiably for a while in the hotel lobby before getting down to business. Dennis reiterated that he'd had particular success with suspended objects such as mobiles and pendulums. He realized that such objects tend to move spontaneously due to air currents and other environmental influences, but he assured me he could influence the objects so dramatically that the movements could only be attributed to PK. To demonstrate his prowess, he had brought along a small mobile, which he assembled and placed on the table for my inspection. I asked Dennis if he'd like to move it right then, but he said that a hotel lobby felt a bit too public. That seemed sensible enough, and besides, a bustling hotel lobby was hardly the quiet environment we'd need to ensure that the mobile wasn't moving normally. So I left Dennis there for a few moments while I located a vacant room.

Although my conference was in full swing, several hotel conference rooms were unoccupied, and I eventually found a suitable location not far from the lobby. It was a large room with several windows, a big table, and an enormous, ornate chandelier, replete with decorative crystals and fancy light bulbs, very much in the grand style of the hotel. We placed the little mobile on the table and waited patiently for it to come to a rest. It did stop, but only briefly. Dennis tried several times to influence the device as soon as it stopped moving, and on each occasion it would start to move again. But we realized that this could easily have been caused by air currents in the room, even though none were evident to us. In fact, the mobile would sometimes start to move again when Dennis was *not* consciously trying to influence it.

But controlling for air currents is a relatively straightforward methodological concern; another problem was more pervasive and much more annoying. No matter how carefully a test is set up and controlled, there's no way to know for certain when a psychic subject's intention or effort begins or ends. At best, we can only estimate roughly when the person's *conscious* willing starts and stops. That's one of the frustrating and unavoidable features of parapsychological experimentation. Obviously, Dennis's efforts took place in a general context of experimenter and subject expectation and desire to see the phenomena occur. It's unreasonable to think that Dennis's desire to influence the test object was something that clearly and unambiguously turned on and off at specific times. And there's no reason to think that only conscious intentions can trigger psychic effects. In fact, there are many reasons for thinking that psi effects can be initiated subconsciously or unconsciously. Moreover, it's not as if we have a "PK meter" that can detect when (or if) appropriate PK emanations leave the body.[1] So for all we know, Dennis might have been influencing the mobile when he wasn't actively trying.

Actually, the ambiguity of the situation was even worse than this. For all we know, if anyone psychokinetically moved the mobile, it could have been me rather than Dennis. After all, I was also eager to see some good PK, and we have no way of determining whether (or to what extent) my desires influenced the mobile. In fact, for all we know the movements could have been caused by someone in another room—say, by means of a PK "accident." Again, there's nothing like a PK meter that can spot stray sources of psychokinetic influence, and there's no barrier we can place around every other potential PK agent (like a lead shield to thwart Superman's X-ray vision). This "source of psi" indeterminacy is a well-known problem in parapsychology, and I was fully aware of it going into our informal experiment. I knew also that this indeterminacy could never be eliminated entirely, no matter how impressive the phenomena were. Still, I hoped that when Dennis tried to move the object it would move so dramatically that this problem would largely recede to the background. Even if others were surreptitiously adding their own PK contributions to the final result, I felt we'd have no choice then but to regard Dennis as at least one of the PK culprits, and probably the primary culprit.

At any rate, we checked to see whether we could detect air coming in from the closed windows or from air vents, and although we felt nothing, we knew that the mobile would respond much more sensitively than our skin to prevailing air currents. Dennis was disappointed but apparently not surprised. Apologetically, he explained that he had no other modestly sized test object he could plausibly have brought with him to the hotel.

I realized, though, that the room's chandelier was the sort of object Dennis claimed to be able to move at will. The light fixture was suspended from the ceiling by a solid-looking metal stem, which if it had any flexibility at all would allow the chandelier to behave somewhat like a pendulum. So I asked Dennis if he'd try to make it sway. Dennis seemed pleased at the idea and apparently started concentrating on the large light fixture. Unfortunately, it didn't move at all, at least as far as we could tell. However, the lights started to flicker during the period when Dennis said he was attempting to move it.

It then occurred to Dennis that he was the cause of the light flickering, and he said he thought he could darken or brighten the lights just by concentrating on them. So he predicted that the lights would flicker and get dimmer, and they did. Then he told me they'd get steady and brighter, and they did. Dennis repeated this for me several more times, and each time the lights in the chandelier behaved exactly as he predicted. Dennis now seemed satisfied; he felt he had compensated for his inability to make the chandelier and mobile move.

I was inclined to agree. After all, the light fixture's heavy and apparently rigid stem may have prevented it from flexing under Dennis's influence. Furthermore, I had found the unoccupied room for us to use. It's implausible to suppose that Dennis knew in advance which room I would choose from the several that were available, or that he'd been able, during or before the conference, to rig the electrical circuits in the conference rooms. Although I didn't search Dennis for some hidden device that would allow him to affect the lights of the chandelier, it was I who suggested trying to influence the chandelier. Moreover, I doubt that Dennis could have known I'd find a room with an appropriate light fixture, one that he could (in principle at least) make swing like a pendulum, and whose brightness he could afterwards alter in intensity and steadiness.

Dennis and I talked for a while after this incident. I explained to him what I expected of a cooperative PK subject and what I believed distinguished good subjects from poor subjects. I gave him a brief history of some of the best cases of macro-PK, and I told him that if we were to work together, ideally I'd like him to wear clothes that we provided, and also that I'd like a continuous videotaped record of the entire session, beginning with his undressing and donning the clothes we supplied. I assured Dennis that the nude scenes in the video would be kept confidential, but that they nevertheless would provide a crucial component of our documentary evidence. To my surprise and relief, Dennis seemed unfazed at the prospect of stripping for the camera, and for me it lent additional credibility to the day's proceedings. Overall, Dennis had impressed me as being both sensitive to the demands of serious research and also genuinely ready to cooperate. I told Dennis I'd see whether I could arrange for him to travel East for some tests.

2. Round 1: Lee vs. Imich

Despite our unfortunate experiences with and disagreements about Joey Nuzum, Alex Imich agreed to bring Dennis to New York. With additional financial assistance from the Parapsychology Foundation, I arranged with both Alex and Steve Baumann (a neuroscientist from the University of Pittsburgh) to conduct experiments with Dennis on three consecutive nights in January 1997.

In my view, Dennis was—at least in one important respect—every bit the "ideal" subject he had promised he'd be. He couldn't have been more cooperative. Throughout the tests he agreed to whatever controls we proposed, including stripping for the camera and wearing clothes we provided. In fact, Dennis often complained that our controls weren't tight enough to insure that evidence of object movements would unambiguously be evidence of PK. Admittedly, we didn't perform or suggest a full cavity search, and Dennis didn't propose it either. We felt it was simply unnecessary given the sorts of experiments we'd planned.

Overall, our tests with Dennis did yield some suggestive but small-scale object movements, enough to merit a second round of experiments. But the entire affair was sabotaged, even before Dennis arrived in New York, by Alex Imich. I don't believe Alex did this consciously. Among other things, he would have been wasting a great deal of his own money, since it was he who paid for Dennis's airfare, accommodations, and meals. But I believe it's clear that his actions betrayed a desire to retaliate against me for having publicly expressed my suspicions about Joey Nuzum.

In retrospect, I suppose Alex's behavior wasn't surprising. He and I had argued many times over the merits of the Nuzum case. But our latest interactions had been cordial, and it seemed to me that we were both enthusiastic and excited about the prospect of obtaining good evidence with Dennis, who (unlike Nuzum) promised to be a most cooperative subject. Still, I blame myself for not having realized that Alex still harbored considerable anger and resentment toward me, and I certainly didn't anticipate that it would outweigh his passionate desire to obtain convincing evidence of PK.

Here are the grubby details. First, Alex booked a flight for Dennis on the red-eye from San Francisco. When he originally informed me of this, I protested that Dennis would arrive tired and not at his best for the experiments. Alex replied that he wanted to keep costs down and that Dennis had said he could sleep on the plane. But I believe Dennis was simply trying to be as cooperative a subject as possible. I also think Dennis made two important miscalculations. First, he underestimated how his anxiety or excitement over the experiments might interfere with his ability to sleep. And second, he failed to appreciate how Alex might have multiplied or deepened his anxieties even before he departed for New York.

I had warned Alex repeatedly that he needed to book Dennis's flight as far in advance as possible in order to get a low airfare. I also reminded him several times that it was important to get Dennis a good seat on the plane, to help ensure that he'd get some sleep. Nevertheless, Alex postponed making a reservation until two weeks before the trip, and then he complained that he couldn't obtain a favorable rate. (And as it turned out, he also failed to reserve a comfortable seat on the plane.) In retrospect, I see this as one of many instances in which Alex didn't take seriously the welfare of our subject. I also see it as the first overt manifestation of Alex's hostile reluctance to cooperate with me, and his (presumably unconscious) wish to subvert the experiments.

As it turned out, Dennis didn't sleep well on the flight. One problem was Dennis's anxiety concerning a crystal he carried with him at all times. The crystal had been a gift from a friend, and Dennis said it had been at the center of some unusual experiences, including (on one occasion) a blinding burst of light. A week before he left California, Dennis told me that Alex had been badgering him to make light appear from the crystal. Dennis complained that he was afraid he'd fail at this, because he never claimed to be able to produce that phenomenon on demand. It seemed to him that Alex was less interested in the phenomena that were supposedly the focus of the test: moving objects in sealed containers at a distance. So I phoned Alex immediately and asked him to stop talking to Dennis about the crystal, because he was creating more anxiety than enthusiasm and confidence in our subject. I urged Alex to emphasize that we were interested in seeing Dennis do what he said he did best—namely, move objects. Alex agreed. Or at least he claimed to agree.

In any case, some damage had already been done. Besides, even if Dennis had been psychologically peaceful enough to sleep on the plane, conditions during his flight weren't conducive to sleep (or even to good rest). The main problem, Dennis said, was that he was seated directly in front of the movie screen, and since he was fairly tall, he had no space to stretch his legs. So Dennis arrived in New York needlessly tired, and also apparently uneasy about Alex's expectations.

Once Dennis and Alex met, Alex talked repeatedly about the miracles of Joey Nuzum and about how Joey was the greatest psychic since D. D. Home. Alex continued to wax enthusiastic about Joey when Steve Baumann met up with the two of them. He showed them the cutlery Joey had allegedly bent and described in detail many of Joey's other alleged miracles (not one of which, as far as I could determine, was ever carefully documented or observed). Alex said nothing about the reasons for thinking that Nuzum was simply a fraud, or even that he faked at least some of his phenomena. And he certainly never mentioned that I had obtained video footage of Joey passing off a magic trick as an example of PK, or that Joey earned money doing magic shows, or that Joey even admitted that he had planned to do a magic show for the audience gathered during my second and disastrous attempt to study him. I'm certain also that Alex never mentioned the various reasons I had for doubting his observational prowess.

Of course, the effect of all this was to make Dennis feel that his phenomena were insignificant by comparison to Joey's, and so Dennis arrived for the first evening's session feeling that nothing he could do would be of much value. To me, Alex's behavior was an outrageous breach both of human courtesy and experimental common sense. Every successful psi researcher has realized the importance of making subjects feel relaxed and safe. However, rather than helping to prepare Dennis by building up his confidence and making him feel as comfortable as possible in a strange and demanding setting, Alex acted as destructively as someone who says to a performer about to go onstage, "You should have seen how great the act before you was!" At one point during our first evening together Alex left the room, and Dennis seized the opportunity to complain about Alex's behavior. When I confronted Alex about the matter, he conceded that his actions had been unwise, and he told me he would be more careful thereafter. But as far as I could determine, that never happened.

In fact, throughout Dennis's visit, Alex apparently made little effort to make Dennis feel even slightly welcome and comfortable. Quite apart from his attacks on Dennis's feelings of self-worth, Alex didn't even make the minimal effort to provide Dennis with coffee, which Dennis drank frequently, and which he repeatedly requested from Alex. I was also surprised and shocked to learn later that Alex made no attempt to compensate Dennis for time away from work. I considered this especially noteworthy because Alex regularly paid honoraria to Joey Nuzum.

The ultimate objective of our planned experiments was to record Dennis influencing objects in sealed containers, and we figured we'd work up to those tests by first asking Dennis to demonstrate his PK in more naturalistic settings, as he was presumably accustomed to do. Therefore, we wanted our initial experiments to be as friendly and informal as possible, avoiding the clinical sterility of a lab setting. And we felt we could do that in someone's congenial residence so long as we had adequate control over the proceedings. So the first evening's session was held at the penthouse of

Dr. Barbara Koopman, a friend of Alex. Present (in addition to the experimenters) were filmmaker Dave Tapper, my video expert and cameraman Karl Petry, and Joanne McMahon, research officer and librarian at the Parapsychology Foundation.

Dr. Koopman turned out to be a major distraction and disturbance. She ignored my request to stay away from the experimental setup, even though I explained that I made the request in order to undercut predictable skeptical suggestions that Dennis was using an accomplice. Moreover, she insisted on playing with Dennis's crystal, placing it on her forehead and other parts of her body, and swooning over its alleged effects. In fact, she did this on several occasions during the evening, consuming at least an hour of our time, despite my repeated requests to back off, assume the role of spectator, and allow the experiments to proceed. I'm sure I explained very clearly why it was important for her to be a passive observer, but she repeatedly returned to the experimental area to chat or to play with the crystal. Because she was Alex's friend and our host, I was reluctant to be more aggressively insistent about having her respect experimental protocols. Alex had already poisoned the atmosphere with his badgering of Dennis, and I didn't want to contaminate it any further and even more conspicuously.

Although Dennis stripped for the camera, wore the medical scrubs we provided for him, and tried to make objects move, we obtained no results that first evening other than some inconclusive movements of mobiles hanging freely in the room. Once I had learned about Alex's various failures to help Dennis feel psychologically prepared for this initial test of his abilities, I suggested to Alex that he uninvite the observers he had contacted for the second evening's session. We agreed, along with Steve Baumann, that it would be best to start over with only the core group of experimenters and observers present.

Evidently, Alex forgot this agreement (or simply chose to ignore it), because more than eighteen observers appeared the next evening in the auditorium at Mt. Sinai hospital. When Dennis arrived and saw the crowd in the auditorium, he became visibly upset and expressed his surprise and dismay. And I was both embarrassed and furious over Alex's apparent betrayal. Dennis said he had expected a small gathering, and of course that is what Baumann and I had told him to expect after our discussion the night before with Alex. Under the circumstances, Dennis naturally felt additional, and completely needless, pressure to perform. And the fact that the crowd had assembled in an auditorium certainly didn't help matters. It made Dennis feel even more on stage and on the spot.

I offered to play the villain and demand loudly that the invited guests leave. But Dennis explained (plausibly) that he would still feel uncomfortable, because that would simply be a different and very dramatic way of letting us (and especially Alex) down. So Dennis felt on the spot whether the guests remained or left. He didn't want to disappoint us, and he didn't want to appear to be a temperamental or "difficult" subject. In fact, I suspect Dennis was particularly wary about being branded a difficult subject because by that time Joanne, Karl, and I had provided him with details of the behavior of Joey Nuzum. (We had discussed that matter in the hope of countering the stifling and unjustified praise Alex had been heaping on Joey.)

Furthermore, when Dennis realized that one of Alex's invited guests was the famous mentalist, the Amazing Kreskin, he became unglued. Kreskin was not there to debunk Dennis; I gather he was genuinely interested in the phenomena. But of course Kreskin was a famous showman, and Dennis had already demonstrated the night before that he was intimidated by the specter of perceived competition. Naturally, I was angry, because Alex could easily have anticipated how inhibiting Kreskin's presence would be. Alex should obviously have asked Kreskin to postpone his observations for a more favorable occasion.

I suspect Dennis could have dealt more calmly with this whole situation had he been more successful during the first evening's experiments, and of course if he had been treated by Alex from the start with more common sense, sympathy, and understanding.

At any rate, the second evening's session continued to deteriorate. Baumann had suspended about a dozen large plastic mobiles on the auditorium stage. Of course, we'd have been happy to see any kind of obvious movement of the target objects. But more specifically, we had hoped Dennis would make the objects rotate in opposite directions, as he claimed he'd been able to do before. Dennis and I sat in one of the front rows, as far away as possible from the invited guests, but it did little good. Although Dennis tried to make objects move, people in the audience kept whispering, moving about, and entering or leaving the auditorium. Dennis found the bustle distracting, and in addition to air currents generated by the ventilation system, the opening and shutting of the auditorium doors produced breezes that disturbed the hanging objects Dennis was trying to influence. Furthermore, Alex moved constantly from guest to guest, talking audibly behind Dennis's back. And frequently, one of the guests would interrupt Dennis and talk to him while he was concentrating on his task. Of course, Alex should have known better than to allow this sort of interference. Since I don't believe he's either that ignorant or stupid, and since I'm absolutely certain that few things mattered more to Alex than obtaining undeniably convincing proof of PK, I can only conclude that his failure to control the audience was another instance of his veiled hostility toward me. At any rate, we witnessed nothing but a few inconclusive movements of hanging objects.

As the company dispersed for the evening, Dennis confided to me that Alex had been hounding him during the day. Apparently, he had tried on several occasions to make objects move for Alex, and according to Dennis, when the objects began to move, Alex would shout at him to produce bigger effects. And later Dennis told me that Alex had been complaining about me throughout this period, saying "It was Stephen Braude who ruined the Joey Nuzum experiments" and "Joe Nuzum is one of the great psychics." Toward the end of the evening Dennis asked, quite poignantly, if he could go home with me that night rather than remain with Alex. Unfortunately, I had booked a very small hotel room for myself near Times Square; it was so small that (as Daffy Duck once said) "I had to step outside just to change my mind." If I had been able to accommodate Dennis, I would have done so gladly.

On the third day, Alex displayed open hostility toward Dennis. This was obvious during our attempted experiments in the evening, but apparently it occurred during the day as well. Dennis told me that he and Alex had gotten into a shouting match during which Alex complained, "Why can you get good results in California and not here?" Dennis said he responded by pointing out that even Uri Geller couldn't produce phenomena whenever he wanted—for example, on the Johnny Carson show. Alex responded (quite foolishly in my opinion), "Once; only once." The Geller example was probably unfortunate, since there's good reason to doubt the genuineness of some of his phenomena. But Dennis knew too little about the great mediums to retort with a better example. In any case, Alex should have known better. He should have known that the Geller example is controversial, and he certainly should have known that psi seems to be situation sensitive and that even the greatest psychics seem to have off-days, just as great athletes or musicians have off-days.

In a conversation with Dennis several days after he returned home, Dennis told me that not once did Alex say an encouraging word to him during his New York visit. I find this thoroughly credible. Alex was anything but supportive in all the interactions I observed, and his behavior stood in stark contrast to the blind support he offered Joey Nuzum, who wouldn't even allow me to examine his props. That makes it all the more amazing that

Alex showed no support to a subject who, in the interest of obtaining good evidence, was willing to be videotaped removing all his clothes.

The third evening's session was held in the auditorium of the Blessed Sacrament School on West 70th St. (the location where I had twice tested Joey Nuzum). It's a large room with no drafts (as Karl Petry ingeniously helped determine with the use of a fog machine). On this occasion Alex's hostility toward Dennis was strikingly overt. This was the session during which we had originally planned to ask Dennis to influence hanging objects in sealed containers. At one point, Dennis was seated at a table with various objects in glass containers. Alex sat down directly in front of Dennis and scowled at him (the video footage and still photos leave no doubt about this). Dennis requested that observers be stationed behind him so that he wouldn't be distracted, although he confided to me later that he really just wanted Alex's negativity to be out of his range of vision. I asked Alex if he would move off to the side of the table, where he could still enjoy a good view of the test objects. But Alex refused. He shook his head emphatically and said "no," and he remained in his chair. I had to ask him twice more, quite insistently, and finally he agreed to move.

We did get some apparently genuine movements of a mobile placed under an aquarium. The video footage looks intriguing, if not compelling. But the movements were small, and because this happened rather late in the proceedings and we were feeling fatigued and somewhat discouraged after the tense interactions between Alex, Dennis, and myself, we hadn't sealed the aquarium. However, it's clear that small drafts couldn't have moved the mobile, and besides, our fog machine had shown there were no such drafts. Steve Baumann tried but couldn't duplicate the results as he waved his hands vigorously near the aquarium.

Of course, it would have been preferable to have Dennis sit at least ten feet from the object, as we had originally planned. But at that stage in the proceedings, we were hoping simply to grease the wheel and get something started before we completely ran out of time. In fact, Dennis was drinking some cognac offered to him by Michaeleen (Mikki) Maher, who attended the session that night, and that did seem to loosen Dennis up a bit. When he relaxed (and ignored Alex), he seemed to get object movements. In fact, when it looked like the evening's work had ended, Dennis was sitting across the room from the test objects, and he predicted that when he glanced at the mobile (still in the aquarium), it would start to move. That it did, on the several occasions when Dennis predicted the movements.

Alex ended the evening's proceedings at a time when Dennis (who by then was pretty loose from the alcohol) was getting small but regular movements of the mobile, sitting quietly at varying distances from the table. Alex walked up to the table, blew forcefully under the aquarium and pounded on the table, producing movements in the mobile, and then declared "no good." Needless to say, the movements obtained prior to that time were not produced in the presence of comparable perturbations.

I was relieved to speak to Dennis the day after he returned home. I had feared his confidence would be too shaken to try again under more favorable conditions. But to my relief, his determination to succeed had apparently only been reinforced. He claimed he was eager to try again, under the tightest conditions we could provide, and he promised to practice the phenomena at home. He also said he'd send me a videotape showing the magnitude of phenomenon he could produce (although he recognized it wouldn't count as evidential), and he said he'd prepare himself for dealing with the pressure of a real test situation, whose dynamics he admitted he hadn't fully appreciated.

3. Round 2: At the Parapsychology Foundation

Joanne McMahon, Steve Baumann, and I agreed that Dennis's trip to New York provided enough tantalizing suggestions of real macro-PK to merit a second round of tests—that is, so long as we could bypass the "cooperation" of Alex Imich. So the Parapsychology Foundation (PF) agreed to finance another series. Because we could no longer count on Alex's connections to find venues for our tests, and because we needed to keep costs down, we agreed to hold the next series with Dennis on the premises of the PF.

After our earlier and frustratingly inconclusive tests with Dennis, Steve Baumann and I were determined to make the new experimental conditions as tight as possible—without, that is, strangling the phenomena to death. In fact, Dennis himself continued to insist strongly that his test results needed to be as unambiguous as possible. So Baumann and I felt that Dennis shared our goals, and we were confident that Dennis would continue to be a cooperative subject. On that score, at least, Dennis never disappointed us. As before, he expressed his willingness to submit to all controls, including stripping for the camera. As far as I know, that degree of cooperativeness is nearly unprecedented in contemporary PK subjects,[2] and it was one reason why I felt we should persevere in our efforts to test Dennis.

However, if we were to succeed with Dennis in this round, I realized that we needed to heal the wounds inflicted previously by Dennis's interactions with Imich. It had become clear that Dennis had overestimated just how perfect a human guinea pig he was, and in fact that his psyche was considerably more fragile than he had appreciated. Obviously, Dennis's confidence had been deeply shaken by his previous trip, not only because of his inability under unfavorable conditions to produce compelling object movements, but also because of Alex's relentless efforts to make Dennis feel that his phenomena (even if genuine) were relatively uninteresting and unimpressive.

All tests were conducted at the PF on June 7 and 8, 1997. The PF was located at that time in an old brownstone on New York's upper East Side, and its rare book room seemed to be the best location for the test objects. That room was small and apparently easily sealed, and although it was an interior room with no window to the outside, it did have a large window that looked out into the hallway. Thus, Dennis would be able to view the test objects from outside the room.

I had also asked Dennis, before his trip, whether he felt he could work using closed-circuit TV feedback rather than looking at the objects directly. He understood that this procedure, if effective, would permit us to isolate him from the test objects in virtually any location. And although Dennis didn't know how successful he'd be under these conditions, he was at least willing to give it a try. Karl Petry assured Baumann and me that he could make the appropriate arrangements.

As before, I was assisted throughout the experiments by Joanne McMahon, whom Dennis both trusted and liked, and also by Mikki Maher, with whom Dennis had also established some rapport during the earlier series of experiments. Furthermore, Mikki had agreed to supply cognac once again, just in case Dennis felt he needed an additional aid to relaxation. We also had the welcome assistance of a husband-and-wife team of photographers, Andrea Robbins and Max Becher. They provided another high-resolution camcorder, and Andrea also documented the proceedings with still photographs. Even more important, they provided lodgings for Dennis and Steve Baumann in a vacant apartment in the same building as their Soho loft, and they accompanied Dennis as tour guides and in his trips back and forth between Soho and the PF. More generally, they helped greatly in making Dennis feel comfortable during his visit.

That assistance was needed right from the beginning, when it looked as if this second series of experiments would be as psychologically debilitating to Dennis as the first. For one thing (and against my better judgment), Dennis insisted on flying to New York on the red-eye again. He said, very thoughtfully, that this would help reduce our expenses, and he claimed that if he had adequate leg room he'd be able to sleep. I made sure Dennis had plenty of leg room, but I couldn't have foreseen that he would be seated next to an elderly, corpulent, and sick passenger whose tubercular hackings and profuse sweating—not to mention the additional intrusions of his sleepy head on Dennis's shoulder (and spilled drink on Dennis's lap)—conspired to keep Dennis awake and irritated throughout the flight. Dennis arrived in New York convinced that Alex Imich had assigned seats on the plane. Moreover, Max and Andrea had arranged for Dennis to be met at the airport, but the limo service didn't appear as scheduled, and Dennis spent at least two frustrating hours wondering what was going on, as Andrea, Max, and I tried in vain to coordinate a backup plan with Dennis. Eventually, Dennis simply took a taxi into town. (So much for saving money on the red-eye.)

Once Dennis got settled into the Soho apartment, we had some encouraging signs that his positive attitude and PK abilities had survived his flight and arrival. On the morning of June 7, Andrea took Dennis sightseeing, hoping to relax him before the experiments later that day. They went to the Guggenheim museum at Broadway and Prince Streets (now closed), where they saw a fashion exhibit, with cloth mannequins, probably newly made, but in the old-fashioned style once used by seamstresses. They were fabric torsos with no heads, arms, or feet. Andrea provided me with an account of what happened.

> Instead of being mounted on a pedestal each [mannequin] was suspended by a wire from the ceiling and displayed in a line (three or four feet apart). We stopped to look at them and a few started to move, and then Dennis told me to look at the blue sequined one and it started to turn (partially revolve and then go back the other way). Quite a few of them were moving back and forth at different speeds, [and] after a couple of minutes a guard came up to us and asked us not to touch them, but neither of us had touched them—I can vouch for that.

Of course, this was exactly the sort of apparently spontaneous PK that Dennis claimed happened to him all the time. So when Andrea arrived with Dennis at the PF and told me what had occurred, I was hopeful that Dennis would be able to bring some momentum into our tests. Dennis also seemed buoyed by the episode. He seemed to be in a very positive mood, and even more voluble than usual. In fact, Dennis wouldn't stop talking, and that worried me somewhat. Dennis's speech seemed a bit like nervous, incessant chatter. I thought he might be trying to convince himself (or us) that all was well, that he was psychologically at ease, and that the damage from the previous New York visit had been put to rest. I worried that Dennis was still all too aware of how badly things had gone before, and that he was trying to suppress those memories as he embarked on his new series of experiments.

Steve Baumann and I wanted to try two different kinds of tests. The first would be to see if Dennis could influence the movement of an anemometer (a device for measuring wind speed) inside the rare book room. The second would be to see if Dennis could influence mobiles sealed inside the room. For all tests, Karl Petry placed a Super VHS camcorder inside the rare book room pointing out through the window into the hallway. It was located so that its field of view included the test objects as well as people in the hallway looking into the room. Output from the camera was also fed to a TV monitor in PF Director Lisette Coly's office down the hall, from which viewpoint the experimenters, onlookers, and Dennis could view the objects. Karl operated an additional camera stationed outside the rare book room looking toward the offices on the second floor of the PF. It provided another perspective on Dennis as he stood outside the room attempting to influence the test objects.

The results with the anemometer were clearly negative. This test was Steve Baumann's idea, and it was a clever variation on the sort of experiment Dennis preferred. Steve knew that Dennis never claimed to be able to influence such an object, but because the anemometer responds sensitively to wind, he felt (and Dennis agreed) that it was worth a try. But Dennis was unable to make the device move from a position of rest, and we were unable to determine whether he could speed up or retard the anemomenter's movement once it had been set in motion. The anemometer was connected to Baumann's laptop computer, which displayed the wind speed produced by a small electric fan stationed nearby. Unfortunately, we were unable to produce a wind speed that varied less than $\pm$ .5mph. Typically, we recorded speeds between 2.1 and 2.6 mph. Once, during one of the tests, the computer registered a speed of 2.7; but that is clearly not enough to demonstrate Dennis's influence on the anemometer (or wind). Perhaps a more expensive anemometer and precision wind source would have erased the ambiguity of our results, but those devices would have greatly exceeded our modest budget.

For the second experiment, three test objects were hung inside the sealed-off rare book room. Two mobiles rotated on their suspended strings, and they contained various objects (e.g., cardboard dinosaurs) that also rotated. The third object was a sort of plastic windsock, with many forty-eight-inch long plastic streamers that simply hung and did not rotate. We tried influencing the mobiles from outside the room by jumping on the floor, but our efforts had no effect.

The results with the two mobiles were less than compelling, although (depending on one's degree of natural optimism) perhaps somewhat encouraging. When Dennis tried consciously to influence the three test objects, the two rotating mobiles moved visibly, albeit slowly. But although it appeared to the experimenters that the mobiles were motionless when Dennis was given the go ahead, subsequent viewing of the video (especially in fast-forward) confirmed that those objects moved very slowly and intermittently when Dennis didn't overtly try to influence them. My initial assessment of those tapes was that the mobiles moved more (or at least more rapidly) during the test periods than during Dennis's periods of "official" inactivity—and that's certainly consistent with the impressions Baumann, Petry, and I had at the time. Although we saw no dramatic movement in the mobiles, it had seemed to us that there was conspicuous (if unimpressive) activity in those objects only during the test periods.

Of course, as in my initial meeting with Dennis in San Francisco, the "source of psi" problem presented a constant and confounding annoyance. If we grant (plausibly) the possibility of unconscious psi, then it's impossible to know whether Dennis was exerting any psi influence during periods when he was not explicitly attempting to do so. It's also impossible to know how the attitudes of the rest of us might have affected the test objects, positively or negatively. Presumably, many (I'd like to think all) of us were hoping Dennis would get some results. So we were all concentrating on (or at least thinking about) the mobiles, whether or not it was an official test period. And since those thoughts could, in principle, be linked to our own PK influence, for all we know our combined (or individual) influences could have perturbed the mobiles during non-test periods. In fact, they might even have interfered inadvertently with the effect created by Dennis. Moreover, if any of us had secretly hoped for Dennis to fail, that might have triggered an inhibiting influence during Dennis's official test periods. Put all of those potential influences together, and it's not clear what might result, especially when the observed effects are modest.

Actually, since we're speculating here in logical space, another option must also be considered. It's likely that Alex Imich had learned (normally) that a second round of tests with Dennis was taking place without his participation. Word of this could easily have reached him through the grapevine. And it's at least possible that he was aware of the fact only by means of ESP. But no matter how he acquired the knowledge, he too might have exerted an inhibiting influence on the results. Certainly, it's plausible to suppose that he would have sabotaged the tests if he could have done so. His rancor toward me continued unabated for several years after our sessions with Nuzum, and I believe it poisoned my relationship with several other parapsychologists (including Bert Schwarz).

In any case, the fact remains that we failed to see a dramatic difference between the test and "control" periods. Baumann and I agreed that the tapes would need to be examined painstakingly to determine whether the movements during test periods were significantly different than those during control periods. But neither of us had the time or resources to make such an analysis, and besides, the whole point of working with Dennis was to obtain a type of PK result for which statistical analysis would clearly be irrelevant.

The windsock results were also a disappointment. The streamers showed no movement at all, either during control or test periods. But ironically, that result had an upside. It suggested that stray breezes were not responsible for the movement of the two mobiles—at least during the test periods, because the windsock's plastic streamers moved very easily in response to the slightest breeze. All three objects were very close together in the small rare book room. So if stray breezes were moving only the two remaining mobiles, they would need to have been extremely localized. But given the care with which the room was sealed, that possibility seemed safely to be ruled out.

So despite never having carried out a statistical analysis of the results with the mobiles, I have to judge that portion of the test as a modest success—as providing some evidence of PK. The two mobiles and the windsock's streamers were all very labile, very easily perturbed. But only the mobiles moved. They were the sorts of objects Dennis preferred to work with, the room was carefully sealed, and the nearby windsock showed no influence at all. In the absence of PK influence, I think we should have expected no movement of any of the objects, or at least none of the clearly increased movement of the mobiles during the test periods. So even if the video revealed that there was some slight rotational momentum in the mobiles that couldn't be eliminated entirely, that wouldn't explain why the movement of the mobiles moved faster on several occasions—notably when Dennis tried consciously to affect them.

Despite our failure to obtain dramatic evidence of PK—which, after all, is what Dennis had initially and confidently promised to deliver—Dennis was satisfied and encouraged. I guess he felt that he had at least demonstrated his ability to move the mobiles under well-controlled conditions, even if he had not managed to dazzle us with large-scale phenomena. So he was disappointed and somewhat puzzled that Baumann and I couldn't share his enthusiasm after we viewed the tapes. Granted, Baumann and I initially shared Dennis's optimism, because it had seemed that we got movement in the mobiles only when Dennis consciously tried to affect them. But later we realized that even if the phenomena were genuine, establishing that fact beyond all reasonable doubt would not be nearly as easy as we had hoped.

I tried explaining the situation to Dennis via e-mail. Dennis had suggested to me that the problem with the video was due to a less-than-optimal camera angle. I disagreed and wrote that the deeper problem was that mobiles—perhaps especially very lightweight ones like those we used—are inherently unstable and subject to a great deal of random motion. I reminded him that we had hoped to gather evidence of PK that wouldn't require statistical analysis. But it looked as if the only way to make something genuinely convincing out of the video footage would be by means of a painstaking analysis of the mobiles' amount or speed of rotation during control as opposed to test periods. I assured Dennis that I hadn't lost interest in his case, but I suggested two things that I felt needed to be done before I'd be able once again to make a case for research funding. First, I endorsed Dennis's proposal to have a camera follow him around in the world, to see what sorts of anomalous object movements occur in his presence. I realized that no such video would be conclusive, but I suggested that, depending on its content, it might provide grounds for moving forward with more tests. Second, I proposed that Dennis try working with any of the skilled researchers in the Bay Area. Dennis also told me he was practicing with moving objects in sealed containers. He said he would videotape his sessions and send me tapes of his progress. I encouraged this strategy as well, and I was glad Dennis still seemed eager to subject himself to more testing.

4. Ending With a Whimper

Regrettably, Dennis enjoyed no more success as a psychic subject. He managed to arrange one or two sessions with researchers on the West Coast, but nothing came of them, and Dennis seemed to grow increasingly bitter over the way Bay Area researchers were treating him. I don't know the details of these encounters, and so I can't judge whether Dennis's complaints have any merit. In any case, Dennis contacted me frequently in the months following his June trip to New York, and then he continued to write me more occasionally. Each time he expressed his desire to work with me again, though not necessarily with Steve Baumann, whose demeanor Dennis now claimed he found too dour. And each time, Dennis promised to send me video of dramatic effects he claimed to be producing out in the world.

I never received any of the promised tapes, even though I reminded Dennis that I needed something from him, either tapes or endorsements from other investigators, before I could reasonably apply again for research funds. Over the years that followed, I continued to hear occasionally from Dennis, and then, after a long period of silence, I received word that Dennis had died on March 20, 2004, from heart failure.

Now I understand more about what was going on during this period. Dennis's wife Jill later told me of the gut-wrenching ordeal suffered by Dennis and his family. Not too long after our second series in New York, Dennis was bitten by an opossum, which forced him to undergo a painful series of rabies shots. Evidently, he was given an overdose of the serum, and according to Jill the live virus settled in Dennis's heart. Soon thereafter Dennis became ill, and after two years of misdiagnoses and various medications that only worsened his condition, he was told he needed a heart transplant. But Dennis began to suffer kidney failure before that could happen, and then he developed both diabetes and gout. According to Jill, the medications needed for Dennis's several conditions were not all compatible, and so Dennis's health continued to decline. This terrible saga lasted seven years. On March 16, 2004, Dennis suffered a heart attack. His doctors sent him home on the 19th, telling Dennis that he needed to get his affairs in order. He spent the night enjoyably, watching a movie with his daughter. The next day he died.

Jill told me that Dennis's medical problems put an end to his PK work pretty quickly. She wrote, "He just didn't have the strength and after a while the motivation. His life just became an ordeal to just stay alive and that one goal used up all of his energies. He never doubted his abilities or talents, but realized his time had passed."[3]

As far as psi research is concerned, perhaps the saddest aspect of this tale is the way Dennis's confidence was needlessly undermined by our investigations. I can't judge how the psychological battering he received, first from Alex Imich, and then from his less-than-spectacular follow-up sessions, might have penetrated into his daily life back home. Similarly, I don't know whether his inability to produce results for (or even engage the interest of) West Coast investigators added insult to injury. At least in the months following Dennis's second trip to New York, it was clear from our communications that he had both the will and the energy to continue as a PK subject. Nevertheless, my impression is that Dennis was somewhat broken by his encounters in New York.

And for what? Although I believe we saw some real PK, it wasn't impressive enough to make headlines even within parapsychological circles. Dennis was a good man, and unlike Joey Nuzum he was open, honest, thoroughly cooperative, and ready to do anything we asked of him. He deserved better. In fact, if Alex Imich hadn't treated Dennis like shit from the beginning, I believe we could easily and sensitively have prevented Dennis from feeling like a failure, even if he had produced nothing resembling observable PK. For example, we could have stressed the difficulty and artificiality of test conditions. We could have helped Dennis understand that what works out in the world often doesn't work well (or at all) in the context of an experiment, even when the investigators are sympathetic and supportive. Of course, if Imich hadn't treated Dennis like shit from the beginning, I think we might instead have seen and documented some pretty sensational object movements.

K. R., or Who Can You Trust?

1. May the Source Be With You

The history of science is more than a series of discoveries, failures, tests of hypotheses, and so on. To some extent it's also a tale of people behaving very strangely—and on occasion, very badly.[1] Historians and sociologists have shown that scientists often fail to be the models of objectivity, virtue, and clear thinking we'd like them to be. Like everyone else, they have confusions, hidden agendas, fears, and other frailties that sometimes lead to less than admirable—or at least curious—behavior. And not surprisingly, this is as true in psi research as it is within more mainstream areas of science. One recurring example is the way some underestimate, and others overestimate, the severity of certain familiar methodological issues.

Consider this: many parapsychologists believe that formal laboratory experiments can do more than merely establish the existence of anomalies in need of a theory. These researchers hope to learn something from their experiments about *how* psi works—for example, how (or to what extent) it's independent of space and time, or how psi success or failure correlates with personality variables or with experimental conditions. But in fact, that viewpoint is an almost total illusion, and veteran researchers can maintain it only by willfully ignoring an important and well-known mystery. As I mentioned in the previous chapter, parapsychology confronts the so-called source of psi problem: that if psi exists, then *by its very nature* it could evade all conventional experimental controls. For example, we can't erect PK "barriers" around all but the official subject in a PK test. Even if that's possible in principle, at our current level of ignorance we haven't a clue how to do it. Moreover, we have nothing like a PK meter to detect the origin of any PK influence. That's why it's important to seek out and test psychic "superstars," individuals who seem to get good results, reliably, under different conditions, and with different experimenters and observers.[2] But all too often, experimenters conduct their tests with more ordinary folk, and in those cases we can never be sure who's responsible for the test results. Similarly, we can't tell whether subjects or others are exerting a positive or negative influence on the results. The best we can do is to note whatever statistical anomalies occur, secure in the knowledge (or hope) that significant deviations can't be attributed to chance or cheating. This point should be painfully obvious. So it's peculiar (to say the least) that parapsychologists often seem oblivious to it.

Ironically, though, the same researchers conveniently remember this problem and quickly mention it in their own defense, when others attack their test results for being unimpressive and unconvincing. At that point, they alertly remind their critics that—for all we know—experimenters and others could be exerting their own (positive or negative) psi influence on the final results. And they point out that—for all we know—psychic functioning might be activated or inhibited by subconscious states which we can't conclusively identify and which we certainly can't control. But apparently it's only when they're under attack that these parapsychologists remember that there's no way they can distinguish, for example, subject PK from experimenter or onlooker PK—much less figure out how the different individuals might be contributing to the final result. When they're backed into a corner, they grudgingly acknowledge that we know almost nothing about what happens under the surface during parapsychology experiments. Unfortunately, that insight dissipates quickly. Before long the researchers resume the same sorts of experiments they conducted before, and they continue to make the same naive claims about what they hope to learn from them.

I suppose the charitable (or least sinister) way of describing this foible is to say it results from an excess of optimism. And if so, we could say that some critics of parapsychology (in fact, even a few parapsychologists) suffer from the reverse handicap: unconstrained pessimism. But this is no place for charity; it's probably more accurate to say that critics, too, have their convenient blind spots. The most notorious example is the way they make a needlessly big deal about the fallibility of human testimony. Although that's a handy strategy for rejecting the enormous number of eyewitness accounts of psychic phenomena, it's also very shallow. In fact (as we noted in chapter 2), it's not difficult to rely on ordinary observation and testimony when it comes to evidence in parapsychology. Contrary to what critics like to insist, these can be highly dependable indicators of authentically paranormal phenomena. Of course, not *all* observation and testimony are trustworthy, and skeptics justifiably (but tritely) point out that these sources of evidence shouldn't be trusted blindly. But it's simply stupid to reject observation and testimony altogether. To see why, we need to keep a few things in mind.

First, we must remember that—with the possible exception of certain internal states to which we have direct and privileged access (e.g., being in pain)—*no* source of evidence is infallible. All other evidence comes to us through channels of information that can be misleading or misinterpreted. In fact, testimony isn't the only thing that's not completely reliable. Things can go wrong even when data are recorded mechanically. Machines can malfunction or be tampered with, and extremely delicate and fine-tuned equipment may easily fall out of adjustment. Moreover, machine-derived data still need to be observed. In fact, they still need to be interpreted, and that process is anything but simple or inherently dependable and uncontroversial. So if we reject parapsychological evidence simply because it's fallible, or because we might incorrectly interpret the data we've collected, then for the same reason *all* scientific evidence should be rejected.

Second, observation and testimony vary considerably in quality from one context to another. Granted, under certain conditions they may be highly unreliable, and it's obviously important to know what sorts of conditions those are (whether or not one is doing psi research). But it's equally important to recognize that in certain circumstances observation and testimony can be very good indeed. In fact, our legal system depends on it. But so do our everyday dealings with others. In order to get through life with as few interpersonal calamities as possible, we need to discern a great variety of things—for example, who can be trusted and when, what sort of response is appropriate in a conversation, and which people have character or personality traits that are likely to gel nicely at a dinner party. These judgments all rest on observational prowess, often of very subtle facts, and some people are undoubtedly better at it than others.

Fortunately, some types of events are relatively easy to observe reliably. For example, matters are often more straightforward in the case of simple physical movements than when we're dealing with subtleties of behavior. But even so, we need to hold eyewitness testimony to certain obvious standards or requirements. These go a long way toward insuring that the events occurred as reported. For example, it helps when the conditions of observation are controlled by the observers, when there are multiple observers, when the light is good, when observers are prepared for and not surprised by the events they witness, when observation is at close range, when the phenomena are large enough to be easily observed, and when they linger long enough to be examined while they occur. The best reported cases of large-scale psychokinesis easily meet all or most of these requirements, and that's why we can't glibly dismiss non-laboratory evidence of PK just because it's based on admittedly fallible, or only conditionally acceptable, sources.[3]

Of course, attention to these requirements can also help us identify weak or bogus claims that something paranormal has occurred. The following is a case that illustrates how. In particular, it illustrates why a single observer's report needs to be scrutinized very carefully. Moreover, it raises interesting and important issues about the distribution of observational skills.

2. May the Force Be With You

Probably, many of us think we know which persons are likely to be keen observers. We suppose that some people are especially sharp and reliable, or at the very least that some people have different kinds of "perceptual antennae" and are more keenly attuned than others to certain kinds of happenings. In fact, that seems clearly to be true; people are seldom just good observers of *everything*. It's part of a person's psychological profile to have idiosyncratic sensitivities and to be more acutely aware of certain kinds of things than others. Some, for example, always accurately notice the color of people's eyes or hair, whereas others are oblivious to these things and might instead be more attuned to certain regularities in behavior—say, fear of intimacy, manipulativeness, or the ways people veil their anger.

We know, too, that observational powers can be sharpened with training and practice. That's why sports announcers and professional athletes notice subtleties in a game that more casual observers don't see at all—say, when a baseball pitcher threw a slider rather than a curve, or whether a basketball collision resulted from an offensive rather than a defensive foul. It's why people are able to refine their perceptions of the subtle properties of wine, chocolate, coffee, and audio equipment. And it's why professional acupuncturists, independently questioned, will agree on the hue of a patient's skin, the quality of the patient's voice, or diagnostically relevant odors, features of those individuals which others don't detect at all as distinct characteristics, or even recognize as descriptive categories.

Also, probably many of us suppose that some professions either attract keen observers or else train a person's perceptual acuity. And presumably that's because we also suppose that observational prowess is either a requirement or at least a specially prized virtue in certain occupations. Now these assumptions may be true as well, but if so, they must still be handled with care.

I admit, I assumed that certain professions tend especially either to attract good observers or at least train and sharpen people's observational powers. That's why I was particularly intrigued by a phone call I received in June 1997 from an Annapolis policeman whom I'll call K. R. This law enforcement veteran claimed that he had made a startling discovery. He found that he could place a photograph on his arm, leg, or on his bedspread, and then the image from the photo would "bleed" onto that other surface. In fact, K. R. said that sometimes the newly formed image would complete the picture by filling in details not in the original photo, and occasionally (he said) the new image would provide additional material merely *relevant* to the photo. For example, he said he placed a photo of two of his police buddies on his arm. The photo showed them only down to their waist. But the image appearing on his skin showed them, as they had been, on two bicycles facing each other. K. R. also claimed that the images on his bedspread were semipermanent. He said he could make them go away only by putting the bedspread in the dryer with a wet towel and tossing them for a while.

I had never before encountered claims for this particular psychic phenomenon, and although I was incredulous, I was intrigued, mostly because K. R. was a policeman. I was willing to give him more benefit of the doubt than I might otherwise have done, because, after all, he was a cop and a detective, and (I supposed) a better trained and more critical, reliable, and objective observer than the average person. I didn't think K. R. contacted me in the hope of gaining some kind of notoriety. In fact, he insisted that we keep this to ourselves. He even emphasized that we shouldn't talk to his colleagues on the force. He felt certain that they wouldn't share his tolerance for things that seemed paranormal.

I asked K. R. if he could easily demonstrate this phenomenon for me. He said he could. I then asked if it was something so obvious that still photos and video footage would reveal it clearly. He insisted they would. So I arranged to meet K. R. at his home, and in addition to a good still camera I brought with me my wife[4] and a friend of hers who owned a high-resolution camcorder. I wanted extra pairs of eyes for this, and if possible I wanted to photograph the phenomenon from multiple angles.

3. I See, You See

When we arrived at K. R.'s house, my companions and I were eager to witness what he had described to me on the phone. But K. R. said he first wanted to show me something impressive he'd been doing with video recorders. He claimed he'd been getting anomalous images on videotape by dubbing them multiple times. This was my first hint that the visit wouldn't go well. As readers may know, when you copy an analog video or audio tape, you add electronic noise that didn't exist on the original. And if you make copies of the copies, you keep adding noise. So late-generation audio cassettes have more audible tape-hiss than both the original tape and the first copy, and videotape copies similarly increase in video noise, which we experience as increased graininess in the image. So, since VHS is a rather low-resolution format to begin with, the late-generation videotapes K. R. showed me were extremely grainy, so much so that it was often difficult to tell what the original images had been.

To my surprise and concern, K. R. insisted that significant images were appearing on the tape, emerging out of the easily discernible grains on the screen. But my companions and I saw nothing, and we certainly saw nothing we could all agree was there. We could each imagine how certain clumps of the grains could be interpreted in various ways—say, as figures of different sorts. But we realized that this was like seeing figures in the shapes of clouds. We knew we were just exercising our creative energies, not seeing what was objectively there on the tape. I told K. R. that he seemed merely to be conducting a kind of Rorsach test, by producing inherently noisy media and then looking for patterns on them.

K. R. was frustrated and unconvinced, and he appeared perplexed that we couldn't see the images that were so evident to him. But undaunted, he said it was time to see what would happen with photos. So I handed him a photo I had brought, and he placed it on a pillowcase spread out on the seat of a chair. Then he invited us to see how the ripples in the less than perfectly flat pillow case started to assume the shapes on the photo. My companions and I looked very carefully and waited patiently, but again we saw nothing. K. R. seemed astonished that we couldn't see what was happening. He kept pointing enthusiastically to areas on the pillowcase where he said images were taking shape. But the rest of us still saw nothing. I suggested to K. R. that he might be using the ripples on the pillowcase's surface the way he used the grains in the videotape: as a source of "noise" onto which he could project images or patterns from his own imagination.

K. R. was still unconvinced and still undaunted. So he invited us to try the test again, first with a blanket, then with a paper lamp shade, and then with a piece of paper. But the farce simply repeated itself each time. The blanket, like the pillowcase, was less than perfectly smooth, and after placing the photo on the blanket, K. R. seemed merely to imaginatively project images onto variations in the blanket's surface. Again, he insisted that the shape of the ripples was evolving before our eyes, and once again my companions and I saw nothing. If something was happening, it was far too subtle for the rest of us. The tests with the lamp shade and paper presented an analogous situation, even though the surface of both objects was smooth and the paper's surface was also flat. In these cases the "noise" was supplied not by ripples but by nonuniformities in the lamp shade's texture and by the clearly visible grain in the heavy bond paper. My companions and I could all see that the two surfaces weren't perfectly uniform, and again we could imagine how various areas on the surfaces could be interpreted as familiar shapes. But we again found nothing we could agree was objectively or clearly on the two objects, and we certainly saw no change in their surfaces when the photo was placed on them (much less something resembling images in the photo). Of course, I conveyed these disappointing results to K. R., and I tried again to explain what I thought might really be happening. But despite my best efforts, I couldn't get K. R. to grasp that he might simply be projecting images onto an inherently noisy medium.

So K. R., bless his heart, was still unconvinced and still undaunted. He thought the problem might be due to the fact that we were conducting these tests in the poorly illuminated interior of his house. Since it was a warm day, he proposed that we go outside onto his deck, where (he claimed) he would show us what happened when he placed a half-photo on a surface. And since he was wearing shorts, he suggested we try the experiment on his leg.

Now I had prepared for this. Before leaving for K. R.'s house, I had cut in half two photos which I thought would be good for a test. One showed my wife walking our pet potbellied pig on a leash (don't ask; that's another story). I cut the photo so that one half simply showed my wife holding a suspended leash. The other photo was of my wife looking over the wall of one of the famous bear pits in Bern, Switzerland. In the original photo you could see the bears at the bottom of the pit. But I cut the picture so that one half simply showed my wife looking over a wall. I took the revealing second halves of the cut photos and placed them in an opaque sealed envelope.

Of course, we would have been happy to have any image at all appear on K. R.'s leg, never mind if it was the missing half of the photo placed there. But K. R. had said that we'd see the image of the other half of the picture. So I gave him the photo of my wife holding the leash. Shortly thereafter, K. R. alerted us that something was happening on his leg. My companions and I again saw nothing, and so I asked K. R. for guidance. Where, exactly, was the change happening? What should we be looking at? K. R. said the configuration of the hairs on his leg was changing. But the rest of us couldn't see it, and I had to point out to K. R., once again, that he seemed merely to be finding patterns in the "noisy" arrangement of leg hairs (the care with which we were now examining his leg was getting a little gross).

But maybe my companions and I were perceptually impaired. Perhaps K. R. could see something we couldn't, and so I asked him to identify the image he claimed to see on his leg. If he said he saw a pig on a leash, that would be something—arguably, a kind of ESP. After all, that half of the photograph was still in the sealed opaque envelope, and it was highly unlikely K. R. would come up with that answer as a lucky guess. Unfortunately, I can't recall now what K. R. claimed to see in the arrangement of leg hairs; but I do remember it was certainly not the image of a pig.

K. R. may now have been bent, but he wasn't broken. There was still one more half-photo we hadn't tried. So K. R. placed the half-photo of my wife at the bear pit on his leg. But the now familiar scene was repeated once more. K. R. saw an image; we didn't. I again asked K. R. what the missing part of the photo was, and he got it completely wrong. He clearly tried to guess, presumably based on his own experience, and so he claimed that my wife was watching mechanical objects such as cars. Not bears.

That should have been the end of the story. My companions and I left, and K. R. was clearly disappointed. More astonishingly, however, he was still puzzled. He still didn't understand why we couldn't see what was so obvious to him. Apparently, he couldn't accept the possibility that this "phenomenon" was a creation of his own imagination. For several weeks after this expedition he sent me photos, and also Xerox copies (very "noisy") of some other photos. In each case he insisted there were anomalous images clearly visible to the naked eye, but I saw nothing. For a reality check, I gathered up the photos and showed them to those lucky enough to be hanging around the philosophy department, asking whether they saw the images K. R. claimed to see there, or whether they saw anything of interest at all. Again, nothing.

I don't pretend to know K. R. well enough to say that he was delusional, much less in need of clinical intervention. Maybe he was simply naïve and (for reasons unknown to me) deeply eager for something miraculous to be happening in his life. It's not uncommon for people to invest very ordinary events in their lives with far more significance than the events deserve, and (as we'll consider in more detail in chapter 7) it's not uncommon for people to mistakenly interpret random events—or events having nothing to do with them—as both miraculous and profoundly relevant. No doubt there's a story here that would shed some light on K. R.'s motivation and beliefs. And although I realize it's not fair to generalize from this one subject, I have to say that the experience didn't serve as a confidence-builder in the Annapolis police.

The Thoughtography of Ted Serios: A Postscript

1. Background

One of parapsychology's more interesting byways is the evidence for so-called *psychic* (or paranormal) *photography*. This material divides easily into two classes, the first of which is commonly called spirit photography. The Spiritualist movement began and really kicked into gear shortly after the invention of the daguerreotype in the mid-nineteenth century. So when anomalous figures, appearing to be images of the deceased, started showing up unexpectedly in photographs, it helped spread the spiritualistic fever sweeping across the US and Europe. Some photographers even opened studios specializing in spirit photography. Although spiritualists and some others believed these "extras" were caused by, and helped prove the existence of, corresponding surviving spirits, many of the images were undoubtedly fraudulent. And of course, some argued that all spirit extras were produced by darkroom tricks.

The second type of apparent paranormal photography is usually called *thoughtography*, and it has no direct connection with the issue of postmortem survival. The term "thoughtography" was introduced in 1910 by Tomokichi Fukurai, a Japanese psychology professor who encountered the phenomenon accidentally, while working with a clairvoyant. Fukurai had asked his subject to identify, by ESP, a calligraphic character that had been impressed onto a still-undeveloped photographic plate. But later, he discovered that this character had also been impressed onto a different photographic plate, one that had simply been in the vicinity of the experiment. Because Fukurai suspected that his subject had psychically—but inadvertently—caused this to occur, he decided to see if the subject could get the same result deliberately. Accordingly, Fukurai selected specific calligraphic characters and asked his subject to imprint them onto photographic plates. The resulting series of tests yielded positive and interesting results, and some of the successful tests were very clever.[1] For example, in one trial Fukurai asked his subject to imprint half of a selected character onto one photographic plate and the other half onto a different plate. On another occasion Fukurai placed three stacked photographic plates into two boxes, one box inside the other, and he asked his subject to imprint a character onto only the middle of the three plates. However, despite his care in designing and implementing these experiments, Fukurai was severely criticized, and eventually he was forced to abandon his research and resign from the university.

Nevertheless, thoughtographic experiments continued in America and Europe. But after a brief flurry of activity, allegations of fraud helped snuff out this form of research for several decades. Then, beginning in the 1950s, Ted Serios sparked a renewed interest in paranormal photography, primarily because his thoughtographs were produced in ways that ruled out the usual opportunities for fraud. Previously, printing photos required several darkroom procedures, any one of which (critics alleged) could be manipulated surreptitiously. But Serios was apparently causing images to appear on the newly invented Polaroid system of so-called instant photography. Experimenters would observe him closely while the pictures were taken, and then everyone could watch the print appear as the film was removed from the camera. As a result, many consider the case of Ted Serios to be not simply the most impressive and best documented case of thoughtography, but one of the most impressive cases ever of psychokinesis generally.

When Serios was in his mid-30s and working as an elevator operator in a Chicago hotel, he began to experiment with hypnosis. During this period, he found that he could produce images onto film, at first using an ordinary box camera, and then eventually onto Polaroid film. After several years of demonstrating his apparent gift to various people and some researchers in the Chicago area, Serios came to the attention of Denver psychiatrist and psychical researcher, Jule Eisenbud. From May 1964 until June 1967 Eisenbud supervised thousands of trials, witnessed by at least one hundred different observers, most of them scientists and academics, and some of them experienced conjurors. These trials yielded around one thousand anomalous Polaroid photographs, the entire collection of which now resides in the Special Collections section of the library at the University of Maryland Baltimore County. Eisenbud reported this research in detail in his book, *The World of Ted Serios*.[2]

More than 400 of Serios's psychic photographs contained specific images. These images, usually of buildings, were typically somewhat blurry or distorted, but they were nevertheless often recognizable. And on some occasions Eisenbud or another experimenter selected a "target" image beforehand but concealed its identity from Serios (e.g., by sealing the image in an opaque envelope). They wanted to see if Serios could psychically identify the target and reproduce it onto Polaroid film. Some of these trials were judged to be successes (or "hits"), although the correspondences were generally not very close. However, Eisenbud suspected that the results probably revealed something about the working of Ted's unconscious, and more generally, about the subtle psychodynamics of psi. It's worth reading Eisenbud's thoughtful and penetrating discussions and interpretations of Ted's efforts in these cases. But for present purposes, it doesn't matter whether the correspondences between the anomalous Polaroids and the hidden targets are especially clear. The fact remains that the Polaroid photos were produced under conditions which seem clearly to rule out fraud, and accordingly which seem to require a paranormal explanation.

In any case, not all of Ted's attempts to reproduce hidden targets require depth-psychological scrutiny. For example, on one occasion the resulting photo seemed clearly to connect with Ted's preoccupation at the time. The hidden target in this case was a photo of the French chateau Maintenon. Ted was in a room about thirty feet away, but not especially interested in the experiment. He was more concerned with the arrival of the spacecraft Mariner IV in the vicinity of Mars. The photo produced on this occasion was a bottle-shaped object, which indeed looks very much like the shape of the spacecraft.[3]

However, some of Serios's most important and puzzling results don't involve the production of images at all. Serios also produced hundreds of so-called *blackies* and *whities*. The former photos were apparently either not exposed or at least greatly underexposed, and the latter were apparently severely overexposed. The blackies are perplexing because there's no reason to think that for those trials light had been prevented from reaching the film. So something should have appeared on the Polaroid film when it was removed from the camera. And the whities are puzzling because they were obtained when all visible light sources *had* apparently been blocked from the camera lens. Those Polaroids *should* have been dark.

In June 1967, Serios's productive three-year period of work with Eisenbud came to a sudden close when Ted produced an image of curtains. Eisenbud quickly grasped the symbolism of this image—"finis." He recognized that the curtain had indeed fallen, both on this fertile phase of Ted's psychic productivity and also on his own research with Ted. From this point on, Serios sporadically produced blackies and whities and some other anomalous effects, but he had apparently lost the ability to produce identifiable images on film.

Another reason this case is so fascinating is that Serios himself was an intriguing character—and hardly the ideal subject. For one thing, he was an alcoholic, and he preferred to work in a state of considerable inebriation. Eisenbud estimated that, during the three year-period of 1964 though '67, Ted consumed "several thousand quarts of hard liquor and beer as heavy drinking turned out to be a regular part of the picture taking ritual."[4] As a result, Ted often became more difficult to manage as the sessions progressed. This undoubtedly fueled the skepticism of some critics.

To complicate matters further, Serios also liked to work with what he called a "gismo," a short open cylinder, about an inch in diameter, typically created during the experimental sessions from the black paper packaged with Polaroid film. Ted often liked to place the gismo in front of the camera lens, holding it with his thumb and forefinger. Apparently, he had developed the habit of using a gismo from his early Chicago experiments, and now he felt comfortable with it, as if it helped him to concentrate (or, if you'll pardon the expression, focus) on the task at hand. Not surprisingly, critics found this highly suspicious. They charged that Ted used the device to conceal an image—for example, a transparency, which (they claimed) could then be projected onto the film.

The primary source of this skeptical allegation was the article, "An Amazing Weekend with the Amazing Ted Serios," in the October 1967 issue of *Popular Photography*, written by David B. Eisendrath and Charles Reynolds. I remember reading this article as a teenager, thinking that the authors had successfully exposed the pretensions of an alleged psychic. I had no idea at the time how misleading that article was, and I was certainly unaware that no one had accepted Eisenbud's challenge (in the following November issue)[5] to duplicate Serios's results under conditions similar to those imposed on Serios. Before long, Eisendrath's and Reynolds's criticism morphed into the unverified assertion that Serios's feats had been duplicated easily by the magician the Amazing Randi, and soon many people had accepted this falsehood as an established fact. The noted science author Martin Gardner undoubtedly moved this process along by repeating the allegation in his book, *Science, Good, Bad and Bogus*,[6] and by claiming in the journal *Nature* that Randi "demonstrates it [the Serios phenomenon] regularly and with more skill."[7] However, as I mentioned in chapter 1, Gardner's claim is completely unsubstantiated. Randi has never even attempted publicly to duplicate the Serios phenomenon under conditions resembling those that prevailed during Serios's tests. He did, however, fail to duplicate the phenomenon under the much looser test conditions allowed on the television show *Today* on October 4, 1967.

In any case, suspicion over the gismo persisted. Of course, it's understandable how people only casually acquainted with the evidence might think that concern over the gismo is warranted. But it's simply unacceptable when presumably authoritative critics try to dismiss the Serios case by claiming that Ted used the gismo to fake his results. In fact, that skeptical strategy betrays either gross and inexcusable ignorance of the evidence or outright dishonesty in reporting it. There are several reasons for my cynicism here. First, Serios often produced multiple images in one experimental session (e.g., as many as fifty separate images during a series of sixty to eighty trials, or ten to twenty images in a shorter series of trials). So even if Ted had been concealing images in the gismo, he would have needed to replace those hidden images many times throughout the session while somehow avoiding the detection of observers who watched him closely. At any rate, the gismo was usually examined before, during, and after shooting, and no images or other devices were found inside. Second, experimenters often held the gismo until the photo was taken. That drastically reduced the time in which Ted could place an image within the gismo, and of course that would make it all the more difficult for Ted's alleged trickery to escape detection. And third, Ted sometimes produced images under conditions of complete darkness and also on unexposed, opaquely wrapped film. (Significantly, critics ignore discussing this and other test conditions in which the appeal to hidden devices would appear ludicrous.)

But most important, Serios produced more than thirty-six images when he was separated from the camera at distances of one to sixty-six feet. Those effects were observed on twelve occasions in nine different locations by fourteen witnesses including Eisenbud. Moreover, on these occasions thirteen witnesses besides Eisenbud and Ted held and triggered the Polaroid camera. Now to appreciate fully just how lame it is to explain away Ted's results by appealing to images hidden in the gismo, consider this: for the hidden-image-in-the-gismo hypothesis to have any credibility, Serios would have needed to be located no more than a small fraction of an inch from the camera lens. Otherwise, the camera would take a picture of the gismo, not the image allegedly hidden inside it. This should be painfully obvious, but in any case Eisenbud and his colleagues made the effort to duplicate Ted's effects by placing transparencies within in the gismo. Not surprisingly, they couldn't do it. Moreover, for some trials Ted was dressed in clothes provided by the experimenter (thereby eliminating the presumed hiding place for images to be inserted later in the gismo). And in some cases Ted was separated from the camera by being placed inside an electrically shielded Faraday cage, while the camera was held by an experimenter outside the cage, obviously well outside the range needed for the alleged gismo trick to work. We should also keep in mind that the hidden-image-in-the-gismo hypothesis doesn't account for Ted's ability to produce blackies and whities.

One of Serios's more interesting photos occurred when he tried to produce a picture of the Chicago Hilton Hotel, where he had once been employed. Instead, he produced a photo of the Denver Hilton (for this trial, Eisenbud held and triggered the camera, and he was standing three feet from Ted). That fact is probably remarkable enough. But arguably more interesting is the perspective from which the Denver hotel is shown. According to Eisenbud, that view of the hotel could only have been shot from "a position not achievable with an ordinary seven-foot stepladder but only with some special contrivance for getting the cameraman well into the air."[8] Eisenbud recognized the similarity between this perspective and the reports of many psychics (traveling clairvoyants) who claim to perceive distant objects as if from a floating position.

Possibly the most fascinating, but also dauntingly complex, aspect of the Serios case concerns the way objects appear distorted in many of Ted's images. Predictably, Eisenbud believed these distortions provided further clues about the underlying psychodynamics of psi. But for now, what matters most about them is that the distortions seem to be of a kind that rules out the possibility of fraud. In particular, they seem clearly to rule out (a) prior fraudulent preparation of the images and also (b) improvised manipulation of undistorted images.

An outstanding example of these distortions is a photo Ted produced spontaneously after Eisenbud suggested paying a visit to his ranch. A fresh pack of Polaroid film was used, and Eisenbud created a gismo for Ted on the spot. After some blackies and barely formed images (Eisenbud called them embryonic), Serios produced a recognizable photo of Eisenbud's property, showing Eisenbud's ranch house and nearby barn. However, the photo didn't resemble Eisenbud's house and barn as they were at the time. The image more closely resembled Eisenbud's ranch at a period before Ted had ever seen it, and parts of the barn were depicted in a condition in which it had never existed (see figs. 6.1 and 6.2).[9]

The house in Ted's photo had no shutters on the windows. Now the windows had in fact been shutterless many years earlier, but Eisenbud added

FIGURE 6.1

FIGURE 6.2

shutters to the windows several years before he and Ted met for the first time. Moreover, in Ted's photo, most of the lower level of the barn appears dark in color. But that had never been the case when the ranch house had no shutters. Also, the barn in Ted's photo apparently has no Dutch door on the lower left, which was not the case at any time. In fact, in Ted's photo, that portion of the barn was solid white. That would almost have accurately depicted Eisenbud's barn if both parts of the Dutch door had been closed, although the door had dark borders on the outside which should then have been visible. But in any case, the upper portion of the door had been removed years before Ted ever visited the ranch, and any photo of that doorway would have shown a dark patch in that location. To Eisenbud, the Serios distortions were suggestively similar both to the dream distortions of his psychiatric patients and to the distortions in drawings of target figures noted throughout the history of ESP research.

Another interesting group of distortions appeared in an image Ted produced of Williams's Livery Stable in Central City, Colorado (see figs. 6.3 and 6.4).[10] On this occasion Ted produced two images in two different cameras, held by two different investigators. The investigators kneeled in front of Ted, who was seated on a sofa and who held a gismo up to (but not quite touching) the lenses. In Ted's photo, the windows of the building are elongated, and the building's archway and windows appear to have been bricked in. (Research conducted at the Western History division of the Denver Public Library produced no evidence that those structures had ever been bricked in.) Furthermore, the masonry of the building in Ted's image is quite different from that of the actual building. The actual livery stable is made of old pressed brick, whereas Ted's Polaroid shows it as being a kind of embedded rock. Also, Ted's image fails to show the large letters, "WILLIAMS'" above the lower window, and it shows a playbill to the left of that window to which Eisenbud was unable to find any match.

I should emphasize that despite Eisenbud's repeated—and financially generous—challenges to conjurors to duplicate the Serios phenomena *under conditions similar to those prevailing during the experiments*, no one has come forward. As I mentioned earlier, some have claimed to produce Serios-like effects, but those claims have never been supported by public demonstrations or any other hard evidence. In fact, as I mentioned in chapter 1, James Randi flamboyantly accepted Eisenbud's challenge on national television (even though he failed to duplicate the phenomenon for an on-camera trial), and then once the program was over refused to make good on his wager. It's also worth repeating that this can easily be confirmed by examining the

FIGURE 6.3

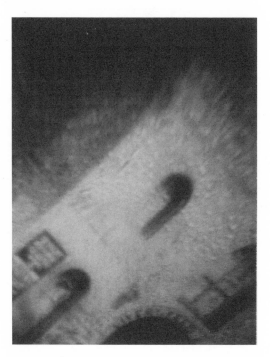

FIGURE 6.4

Eisenbud-Randi correspondence, finally available for public scrutiny in the Special Collections section of the UMBC Library.

2. Meeting of the Minds

I met Jule Eisenbud in 1978, but only casually, at a meeting of the Parapsychological Association. However, the following year I visited Denver for a conference on philosophy and parapsychology, and that occasion allowed me to spend extended time with Jule at his home and ranch. We quickly discovered that we were kindred spirits who admired each other's work, and soon we became very close friends. Jule was an exceptionally impressive person. He had a remarkably thorough grasp of many different fields, including philosophy, physics, mathematics, history, anthropology, art, and music. He also had a prodigious memory and could quote extensively from Freud, Shakespeare, the letters of Mozart, and Wittgenstein. I managed every year thereafter to visit Jule at least once, for extended discussions on a wide range of topics, detailed critical examination of our most recent manuscripts, and also for very enjoyable hanging out with Jule, his wife Molly, and Jule's children and their families. I couldn't share Jule's enthusiasm for psychoanalysis, but I had great respect for his subtle and penetrating application of its principles. In any case, our views on many other subjects were quite similar or at least complementary, and so conversations with Jule were invariably stimulating.

Not surprisingly, Jule and I often discussed the Serios case, especially the way that work had been, and continued to be, misrepresented in both the popular press and in specialized scientific publications. The original edition of *The World of Ted Serios* had sold briskly until the *Popular Photography* article appeared. But afterwards, sales ground to a halt, and thousands of copies were returned to the publisher. Of course, Jule was deeply disappointed and frustrated by his inability to get a fair hearing for his work with Ted. Eventually, after relentless prodding from me, he published a second and revised edition of the book, in which he described and responded to the shabby treatment he received at the hands of his critics.

Although Jule's research with Ted had ended, his involvement with Ted had not. Serios sometimes remained in the Denver area for extended periods, sometimes finding work, often getting into trouble and needing Jule to bail him out of jail, and periodically returning (or fleeing) to his old territory in and around Chicago. Because Ted's alcoholism frequently interfered with his holding down a job, Jule established a foundation to provide him with a modest monthly income and a reasonable measure of security. Among other things, Jule feared that if Ted found himself unemployed and with no funds for alcohol, he might easily be lured into a false confession of fraud.

I first met Ted on one of my regular visits to Denver. Ted had been in town for a few months, living in a battered truck with several dogs, and one evening he came to the Eisenbud house for dinner. Although Jule doubted that Ted would regain his abilities (especially the power to produce recognizable images), he never entirely lost hope that Ted's mid-1960s magic would return. Jule would have dearly loved one more chance both to put the evidence before the public and also to restore his damaged reputation. Besides, he was always ready to understand more about what made Ted tick. So he usually had several Polaroid cameras near at hand, especially when Ted was in the vicinity, just in case Ted felt ready to experiment.

I'm not sure how much alcohol Ted had consumed before appearing at the Eisenbud house that evening. Most likely it was enough to disable the average person. But whatever the amount, Ted enjoyed some additional lubrication with dinner, and eventually he said he wanted to try getting results with one of Jule's cameras. But I'm not sure what prompted him to do this. Since arriving in Denver, Ted had shown no interest in resuming tests of his abilities; instead, he'd been preoccupied with personal issues. My guess is that because Jule had been saying very flattering things about me, Ted now wanted, competitively, to show off a bit.

At any rate, while the rest of us remained seated at the dining room table, Jule held the camera and followed Ted as he paced around the room. After a few minutes, Ted scrunched up his face and tried to summon his old mojo. (He used no gismo, by the way.) The camera was pointed at Ted, and on Ted's signal Jule tripped the shutter. The first couple of shots were unremarkable and showed part of Ted's face and part of the dining room. So Ted tried twice more, and in both cases part of the image was blanketed by a large bright area, more yellow than white, but almost as if the Polaroids were whities in the making. In the second of the two images, the bright area covered nearly a third of the picture. But nothing in the camera's field of view would ordinarily have produced that effect. The bright areas didn't look like the sorts of streaks that might be produced if the camera had been pointed at a nearby light source. The room was illuminated only from a light fixture over the table; that light was rather muted; and besides, the camera wasn't facing that direction. After these two pictures emerged from the camera, Jule took another shot, as a control, to see what would appear if Ted wasn't trying to influence the results. Again, we got an unremarkable picture of the room.

Although Ted wasn't happy with the outcome, Jule seemed pleased. And I had to agree with Jule that under the circumstances, the bright areas shouldn't have appeared in the Polaroid photos. No light source near the camera could have produced them, and the camera seemed to be operating properly, as the first two pictures and the final control shot had demonstrated. (In fact, Jule had used the camera the day before to photograph his ranch, and he encountered no problems at that time either.) Moreover, Ted neither held nor operated the camera, so it seemed highly unlikely that he had managed to rig the results.

As Jule's health declined in the 1990s, he realized the urgency of finding a safe haven for the original Serios photographs, numerous signed affidavits, and other documents pertaining to the case. Probably because Jule was something of a celebrity in the Denver area, the Denver Public Library apparently came to the rescue. They offered to hold and protect the Serios materials and also digitize the photos as a backup. So even though Jule died unsatisfied about the public response to his work with Ted, he was comforted in his final months believing that the evidence would survive and be accessible to researchers willing to study it fairly.

3. The Hotel Series

Jule died in March 1999, and his son Eric (Rick) assumed responsibility for watching over Ted and managing the foundation funds. Rick learned quickly what his father had discovered a long time before: that keeping on eye on Ted could be a full-time job. Two months after Jule's death, Ted made the first of several extended return visits to Denver. At first, Rick found lodging for Ted in a nearby hotel, but two weeks later he managed to place him in a supervised residence. When I visited Denver the following September, Ted was still in town.

I had come to Denver on this occasion to help the family sort through Jule's letters, papers, and books. Jule's children were uncertain which personal items were worth preserving for posterity and which books or journals might be of interest to other scholars or research institutions. This turned out to be no small task. For one thing, Jule's library was enormous, and for another, he had apparently preserved all his written correspondence, both personal and professional, since the 1930s. His files were a real testament to the durability of carbon copies. Moreover, Jule wrote lots of letters; in fact, he was a wonderful correspondent. So it took me at least five more visits over the next few years to finish wading through the material. The process was interesting, often painful, and definitely intimidating. As glad as I was to help the Eisenbud family with this matter, I wasn't entirely comfortable trying to decide which of Jule's (sometimes very) personal items should be retained, and in general which of them might turn out to be of scholarly interest. The only easy decision was to keep everything pertaining to the Serios case, and there was quite a lot that hadn't been deposited at the Denver Public Library.

At any rate, soon after I arrived in Denver, Rick Eisenbud told me that Ted was in town. He informed me that Ted claimed to have been sober for the past four years and was curious to see if he could produce thoughtographs while alcohol-free. Of course, that was an intriguing prospect. So one evening Ted and Rick came to my hotel room, armed with a Polaroid camera and several fresh, sealed rolls of film.

Ted and I chatted amiably at first and reminisced with Rick about Jule, just to break the ice and apparently get reacquainted (though I didn't believe Ted when he said he remembered who I was). However, I did believe that he was sober. He was less manic and scattered than on our previous encounter; he showed none of the aggression and bravado that had characterized his intoxication over the years; and apart from needing periodically to satisfy a clearly gnawing nicotine craving, he was pretty relaxed. I can't confirm Ted's claim that he'd been on the wagon for four years, and he may well have been exaggerating. Still, although it would have been in character for Ted to overstate his success, he had no reason to lie to us simply about having been sober for a while. After all, it's not as if his security depended on it. He knew that the foundation would provide for him no matter what. Besides, nothing else that evening suggested that Ted had any interest in impressing either Rick or me. Apart from our informal experiment, the occasion was more like a male bonding session in memory of Jule.

Eventually, Ted seemed comfortable enough to see what he could do with the Polaroid camera. He'd been sitting on a chair near my bed and I'd been sitting on the side of the bed, a few feet away. After Rick and I rolled paper from the film pack into an impromptu gismo, Ted pulled the chair closer to me while I loaded the camera. Ted never held the camera. Instead, he held the gismo with one hand and placed it around the camera lens. Then with his other hand on my forearm, he guided the camera into a position close to his face and instructed me to trip the shutter at his signal. Rick was seated to Ted's right, where he could see clearly whether Ted tried to obscure or place another object (e.g., a transparency) in front of the camera lens.

We didn't have time to take some initial control shots; Ted was ready to go. But the first ten shots were nothing special. They showed a blurry image of Ted's face (caused primarily by his movement as he signaled me to take the picture) and often an easily recognizable portion of the floor lamp or the curtains behind Ted's chair.

However, picture no. 11 was a blackie. It was the third of four shots taken in rapid succession and under virtually identical conditions. The other three shots show, in varying degrees of blurriness, part of Ted's face and the curtains behind him. At that point I was quickly taking the exposed photos as they emerged from the camera and placing them on the bed where they could develop. And because it took about a minute for the pictures to finish developing, we didn't realize that no. 11 was a blackie until after we had taken the next picture. So I shot picture 13 as a control (with Ted's hand removed from my forearm), and the camera clearly registered Ted, part of his chair, and the curtains behind them (see fig. 6.5).

10   11

12   13

FIGURE 6.5

We then resumed taking pictures. First we got two more blurry shots of Ted's face. However, the second of these was covered by splashes of streaking light, possibly more than could have been produced by the floor lamp behind Ted. We weren't using a flash with the camera, and the floor lamp was off to Ted's left and not visible in the photo. But the splashes of light covered most of the picture, including the area to the right of the blurry outline of Ted's face, and it partially obscured the clearly visible curtains behind and to the right of Ted. Although I can't confidently rule out that these effects resulted from a combination of Ted's movement and light from the lamp, I'm inclined to doubt it. In fact, the bright streaks reminded me of the effect obtained several years earlier in Jule's dining room, when there was no nearby light source.

In any case, the next shot (no. 16) was more impressive—another blackie (fig. 6.6). So I immediately took a control shot, and again, we got a clear image of Ted, his chair, and the curtains. Then, after getting yet another blurry shot streaked with bright areas, I asked Ted to place his finger over the gismo, to see whether that would produce a blackie. Ted used the thumb of his right hand, which still held the gismo around the lens. His left hand remained on my forearm. The resulting shot, no. 19, was a picture of the corner of the room behind Ted, with a mostly underexposed lower two-thirds of the frame (fig. 6.7). But the underexposed portion wasn't nearly as black as the blackies obtained in images 11 and 16. That's not surprising, because Ted's thumb wasn't as large as the opening of the gismo, and since the gismo kept the thumb at least an inch from the lens, it couldn't obscure the lens entirely. Moreover, when Ted repositioned his hand to comply with my request, he shifted his body somewhat. That forced me to move a bit as well, and as a result the camera ending up facing in a slightly different direction from the one in which we had obtained the previous images and blackies. That's why this control image, unlike those that preceded it, reveals the room's corner, where a bare wall meets a curtained window. Also, if Ted had managed to cover the entire gismo with either the hand still holding the gismo, the hand on my arm, or his body, presumably he would have needed to move in a way that would have been obvious to either Rick or me. So I suspect that Ted didn't produce the two blackies by blocking the front of the gismo.

Finally, we ended our session with six more shots, all of them blurry and most of them featuring splashes of light. Our penultimate shot, no. 25, was particularly amorphous, with no visible outline of Ted's face (fig. 6.7). In fact, in the final series of shots, Ted's face became progressively unrecognizable, and I doubt that this was caused entirely by either Ted's movement or

15   16

17   18

FIGURE 6.6

camera shake, especially in the case of shot 25. Assuming (reasonably) that the camera's non-flash-sync shutter speed was at least 1/30 of a second, Ted's movement would have been recorded as streaks of partially recognizable facial features—precisely what we saw in most of the preceding shots. In fact, some signs of (relatively minor) facial movement were evident in the final images. But in shot 25, and to some extent in the other shots as well, Ted's facial features were obliterated and replaced by cloudy or foggy patches. In fact, shot 25 is almost entirely fog. I should add that Ted never yanked the hand he placed on my arm, and (as a veteran and occasional professional photographer) I'm well aware how to trip a shutter smoothly.

Of course, unlike Jule's earlier work with Ted, these were very informal trials, and I don't want to overestimate their importance. If the Serios case depended on evidence of this quality, it probably would never have

19   20

FIGURE 6.7

risen above the status of a curiosity. Still, the splashes of foggy light and the blackies shouldn't have occurred under our modest controls. Moreover (as I mentioned earlier), I don't believe Ted felt he needed to impress Rick or me. In fact, I'm confident he knew that nothing of any consequence hinged on the outcome of our informal tests. The three of us were simply hanging out, talking about life and sharing fond memories of Jule, and Ted merely seemed curious to see whether he still had it in him to get some results, especially in his unprecedented state of extended sobriety.

If, as I suspect, our informal tests reveal Ted's PK influence on Polaroid film, they're at least an interesting footnote to a rich and undeniably important case. Jule had already noted that, after the "curtains" fell in 1967 and Ted could no longer produce recognizable images on film, he still got occasional blackies and whities. So our results seem to indicate that Ted's reduced powers still lingered. Actually, his career as a whole looks intriguingly like the careers of some mathematicians, athletes, and musicians, who enjoy spectacular spurts of creativity or productivity early on, but then settle down to something less dazzling.

In fact, it wouldn't surprise me if Ted's post-1967 career contains clues to one of parapsychology's major mysteries: the so-called decline effect. It's well-known that the abilities of even parapsychology's superstars often seem to fade over the course of their careers, and this is clearly not because investigators imposed ever-tighter experimental conditions as time went on. Moreover, short-term declines have been observed repeatedly *within* quantitative experiments. That is, non-chance scoring in psi tests often drifts toward chance during a single session or over a series of trials, even when the overall results remain significantly non-chance. It's far from clear why these declines occur, although (of course) conjectures abound. Hopefully, at some more enlightened time in the future, we'll have learned enough about psi to make fine-grained observations about its natural history and explain this phenomenon in particular. And perhaps then we'll then know what to make of the apparent vestiges of Ted's power displayed in my hotel room.

4. Recent Developments

Near the beginning of 2002, the Denver Public Library informed Rick Eisenbud that it had decided to divest itself of its Serios holdings. The Library's management had changed, and those now in charge evidently felt no need to honor their earlier commitment to Jule to maintain and protect his donation. Because Rick and his siblings were often traveling or otherwise difficult to reach, Rick asked the Director what they would have done with the material if they hadn't been able to reach him. To his astonishment, the Director replied that they would probably have thrown the material away. Of course, Rick was angry over the Library's cavalier attitude, and it added to the anxiety he already felt about finding a good home for his father's scholarly legacy. I'd already set aside many boxes of letters, papers, and photos from my several years of sifting through Jule's stuff, and to that we now had to add the substantial material from the Denver Library.

Beginning long before Jule's final illness, Jule and I had occasionally discussed where the valuable Serios material should eventually be housed. We'd considered offering it to one of the parapsychological research organizations in the US—primarily, the American Society for Psychical Research (ASPR), the Parapsychology Foundation (both in New York), or the Rhine Research Center in Durham, North Carolina. Patrice Keane, director of the ASPR, had even lobbied actively for the material. But Jule and I agreed that all those organizations were too unstable financially to be entrusted with the material. Moreover, both the Rhine Center and the PF were located at the time in old buildings, and most of their archives were housed in areas which we felt were too vulnerable to floods or fires. Furthermore, we believed that the ASPR's management had driven that once respectable and proud organization into the ground—going so far as to sell off some of its valuable artifacts. So entrusting them with the Serios material hardly seemed like a safe bet. In fact, the ASPR had become so disorganized and poorly managed that it was almost impossible for interested researchers to access the material in its collection. That's why Jule was pleased when the Denver Public Library offered to care for at least major items from the Serios archives. Presumably, that institution wasn't going anywhere, people would be able to access the material, and Jule felt he could trust its management.

Rick and I revisited this issue and agreed that the situation was largely unchanged. Although the Rhine Center had finally relocated to a spiffy new building, financially its future was more precarious than ever. So Rick and I agreed that it would still be unwise to donate the material to one of the major US parapsychological research centers. Then it occurred to me to see whether my university's library would be interested in housing the Eisenbud/Serios material. Perhaps it's surprising that I hadn't taken this idea seriously before. But I believe I was justifiably cynical about finding a mainstream academic home for it. I'd had more than my share of encounters with the academic community's irrational resistance to psi research (including skirmishes at my own institution), and I knew that my experiences were similar to those of other university-based parapsychologists. However, the situation was now grim. All the material had been housed temporarily in the office of Jule's other son, John. But John's business was moving to a new and smaller location. So I approached Tom Beck, chief curator of Special Collections at UMBC's Albin O. Kuhn Library and Gallery, and to my surprise and delight, Tom realized what an intriguing and valuable acquisition this would be. He recognized the intrinsic interest in the collection and hoped that it would attract researchers from around the globe. Moreover, Tom felt it would further enhance the library's already very distinguished collection of nearly two million photographs, from some of the world's leading photographers (including Ansel Adams, Lotte Jacobi, and others). Before long, Rick sent him fourteen big boxes.

Tom was right. After the library issued some press releases, the Eisenbud/ Serios material quickly became a magnet to both domestic and European researchers eager to examine it carefully for themselves. For example, in 2003, a team from German television accessed the collection for a series they were producing on the paranormal. The following year, the collection was examined thoroughly by Andreas Fischer, from the Institut für Grenzgebiete der Psychologie und Psychohygiene (IGPP) in Freiburg, Germany. As a result of his efforts, UMBC loaned thirteen Serios thoughtographs to the renowned Maison Européenne de la Photographie in Paris. From November 2004 until February 2005, those photos were part of an exhibit entitled "Le Troisième Oeuil: La Photographie et l'Occulte" (The Third Eye: Photography and the Occult). In September 2005, the exhibit moved to the Metropolitan Museum in New York, where it ran until December under the title, "The Perfect Medium: Photography and the Occult."[11] Each exhibit was accompanied by a handsome and very large catalogue of its photos, many of them extremely rare.

I'm pleased to say I was able to write the essay on Serios for those catalogues.[12] It allowed me to counter the usual falsehoods circulated about Serios and explain (however briefly) why the case is so important. Perhaps my efforts paid off in at least one instance. The September 4, 2005, *New York Times* contained a mostly snide and dismissive review of the Met exhibit. The article even contained a cowardly and shamefully ignorant quote from Nancy Sondow, president of the ASPR, who loaned several photos to the exhibit. Of the exhibit as a whole, Sondow said, "We don't consider it the real stuff, you know . . . I guess it's interesting from the standpoint of the history of photography."

Nevertheless, the author of the article, Randy Kennedy, singled out the Serios photos as an exception. He wrote,

> The 120 pictures in the exhibition are by turns spooky, beautiful, disturbing and hilarious. They are also, by and large, the visual records of decades of fraud, cons, flimflams and gullibility—though there are also some pictures, like those produced by an eccentric Chicago bellhop, Ted Serios, said to be purely from his thoughts, in the 1960s, that have never been adequately explained.

It's too soon to say whether the recent attention given to the Serios case will lead finally to its widespread acceptance and appreciation. Certainly, the history of parapsychology offers little basis for optimism. Skepticism is just as glib and dishonest now as it was in 1882 when the British SPR was founded. In fact, despite sensible and careful dismantling of the traditional skeptical objections, the same tired arguments surface again and again.[13] And those arguments all too easily mislead those who haven't yet heard the other side of the story or examined the evidence for themselves.

It's also difficult to know what will become of the Eisenbud/Serios material after inevitable management changes at UMBC's library. It's unlikely that the Denver library episode is a total anomaly. Nevertheless, it's clear that the Serios case has survived many years of misrepresentation and dishonest criticism. Maybe, in this case at least, the truth will out.

The Synchronicity Confusion

1. Introduction

We've all experienced coincidences in our lives: surprising combinations of events that appear to be causally unrelated. Of course, what surprises us about the events isn't simply that they're apparently unrelated causally. That's true of many (if not most) pairs of events at any given time, and in fact the vast majority of events are completely unremarkable when considered in combination. The event-clusters in a coincidence attract our attention first because something about their combination seems personally noteworthy or strange, and second, because we consider that combination to be more or less improbable. In fact, the more improbable we think the event-clusters are, the more significant and remarkable the coincidences are likely to seem.

Nevertheless, a coincidence will often appear far less interesting after only a little reflection. For one thing, it's usually clear that the coincidental events probably have no *common* cause. And for another, we can recognize that each event probably has its own independent—and perfectly conventional—causal explanation. For example, suppose I find myself thinking about an old high school friend Paul, whom I haven't seen in decades, and suppose that at that moment I run into Paul on the street. On the face of it, that might seem quite astonishing. But I might realize later that there was nothing special or cosmic about our meeting. It might turn out that I was thinking about Paul because I had just read a magazine article about proctologists, and I remembered that good old Paul had (inscrutably) yearned for a career in proctology. And it might turn out that Paul was in town to attend the proctology convention that's held annually at the same hotel. It might then occur to me that I ran into Paul because I often frequent the neighborhood around the convention hotel. In fact, when I consider how often I'm near the convention site and how regularly Paul attends his professional meetings, I might even wonder how I had missed running into him in the previous years. Moreover, since I frequently read magazine articles about medicine, and especially since I might have subconsciously noticed signs and other indicators of the convention as I passed the hotel, it seems considerably less amazing that I was thinking about my physician friend prior to our meeting.

These kinds of considerations will frequently rob coincidences of their apparent mystery. It's often the case that the combination of events in a coincidence isn't as improbable as we initially thought. To take another example, many are surprised to discover that with as few as forty-eight people, there's a 95% chance that two of them are born on the same day and month. But causal and statistical naïveté aren't the only reasons we overestimate the importance of coincidences. Sometimes, our judgments are colored by a kind of egocentric bias—a tendency to overestimate the significance or rarity of an event-combination simply because it happens to us.[1]

Still, some coincidences seem, even after consideration, to be too bizarre and too meaningfully appropriate to our lives to be explained away in normal terms. For these event-combinations, we have trouble believing that they're not really special and that we merely, more or less innocently, happen to find them meaningful and arresting. In fact, in the most impressive cases it looks almost as if the universe is speaking to us. The coincidences have a numinous or awesomely supernatural quality, and they're astonishingly specific and remarkably pertinent to major themes in our lives. We can't help but think that no conventional explanation, no matter how intricate, will successfully normalize the experience. In these cases we're inclined to think that appeals to conceptual naivete and observer bias are simply beside the point.

The psychologist Carl Jung coined the term "synchronicity" to stand for these more potently meaningful coincidences.[2] Unfortunately, his explanation of the concept of synchronicity has some needless and arguably harmful conceptual baggage. One is an apparently naïve and limited grasp of the nature of causality.[3] Jung claimed that synchronicities are *acausal*—that is, somehow outside the realm of causal explanation. But Jung seemed to believe that two events are causally connected only when they're contiguous or adjacent in space and time (like billiard ball collisions), and perhaps also only when there's some rationally evident connection between the events.[4] However, that view has been seriously questioned at least since David Hume's discussion of causality in the eighteenth century, and it's at odds with the way virtually every scientist and philosopher talks about causal connections. So it's not surprising that when Jung analyzed specific examples of synchronicities, he apparently couldn't help but rely on causal language. That is, Jung himself seemed unable to describe synchronicities except in causal terms. Nevertheless, Jung's followers on the topic of synchronicity continue to claim that those coincidences are acausal.

Another problem is Jung's reliance on his notion of *archetypes*, components of the collective unconscious which he claimed are inextricably linked to synchronicities. But Jung's concept of an archetype is quite fuzzy, arguably causal (though not in the needlessly limited sense of "causal" Jung apparently has in mind), and linked to deep confusions (or at least unclarity) about the nature of meaning. But no matter what Jung's actual grasp of the relevant concepts might have been, his treatment of synchronicity has done little more than muddy the conceptual waters and confuse several generations of scholars, many of whom were already naïve or unclear about the concepts of causality and meaning (though not always in the same respects as Jung).[5]

Fortunately, we needn't dwell on matters of Jungian scholarship, although I'll occasionally return to that topic as the chapter progresses. I'd prefer to get right to the heart of the issue concerning synchronicity. And that is: are there in fact deeply meaningful coincidences that resist all conventional normal explanations? And if so, what sort of explanation (if any) *would* be appropriate? This, after all, is the issue Jung and others have tried, often clumsily, to address, and I believe it's the issue most on people's minds when they wonder what to make of the extraordinary strangeness and aptness of their most deeply meaningful coincidences.

2. Examples

To illustrate why people are drawn to the topic of synchronicity, consider the following peculiar case from my own life. First, an important piece of background information. In January 1972 *Esquire* magazine published its

Dubious Achievement Awards for that year. One mind-boggling item in particular caught my eye. A policeman in Jackson, Mississippi, had stopped a car that was weaving wildly down the street. He discovered that the driver of the car was blind and was taking directions from the car's owner, who was seated next to him but who was too drunk to drive.

About nine years later, I was taking a solitary vacation on the coast of Maine, a place where I've often gone both to unwind and to write. On this occasion synchronicity was very much on my mind. Several weeks earlier, a journal editor had asked me to review a new book on synchronicity, and I had planned to finish the book and write the review during my vacation. Unfortunately, the book was disappointing. It was a popular treatment of the topic, and like much of what I had read on synchronicity (including scholarly works), it struck me as confused and conceptually unsophisticated. So by the time I arrived in Maine, I was ready to dismiss the entire topic of synchronicity. In fact, I had already written a disparaging (and somewhat arrogant) analysis of synchronicity for my first book, which had appeared the previous year,[6] and nothing in the interim had changed my mind or my attitude.

Nevertheless, my smugness had been under fire. From the time I began reading the book on synchronicity and preparing its review, the number of coincidences in my life skyrocketed. However, I figured this was because I was preoccupied with the entire theme of coincidences. I assumed I was simply paying more attention to inevitable and endless similarities and correspondences that otherwise would have escaped my attention. But that explanation didn't seem to cover what happened at a restaurant one evening during my Maine vacation.

Usually, when I dined out during these solitary vacations, I took reading and writing materials with me (I get very productive in restaurants). On this night I had the book on synchronicity with me, and as I read it, I again experienced my irritation with the author's simplistic approach to the subject. Now I'm sure I enjoyed feeling superior to the muddled author. But I'm also certain I disliked wallowing in his confusions, looking for ways to explain clearly to others why the book was so unsatisfactory. I felt I had already spent enough time playing deep nonsense police in various publications and in my role as university professor. I preferred coming to Maine for a break from that grind, and I wanted to pursue my own thoughts.

So, to relieve the annoyance and tedium, I struck up a conversation with my waitress, and—probably in an effort to say something amusing and feel even better about myself—I mentioned to her the incident from *Esquire* I had read back in 1972. The waitress said to me, "Oh yes, that was the case in court last week." Surprised, I said, "No, this happened in Mississippi in 1971." But the waitress insisted, "No, this was here, last week. I had to go to court last week for a different case, but the case right before mine was exactly what you described: a blind man driving and taking directions from the drunk owner of the car."

It's easy to see why this seems to be a nifty synchronicity. During this period I was preoccupied with the topic of synchronicity and also largely dismissive of it. And apparently I had been deflecting hints from the universe—the many coincidences I had been experiencing—to treat the subject with more respect. But here was a dandy coincidence that I couldn't explain away by the expedient of heightened vigilance. It was as if the universe was confronting me with a coincidence I had to take seriously. It was so highly appropriate to what was going on in my life, and also so unusual, that it didn't seem merely to be accidental.

Now I can anticipate at least some of the questions readers will raise about this incident. Why did I mention the Mississippi case in the first place? Was it just to impress the waitress? After all (and you'll have to take my word on this), there were other amusing things I could have said instead. So, might I have noticed a newspaper story about the recent case and simply forgotten it? That's unlikely, since I don't like to get my news from newspapers, and I didn't even have a television at the inn where I stayed in Maine. I really did visit there to get away from it all, think about philosophy, and play several pianos that acquaintances in Maine kindly made available to me. I vacationed in Maine because I wanted to be fully absorbed in my own interests and projects. But might I have seen a newspaper headline in passing—say, as I walked down the street? I can't say confidently that I didn't, but that too seems unlikely. Gazing at newspaper headlines as I walk around town is not something I usually do, especially in a small coastal Maine village where there are very few such opportunities and where I go to be lost in my own thoughts. Actually, to the extent I did any strolling around town at all, I'm sure I was very much the distracted philosopher, lucky not to be bumping into things.

But perhaps there's another humdrum explanation for this apparently remarkable correspondence. Perhaps incidents like the ones in Mississippi and Maine aren't so rare after all, and maybe all it ordinarily takes to learn about them is to raise the subject. For example, I have webbed toes, and throughout my life I've found what seemed to be a surprising number of people who also have webbed toes—including people close to me, such as my ex father-in-law, my good friend from next door and his father, and valued friends in the academic community. And I was struck by the fact that I seemed to know a lot of webbed-toed people and that apparently most everyone else didn't. Why was that? Initially, I wondered if webbed-footed folks emitted some sort of vibe and attracted other syndactyl humans into their orbit. But I got over that pretty quickly after learning that the condition isn't especially rare. I then realized that the reason I knew more webbed-toed people than most is that I was more likely than they were to raise the subject in the first place. People who aren't fortunate enough to have webbed toes (the pedally challenged?) are unlikely ever to mention it to anyone. So they're unlikely to discover how many of their acquaintances have webbed toes.

So maybe blind driver cases like the one from Mississippi are also relatively common, and maybe that could easily be confirmed by raising the subject often in conversation. But in fact, I haven't encountered any other blind driver cases in conversation, and I've probably recounted the Mississippi story at least as often as I've mentioned my webbed toes. Ever since my Maine synchronicity occurred, I've mentioned it often, both in the US and in Europe—even during public lectures and to my university classes. And not once have I discovered that anyone else knew of such a case. I know also that between January 1972 and my Maine trip nine years later, I occasionally mentioned the Mississippi incident in conversation. After all, it's a great story. But not once did anyone else tell me they'd heard of such a case.

Furthermore, a recent Web search turned up only three cases of blind drivers, only one of them at all similar to the Mississippi case, and it involves a golf cart rather than a car.[7] A second case is quite different: an undated and unconfirmed Romanian story about a blind driver who stole a car.[8] I even found several stories about drivers who were *both* blind and drunk. One concerned a man from Mainz, Germany.[9] Similarly, the NBC *Evening News* on May 17, 1985, aired a story about a Virginia man, blind since birth, who was arrested for driving while drunk.[10] I also found a recent story about a blind New Zealand man who (after some training and previous races) set the new land speed record, on an airstrip, driving a BMW M5.[11] This apparently makes him the world's fastest blind driver, beating the marks set by the previous record-holders from South Africa and England.[12] But that's it.[13] I certainly found no reports of (or court records for) cases like the one in Mississippi or the Maine case mentioned by my waitress. If such records exist, I found no traces of them on the Web, and apparently, they're not that easy to dredge up. I imagine that if the cases had been considered newsworthy at the time, or cases which people discuss frequently, the better search engines would have come up with something about them, or (like my experiences discussing webbed toes) I would have run across them.

Three more examples of synchronicity will help set the stage for the rest of this chapter, and fortunately they can be described quickly. The first is an apparent double synchronicity, and it's quite well known. In the early 1970s, British actor Anthony Hopkins signed to play a leading role in the film version of George Feifer's novel, *The Girl from Petrovka*. Naturally, he wanted to read the book in order to prepare for the part, but he was unable to locate a copy even after visiting several London bookstores. However, while he was waiting at the Leicester Square underground station for his train home, he noticed an apparently discarded copy of the book lying on a bench. Later, as the movie was being filmed in Vienna, Feifer visited Hopkins on the set. The actor told Feifer about the strange way he had acquired a copy of the novel, and he mentioned that he was baffled by the red marks scattered throughout the book. He handed Feifer the copy, asking, "Might that copy have some personal meaning for you?"

It certainly did. About two years earlier Feifer had lent his last copy to a friend, and unfortunately it was a unique copy, annotated extensively with changes Feifer—who is an American—wanted for an Americanized version of the original English edition (e.g., changing "labour" to "labor"). But within a week of lending the book to his friend, his friend lost it, and despite many searches and offers of rewards, Feifer failed to recover it. But that was the copy Hopkins had found. So the only copy of the book that Hopkins was able to locate turned out to have both sentimental and considerable practical value to its author.

The second example is another apparent double synchronicity.

A certain M. Deschamps, when a boy in Orléans, was once given a piece of plum-pudding by a M. de Fortgibu. Ten years later he discovered another plum-pudding in a Paris restaurant, and asked if he could have a piece. It turned out, however, that the plum-pudding was already ordered—by M. de Fortgibu. Many years afterwards M. Deschamps was invited to partake of a plum-pudding as a special rarity. While he was eating it he remarked that the only thing lacking was M. de Fortgibu. At that moment the door opened and an old, old man in the last stages of disorientation walked in: M. de Fortgibu, who had got hold of the wrong address and burst in on the party by mistake.[14]

Finally, consider this famous example from Jung. In 1909 Jung visited Freud in Vienna, and at one point he asked Freud his opinion on ESP.

Although Freud later changed his mind on the subject, at the time he was unsympathetic to the idea of ESP. According to Jung,

> While Freud was going on in this way, I had a curious sensation. It was as if my diaphragm was made of iron and becoming red-hot—a glowing vault. And at that moment there was such a loud report in the bookcase, which stood next to us, that we both started up in alarm, fearing the thing was going to topple over on us. I said to Freud: "There, that is an example of a so-called catalytic exteriorization phenomena."
> "Oh come," he exclaimed. "That is sheer bosh."
> "It is not," I replied. "You are mistaken, Herr Professor. And to prove my point I now predict that in a moment there will be another loud report!" Sure enough, no sooner had I said the words than the same detonation went off in the bookcase.[15]

3. Philosophy 101

So here's the puzzle we must confront. According to Jung and many others, some coincidences are so improbable and so meaningfully appropriate to our lives that we can't dismiss them as relatively humdrum occurrences whose significance we've simply overestimated for one reason or another. But if that's the case, how are we to account for those coincidences? As I mentioned earlier, Jung apparently thought that no causal explanation would work. But quite apart from potential confusions about what causal explanations are, Jung and most others who take synchronicity seriously seem to agree on one thing—namely, that human agents don't (consciously or unconsciously) cause synchronicities to occur. Of course, humans might be causes of the individual events in a synchronistic cluster. But the point here is that, on the more or less received view of synchronicity, humans aren't responsible for the occurrence of the meaningful cluster itself.

But suppose we rule out the possibility that humans cause events to occur in meaningful combinations. And suppose we also rule out the possibility that we're simply misinterpreting or overestimating relatively normal—and presumably chance—occurrences. That seems to leave two options. The first is that God, or some other individual outside the sphere of human agents, brings together the events making up a synchronicity. Of course, Jung rejected that explanation because it's clearly causal. And others would reject it either because it's crudely anthropomorphic or because it's unfalsifiable and without any empirical credentials. I also believe this option is untenable, or at least superfluous (for reasons I'll explain below), but in any case we can't deal here with the big issues of philosophical theology.

So (if only to see where it leads) let's ignore the intervening God (or supra-human agent) hypothesis for now and consider the remaining option, which (as far as I can tell) is similar to what Jung preferred. According to that option, synchronicity is a principle concerning a basic operation of nature, like so-called *framework* principles in physics—for example, conservation laws, the Complementarity Principle, or Pauli's Exclusion Principle. At least on the face of it, these principles don't make causal claims; they simply require the universe to exhibit certain kinds of order (for example, that no more than one electron can "occupy" an atomic "orbit"). So if synchronicity too is a noncausal framework principle of nature, it would likewise link and organize events in some way. But on what basis? The answer, apparently, is that a principle of synchronicity would arrange events according to certain crucial properties of those events. And which properties? Presumably, those that together constitute the synchronicity—that is, those properties in virtue of which event clusters are strikingly meaningful. For example, Jung's conversation with Freud had the property of being an argument, or an explosive exchange, and the sounds from the bookcase also had the property of being an explosion. So we could say that synchronicity is a principle that links events with respect to their natural meaning or significance.

Now it's important to grasp that when Jung and others talk about synchronistic meaning, or the relevant features of events linked by synchronicity, they don't have in mind properties that we simply *attribute* to events by interpreting them in a certain way. After all, those interpretations might be petty or idiosyncratic, or in some other way merely reflect limited, trivial, or simply temporary personal concerns. But synchronistic connections are supposed to reveal something very deep about the workings of nature. Synchronicity is supposed to be a fundamental natural principle that links events according to the properties that make the events jointly meaningful. So if event clusters aren't synchronistic because of interpretations we merely impose on them, and if no agent (including God) arranges the events so that they appear meaningful to us, then the events must be arranged independently of the way humans or other agents happen to conceive them.

Apparently, then, a principle of synchronicity would need to operate on properties those events have *in themselves*, not properties human beings simply ascribe or assign to them. Presumably, that's why Jung says that synchronicity is a "factor *in nature* which expresses itself in the arrangement of events and appears to us as meaning,"[16] and also "Synchronicity postulates a meaning which is *a priori* in relation to human consciousness and apparently exists outside man."[17] So synchronicity, on this option, is a principle that operates on events on the basis of features *built-in* to the events themselves.[18] Jung even concedes "that synchronicity . . . might occur without the participation of the human psyche."[19] Thus, synchronistic connections exist solely in virtue of relations shared between events, and synchronistic meaning turns out to be a kind of *intrinsic* or *inherent* meaning. In fact (as Jung also noted), synchronicity ultimately concerns an intrinsic "equivalence or conformity" between two or more events.[20]

But at this point, I'm afraid we have to step back and do some remedial philosophy. This second option (that synchronistic connections or correspondences are built-in to events themselves) is actually nonsense. That doesn't mean it's stupid; it just means it literally makes no sense. Of course, some nonsense *is* stupid—actually, there's more than enough of that to go around. But other nonsense is, we might say, *deep* nonsense—that is, claims which might seem intelligible and innocent enough until we reveal some of their hidden presuppositions. I'd like to think that one of the valuable services philosophers can perform is to function as deep nonsense police, exposing hidden assumptions and bringing them up to the surface where their flaws stand out clearly. And it turns out that some very deep mistakes lurk beneath the view that nature organizes events in virtue of their intrinsic meaning or similarity. Once we understand those mistakes, it becomes clearer that the most viable interpretation of synchronicities might be that human agents do, in fact, cause at least some of them.

As Jung seemed to recognize, behind every alleged synchronicity is the perception or assertion that the meaningfully related events are *similar* or *relevant* to one another in some outstanding way. In my blind driver case, for example, the connection was one of similarity between two highly unusual events. But the connection might be more abstract and concern what the events seem to *represent*. For example, the exploding sounds in Freud's bookcase presumably connect with the fact that Jung's argument with Freud was an explosive confrontation about ESP. And in my blind driver case, you might say there's a connection between the appropriateness of my discovering a second such incident when I was feeling particularly cynical about the concept of synchronicity.

But these similarities or correspondences are not static or inherent properties shared by events or by anything else. Two or more objects or events count as similar only against a background of assumptions concerning things we consider relevant or important about them. Moreover, those background conditions are themselves dynamic and fluctuating; they hold only at a particular time, or in a particular situation. That is, things count as similar only within a shifting context of human action, needs, and interests. This point is so elementary and so easy to grasp, it's actually quite amazing when philosophers and others who should know better manage to overlook it.[21]

A simple example from geometry should make the point clearly. Consider the triangle:

A

Next, consider these other geometric figures:

B   C   D   E

Now consider the question: to which of the last four figures is (A) similar? The proper response to that question should be puzzlement; you shouldn't know how to answer it. Without further background information, without knowing what matters in our comparison of the figures, the question has no answer at all. Mathematicians recognize this, although instead of the term "similarity" they use the expression "congruence." In any case, mathematicians know that in the absence of some specified or agreed-upon rule of projection, or function for mapping geometric figures onto other things, no figure is congruent with (similar to) anything else.

Mathematicians recognize that there are different standards of congruence, appropriate for different situations. But no situation is *intrinsically basic*; standards of relevance emerge from living and ephemeral human situations, not from Nature herself. But then no standard of congruence is inherently privileged or more fundamental than others. For example, engineers might sometimes want to adopt a fairly strict mapping function according to which (A) is congruent only with other figures having the same interior angles and the same horizontal orientation. But in that case, (A) would be congruent with none of the other four figures. Of course, only in very specialized contexts are we likely to compare figures with respect to their horizontal orientation. In many situations it would be appropriate to adopt a somewhat weaker standard of congruence, according to which sameness of interior angles is all that matters. And in that case we'd say that figures (A) and (B) are congruent but that (A) is not congruent with the other figures. However, there's also nothing privileged about sameness of interior angles. Perhaps what matters is simply that (A) is congruent with any other three-sided enclosed figure, in which case we could say it's congruent with the three triangles (B), (C), and (D), but not with the rectangle (E). But even that criterion of congruence can be weakened. Mathematicians have rules of projection that map triangles onto any other geometric object, but not to, say, apples or oranges. Of course, the moral here is obvious. If simple geometric figures are not intrinsically similar—that is, if they count as similar only against a background of contingent assumptions about which of their features matter, then we certainly won't find intrinsic similarity with much more complex objects—in particular, the events related in a synchronistic cluster.

But maybe you're still not convinced. Perhaps you think that there *is* a fundamental principle of congruence for this geometric example. You might think that, first and foremost, (A) is similar to just those figures with sides of exactly the same length, the same horizontal orientation, and with exactly the same interior angles. And perhaps you'd want to call that something like "strict congruence (or identity)." But there are at least three serious problems with that position.

First, even if strict congruence (construed in this way) counted as more fundamental than other forms of geometric similarity, that could only be in virtue of a kind of historical accident. The primacy of that standard of congruence would reveal more about us, our conventions and values—in short, what merely happens to be important to us, than it does about the figures themselves. In fact, it's a standard appropriate for only a very narrow range of contexts in which we consider whether things are similar. Second (and as an illustration of that first point), it's easy to imagine contexts in which two triangles have exactly the same interior angles, horizontal orientation, and sides, but don't count as similar. If we're interior designers, for example, it might also matter whether the triangles are of the same color, or whether they're placed against the same colored background, or whether they're made of the same material. If we're graphic artists, it might matter whether the triangles were both original artworks or whether one was a print. Or if we're librarians or archivists, it might matter whether the triangles occur on the same page of different copies of the same book. And third, even if we could decide on some very strict sense of congruence (or identity) which would count as privileged over all other forms of similarity, it would be useless in the present context. Events in synchronistic clusters are never strictly identical (say, with all properties of one exactly the same as all properties of the other). The looser and more complex forms of similarity at issue in alleged synchronicities are classic examples of the sorts of similarities that can't possibly be inherent, static relations between events.

For example, there's no intrinsic similarity, difference, or meaningful relationship between (1) A's punching B in the mouth, (2) A's making demeaning remarks to B in front of B's fiancée, and (3) A's laughing at and walking past an old woman who fell and injured herself. If we're concerned with A's propensity for physical violence, we'd probably say that none of the events count as similar or related. If we're discussing A's antipathy toward B in particular, we'd probably connect events (1) and (2). And if we're concerned with A's general surliness or hostility, we could appropriately link all three events.

It's easy to multiply examples and extend them to a wide range of comparisons. For example, there's no intrinsic similarity or difference between the baseball swing of Barry Bonds and that of a Little League player. They might count as similar in a context where we compare baseball swings to strokes in tennis or golf. But Bonds's swing and that of the Little Leaguer might count as dissimilar when we're comparing the swings of major league players to those of children, or when we're comparing steroid-enhanced to drug-free baseball performances. Likewise, there's no intrinsic similarity or difference in the decor of two homes. They might count as similar if we're comparing contemporary furnishings to those in a home decorated more traditionally; but they might count as dissimilar when we're making finer distinctions between different styles of contemporary decor.

But this is only the beginning of the problem for the Jungian idea that synchronicity is a principle in nature that links events with respect to their agent- or perspective-independent properties. If a principle of synchronicity could do that, it would also have to operate on bits of history that *intrinsically count as events*. After all, synchronicities are event-combinations linked by properties that make the events jointly meaningful *in a particular context.*[22] But for a principle of nature to operate on those properties, it must operate on the events which manifest the properties. So if synchronicity is a basic framework principle of nature that connects events according to properties that, as Jung says, can be picked out "without the participation of the human psyche," then it must also operate on things that count as events, also according to properties determined possibly "without the participation of the human psyche." And that's the problem: there simply is no absolute inventory of events in nature. Just as things count as similar only against a background of human action and purposes, bits of history count as events only against a guiding set of needs and interests.

This is easy to demonstrate. Consider the question: how many events were there in World War II? As with the earlier example concerning geometric figures, you shouldn't have a clue how to answer that question. And that's because it too has no privileged or absolutely correct answer. The answer to the question depends on why and how we want to parse (or divide and identify) the relevant portions of human history. That is, it depends on what's at issue for us and what we're trying to accomplish. So obviously, just as there's no fundamentally correct way to slice a pie, here too there's no inherently basic or right way to make divisions. Independent of a context in which we decide that certain things matter, no parsing is preferable to any other. For certain purposes (e.g., in which we take a very broad view of human history, or simply on military history), we might want to say that the Second World War was composed of only two events, the European and Pacific campaigns. But of course, historians often want to make finer-grained analyses—say, into campaigns linked to specific countries, or into particular battles, never mind the country in which they occurred. They might also count things other than battles as distinct and noteworthy events—for example, particular discussions or conferences held by military leaders or government officials, or the issuing of particular orders to generals in the field, or the liberation of prisoners from concentration camps. And of course, events aren't the only things lacking an inherent inventory. Apart from a background of purposes and interests, there's also no answer to the question, "How many things are in this room?"

The moral, we might say, is that Nature does not parse herself. There's no absolute structure or inventory of events or objects waiting to be discovered and transcending *any* human perspective or point of view. How we divide a bit of history always depends on our objectives, our reasons for slicing it up in the first place, and those motives only emerge against a larger background of activities, interests, and concerns, none of which are essential features of Nature.

Please note that this kind of perspective and inventory-relativism doesn't mean that there's no reality independent of our mental activity. That is, it's not a way of denying the existence of an objective world beyond one's mind. However, we can only grasp that objective world by means of a conceptual framework of some sort—that is, a grid of descriptive categories and principles that we (as it were) place over reality and which accordingly allows certain things and certain configurations of things to pass through. And the relevant point is that this framework is contingent and somewhat malleable from context to context (and certainly over longer stretches of time, as our thinking evolves). Thus all I've been urging is that nothing makes the framework of any person or at any time *inherently* better or more accurate than another, although for a given situation one might be especially appropriate or pragmatically advantageous.

But maybe Jungians can still avoid committing themselves (absurdly) to context-independent relations of similarity and divisions of nature. Jung seems to say that meaningful coincidences count as synchronistic only when they're connected to some *archetype*.[23] So perhaps archetypes provide both the context and the mechanism according to which Nature divides into events and objects, as well as the context according to which two or more events count as similar. But in fact this move won't help at all.

For one thing, archetypes don't seem to be "a priori in relation to human consciousness." On the contrary, they're explained in terms of inherited propensities or patterns of human thought. As Morris puts it, an archetype is:

> a potentially active component of the collective unconscious, the apparent product, at least in part, of repeated universal experiences of humankind, which have occurred so often and with such consistency that the underlying theme has come to take on a life of its own, so to speak, not necessarily with intelligence, but with the capacity to exert influence when activated in an individual in some way, such as by thematically related ordinary events having impact upon that person.[24]

If that description is correct, then archetypes are linked essentially to features of human experience and evolution. But then, even if those features are universal (as Morris says), that doesn't mean they're *necessary*. In fact, they seem quite clearly to be *contingent* (or accidental); human development might have proceeded along significantly different lines. In particular, humans might have evolved, either physically, conceptually, or socially, so that certain archetypes never emerged. For example, if humans had been hermaphroditic, or if we had followed the developmental path of those species for which child-rearing is a male role, or (perhaps especially) if human infants (like infants of other species) were self-sustaining right out of the womb, the archetype of the nurturing mother might have served no useful symbolic human function. This shows that archetypes don't ground synchronicities in features of nature that transcend (or are literally independent of) human consciousness, including the accidents both of biological evolution and the development of human conceptual systems.[25]

But even more seriously, appealing to archetypes only pushes the confusions about similarity and event-identity to another level. Consider: what connects events to the right archetype, or to one archetype rather than another? The process can't be intrinsic or automatic, as it would have to be if the synchronicity principle operated "without the participation of the human psyche." Recall one of the lessons from our earlier example from geometry: for any two things, X and Y, there's always some function (or rule of projection) that maps X onto Y. And in fact, anything can be mapped onto anything, given an appropriate rule of projection. But then, in order for one mapping function to be particularly appropriate—that is, appropriate in a given situation—this must be determined relative to some *wider* context in which certain things (rather than others) count as relevant. However, as we also noted earlier, standards of relevance are not context- or interest-independent pieces of natural furniture.

Fortunately, we can emerge from these various confusions and make some sense of synchronicity. But first, we need to make a few more elementary observations—this time about *meaning*. Evidently, Jung thought it was acceptable to follow in the distinguished footsteps of Plato and Gauss by postulating the existence of what he calls "self-subsistent meaning."[26] But we've seen that we can't attribute a structure to nature (or history)—that is, slice it into elements (or events)—apart from a background of activities within which certain things (rather than others) matter to us. Without the perspective which those activities provide, nothing about nature or history intrinsically stands out from anything else. But meaningful relations between events likewise can exist only within a certain parsing of history— that is, as part of a decision to take certain things rather than others to be events. In fact, we can't identify or posit meaningful relations between things independently of parsing nature somehow into the things in question. So meaningful relations are no more intrinsically parts of nature than the number or kinds of events in a period of history or the number or kinds of things in a room. But then meaningful relations, like ostensibly more elementary relations of similarity, also presuppose a perspective, a contingent background of activities, needs, and interests, from which certain things (rather than others) matter to us and stand out as relevant.

Of course, this last observation applies also to the subset of archetypally meaningful connections. As I noted earlier, archetypes emerge only from a contingent set of background conditions concerning our biological, social, and conceptual development. Those conditions incline us to adopt certain perspectives on our lives from which we identify certain things (rather than others) as events, actions, and objects.

But all this raises serious concerns over the standard view of synchronicity. If synchronistically meaningful connections between events require a perspective relative to which the events are meaningful, whose perspective is it? For those who believe that synchronicities can occur "without the participation of the human psyche," presumably it's not an option to say that *we* actively provide the relevant perspective and parsing of events. I also suspect that many would also rule out the possibility that God (or some other individual outside the realm of human agents) provides that perspective. Moreover, we noted above that the process can't be automatic or mechanical, based on intrinsic archetypal relations holding between the synchronistically related events, because no such relations can exist. So where does the perspective come from? And if synchronistic connections don't simply arise by chance (as Jung and others insist), why, then, do they arise at all?

I suspect that the only way to resolve all this is to make some moves which Jung, with his needlessly limited conception of causality, wanted to reject. I think we can agree with Jung that at least some synchronicities aren't simply chance occurrences which we simply take to be meaningful. But then we must admit that the principle of synchronicity is a *causal* principle of some kind, and I believe that the most acceptable way to do this is to see ordinary human agents as the instruments of synchronistically meaningful connections. To see why, we need to consider briefly only a few more rudimentary philosophical points—this time, about causality and explanation.

4. The Role of Causality in Synchronicity

Jung and others have thought that by appealing to a principle of synchronicity, we can explain *why* certain meaningfully related events clustered together. The idea is that these events didn't clump together simply by chance. Rather, their joint occurrence was in accordance with a certain organizing principle of nature, the principle of synchronicity.

Now ordinarily, when we ask *why* an event or group of events E occurred—that is, when we request an *explanation* of E, we're looking for one of two kinds of answer. Sometimes we want to know what other event(s) caused E, and then we'll feel we've explained E when we've identified that cause. For example, we could explain why Jones crashed his car by noting that his brakes failed or that he fell asleep at the wheel. Similarly, we could explain why Jones had an upset stomach by saying that he had just eaten a very spicy meal.[27] But sometimes we say that *E* is explained, not by another event, but by a law, principle, or regularity that systematically links *E* with other and possibly diverse kinds of events. For example, the laws of gravitation allow us to explain why all sorts of unconstrained objects fall to the earth, as well as the relationship between the sun, moon, and tides, and also the bending of light around massive objects. Similarly, we might explain certain behaviors relative to a "covering law," or overarching regularity. For example, we could explain Jones's choice of sexual partners by noting that he's attracted only to women who remind him of his mother. Or, we could explain his preferences for certain chamber music recordings over others by noting that he can't stand the sound of a fortepiano.

Many believe that some covering laws, principles, or regularities are *ultimate* or primitive in the sense that we can't profitably ask *why* those principles, etc., hold. Usually, the regularities or principles they have in mind here are so-called *framework* principles, like conservation laws in physics, or the Pauli Exclusion Principle. And as I noted earlier, Jung and others have apparently considered the principle of synchronicity to fall within that class. From their point of view, synchronistic connections are fundamental. That is, no fact of nature is deeper than the synchronistic link itself, and there's no point in trying to explain why or how synchronistic connections occur. *That* they occur is simply one of several basic facts about how the universe operates.

Now even if it's acceptable to say that certain framework principles govern the course of nature, there are many reasons for doubting that synchronicity could be such a principle. One problem in particular is worth noting now. There's a significant difference between the way standard framework principles operate and the way the principle of synchronicity is supposed to work, and it's something Jung and others have apparently failed to appreciate. Presumably as the result of his association with Wolfgang Pauli, Jung thought that synchronicity could be compared to the most basic organizing principles in physics. But framework principles in physics have both great generality and predictive utility. For instance, conservation laws apply to a vast range of occurrences, and they allow us to predict in many precise respects how nature will behave in the future. But synchronistic explanations are always *situation specific*. They don't apply to events generally, and they have no predictive value.

Consider again the explosions in Freud's bookcase, which many regard as synchronistically related to the argument between Jung and Freud on the subject of ESP. Remember, Jungians propose that a principle of synchronicity allows us to explain why meaningfully related events clump together. But then, for an appeal to synchronicity to be of any explanatory value, it has to explain why the explosions occurred *as and when they did*, instead of at a time or place where they would no longer be meaningful. So a synchronistic explanation of this event cluster must indicate why the sounds occurred within earshot and during the argument, rather than (say) the following year when no one was in the room, or in a room elsewhere in Vienna. But that can't be done by means of a *general law* connecting arguments to sounds. Synchronicity doesn't specify or require any such law; and synchronistic explanations are always case-specific and without predictive value for future occurrences. In fact, each synchronistic cluster can be unique and thoroughly idiosyncratic. There's no reason whatever to think that Jung and Freud's argument exemplifies a *law* connecting sounds with arguments, or that my blind driver case is an instance of some broader regularity having to do either with blind drivers or with philosophical complacency or arrogance. Moreover, even if partisans of synchronicity tried (absurdly) to formulate such a law, it would arguably be *causal*. It would have the same form as virtually every other familiar causal law in science. It would be a generalization stipulating that certain kinds of events regularly accompany one another.

So let's return to our crucial pair of questions: (a) If synchronistic event-juxtapositions aren't chance occurrences onto which we simply impose or project an interpretation, why do they occur at all? and (b) Who (so to speak) *owns* the perspective or point of view according to which certain slices of history count as events, and according to which those events seem meaningfully related? I think we can begin to get a handle on this by considering persons who regard themselves as *coincidence-prone*—especially those whose coincidences are sometimes quite remarkable. I suspect that the best way to make sense of these individuals' lives is by positing a combination of creative cognition and possibly paranormal influence over events seemingly beyond their control.

We can start with what at least appears to be an easy case. I knew a former psi researcher (let's call her B.) who liked to claim, with tongue partly in cheek, that God was a punster. That is, she believed that she frequently experienced coincidences which could best be described by means of puns. The problem with this, however, is that B. was already disposed to think in terms of puns. Unlike those who find punning to be a low and extremely annoying form of humor (especially when practiced relentlessly), she enjoyed it immensely. Quite probably, then, B. was the relevant punster—not God or the universe. She was prepared to see—or better, to *make*—punlike connections when others would not.

It may be significant that I can remember none of B.'s alleged punlike synchronicities. I know that I and others found them to be both contrived and thoroughly forgettable. Certainly they weren't archetypal, connecting (conspicuously or otherwise) to the grand and pervasive themes Jung had in mind. And arguably, they didn't connect even to large themes in B.'s life. So it seems likely that, for at least many of the coincidences, B. was simply employing her own considerable ingenuity in drawing punlike connections between everyday, humdrum event-clusters. It would merely be an extension of her already pronounced tendency both to make puns and (more important) to *see opportunities* for making puns. Still, if we're willing to grant that people can paranormally influence their lives (sometimes on a large scale), we can't rule out the possibility that B. at least sometimes influenced events to reinforce her belief that God (or the universe) operated on the basis of punlike principles.[28]

Other cases, however, suggest more strongly that people can and do paranormally shape their lives in both subtle and dramatic ways. The cases surveyed in chapter 2 provide some systematic evidence that gifted subjects can, fairly reliably, influence the physical world in conspicuous ways. Moreover, anecdotal cases suggest first that this capacity isn't limited just to psychic superstars, and second, that it may extend to complex arrangements of events.

Mathematician Ivor Grattan-Guinness is another person who feels he's coincidence-prone, and the coincidences he mentions seem more likely than B.'s to have a paranormal component.[29] Moreover, Grattan-Guinness suggests, plausibly, that coincidence-proneness is idiosyncratic—that is, that there are personality-specific regularities in the way coincidence-prone people experience their coincidences. For example, Grattan-Guinness claims, "I am good at unexpectedly meeting people, and also at opening books at the right place,"[30] and he routinely made notes of his experiences. One of his examples is the following:

Melbourne, 8 December 1977. I was sent a paper to referee for a journal. The author had traced an important collection of manuscripts to their probable destruction in a fire at a mine at Vollpriehausen, Germany, in 1945. I read the paper quickly and then had to go into Melbourne to look at the University of Melbourne's holdings of old mathematical books. While in the library stacks, I passed by a bookcase filled with thousands

of booklets. I took one out to see what they were, and found them to be
a series of reports prepared by the British and the Americans about the
German economy and industry at the end of the war. The one that I had
selected was the second of three on the adaptation of existing underground installations. It fell open on page 5—where there is a description
of a mine at Vollpriehausen.

Taken singly, events of this sort can easily be viewed as interesting but
insignificant chance occurrences. But when they happen relatively often,
it's tempting to think that something more is going on—specifically, that
the person experiencing the coincidences plays a role, somehow, in arranging the events. And when normal forms of influence seem ruled out, it's
tempting to suppose that the person is either unconsciously directed by ESP
or else is psychokinetically disposing events to take a certain course rather
than another.

A slightly different type of case reinforces this suspicion. In a way, it concerns coincidences, but not the kind people usually regard as synchronistic.
As I've suggested elsewhere,[31] if we want to get a feel for the way psychic
abilities might operate in life and possibly insinuate themselves subtly into
the normal flow of events, we should look at people who are remarkably
lucky or unlucky. Of course, everyone experiences incidents they regard as
lucky or unlucky, but some seem to do this with exceptional regularity. Now
don't misunderstand me: I'm not suggesting we write a blank check for all
apparent instances of good luck or misfortune and attribute these occurrences to under-the-surface psi. I'm suggesting only that if we can ever hope
to grasp how psychic processes might infiltrate our lives, and if we ever
hope to grasp just how extensive and refined those psychic interventions
might be, our best doorway into the phenomena might be people whose
lives seem unusually marked by good fortune or misfortune.

Admittedly, it's not entirely clear what sorts of unusual regularities we
should be looking for here. But some likely candidates come easily to mind,
and they seem to be externalized versions of the familiar ways we can mentally influence our physical well-being, both positively and negatively. For
example, although we have no idea how to explain it, we know that people
can psychosomatically alter their bodily states. Moreover, the history of
hypnosis shows clearly that people can produce remarkable bodily changes
(e.g., welts on the skin, and even general anesthesia) under nothing more
than the suggestion to do so. Similarly, dramatic bodily changes sometimes
accompany identity switches in Dissociative Identity (formerly Multiple

Personality) Disorder.[32] Now if our psychic influence can likewise insinuate itself into everyday life, it might help explain, say, why some soldiers escape injury (or at least serious injury), despite repeated heroic risks on the battle-field. Similarly, it might explain why some incompetent or reckless drivers never have an accident, and why some careful and competent drivers seem regularly to be victimized either by other motorists' poor driving or by automotive calamities of other sorts (e.g., accidents or damage caused by flat tires, windblown debris, or other falling objects). It might explain why some have a knack for making speculative business decisions and why others (although neither reckless nor stupid) seem repeatedly to fail.[33] It might even explain why some people seem to have "parkma," good karma for finding parking spaces.

However, I suspect that the most revealing manifestations of our under-the-surface psychic influence will be more subtle and diverse. It's clear that we have many normal (and often unconscious) ways of either enhancing or ruining our lives, and it's clear that how we feel about ourselves often plays a large role in this. For example, some people covertly undermine their relationships with others and thereby reinforce their low self-esteem. So assuming that we can paranormally influence our lives in either pervasive or conspicuous ways, we'd expect to see additional indications of relationships between, say, our self-image and our good fortune or misfortune.

For example, I find it striking that some peoples' lives seem to be marked by difficulty, chaos, or disaster—one apparent nuisance or tragedy after another. Wherever they go, whatever they do, they seem to have trouble, whether it's problems with their cars, computers, pets, or gardens, or with the postal service, credit cards, personal injuries, ordering products on the Internet, using household appliances, making routine repairs around the house, or making everyday purchases. Why are some people consistently beleaguered in these ways, while others lead lives of relative tranquility?

There's even a Yiddish term for a person who suffers so regularly and conspicuously: *shlemazel*. This should not be confused with a *shlemiel*. A shlemiel is someone who spills soup on himself; a shlemazel has it spilt on him. So shlemazels are what we might call unlucky souls, people who seem to be victimized by impersonal forces or by the universe at large. And it seems to me not only that shlemazels really exist, but that they're ideal subjects for study by parapsychological naturalists. (Of course, shlemazels might feel that any such investigation would be another annoying intrusion into their lives; so researchers would need to be careful to minimize the imposition created by their inquiries.)

One reason I take this seriously is that I've known a number of shlemazels. In fact, I believe I was once married to one (actually, many in her family seemed to be lightning rods for misfortune). But for various reasons, it's probably wiser that I tell you instead about some former neighbors. I wish I knew whether this man and woman had been shlemazels before they married. It's worth pursuing if we want to understand paranormal pathology, but unfortunately there's no reasonable way for me now to uncover their history. In any case, there's no doubt that this couple's married life was a living hell of aggravations and annoyances, and I'm quite sure that, from my remote perspective, I had merely scratched the surface of their problems. Nevertheless, what little I knew was impressive enough. For example, it seemed as if nearly everything my neighbors bought was defective. Brand-new appliances and other electronic equipment routinely failed to work and had to be returned or exchanged; an apparently solid rocking chair collapsed within the first days of ownership (with their infant sitting on it); and their cars frequently needed repair, even though they owned brands noted for reliability.

However, my favorite example concerns the poster-size photo the wife had purchased and then framed and mounted on her living room wall. She told me she had just bought a lovely photo of the Golden Gate bridge, and she proudly invited me over to see it. But in fact, the photo was of the Brooklyn Bridge. Now first of all, the Brooklyn Bridge is not nearly as elegant or romantic a structure as the Golden Gate Bridge. So first of all, what my neighbor purchased was not what she thought she had purchased; although the photo was dramatic, it was not as lovely as what she had wanted on her living room wall; and she even paid extra to have it framed. But more significantly, at least older readers will know that a classic—though now quaint—image of the gullible "sucker" or "loser" is someone who falls for the trick of being sold the Brooklyn Bridge. So it seems that my neighbor both symbolically and (in a sense) actually bought the Brooklyn Bridge.

Therefore, I'm suggesting first that shlemazels might be people whose misfortune is actually a psi-mediated expression of their own self-destructiveness. And I'm suggesting it's something they might accomplish with the same degree of subtlety and thoroughness found in normal and more familiar forms of self-destructive behavior. Of course, an equally disturbing alternative is that *other people* might be psychic agents in this apparent misfortune. That is, shlemazels might suffer occasionally through the (conscious or unconscious) psychic interventions of people who wish them harm. Like it or not, once we've opened the door to our own psychic influence on the world around us, we can't arbitrarily deny the possibility that others can psychically influence our own lives. It's all part of the same package. After all, if we can psychically alter events in ways that either promote or subvert our own welfare, there's nothing in principle to prevent this influence from affecting others as well. So for example, perhaps my unlucky neighbors' hellish existence had less to do with their own negativity and more to do with (say) antagonistic in-laws, or perhaps even the churlish philosopher living next door.

Of course, if we're willing to go this far in speculating about the reach of psi, there's no reason to limit it to those who are either lucky or unlucky. However mysterious the underlying causal picture might be, we have no choice but to consider the possible role of psi in a wide range of everyday affairs, both sporadic and recurrent. So for all we know, at least some of the more outstanding alleged synchronicities might be caused, at least in part, by our own or others' psychic influence.

I realize these sorts of conjectures inspire fear and loathing among many. They see it as an unjustified and intolerable regression to the kind of magical thinking we usually associate—condescendingly at that—with so-called primitive cultures. Now I'll agree that my suggestions fall within that tradition, although I wouldn't describe this as "magical" thinking. After all, what's at stake here are serious issues about the nature of causality generally and the reach of our personal influence in particular. And no matter how uncomfortable we may feel in taking seriously the possibility of wide-ranging psychic influence, the discussion has a substantial empirical backbone. There's a wealth of respectable data to consider, both experimental and anecdotal, and (as far as I can see) no reason, other than our discomfort, for refusing to look carefully and courageously at what the data seem clearly to suggest. Significantly, I think, our resistance to the idea of extensive psi primarily concerns its potentially negative applications—for example, what we'd call "hexing" or "the evil eye." Relatively few people bristle over the suggestion that we can (say) promote healing at distance, even though the possibility of harming at a distance is logically bound up with it.[34]

Of course, defending and working out the details of this point of view is a complicated business and more than I can undertake here. (However, I've dealt with the matter in somewhat more detail elsewhere.[35]) For now, it's sufficient to note that if we accept the existence of psychic influence (especially unconscious psychic influence), and if we believe that some meaningful coincidences can't be dismissed as chance occurrences onto which we simply project personal significance, no real option remains.

5. Final Thoughts

So where does this leave us regarding my blind driver case? Should I really accept that I psychically and unconsciously helped orchestrate that peculiar cluster of events? And if so, just what kind of causal story would I be endorsing? Initially, it might seem as if I'd need wide-ranging and very specific ESP to acquire information that would allow me to arrange a meeting (psychokinetically or by telepathic influence) with someone who would tell me about a recent blind driver case. So somehow I would have needed to determine who would be waiting tables at various restaurants, which of those people had the appropriate experiences with the local legal system, and (for that matter) what cases had been brought before courts in that part of New England. But is that at all plausible? Would even the firmest believers in psi accept so much unimpeded psychic virtuosity? Also, it's hard to imagine that I could have psychically arranged to have the right person with the right history wait on my table, even if I had been able psychically to dig up all the necessary information. Can we really exert such thorough control over the actions of others?

I admit, it's certainly a stretch to suppose that anything like this actually occurs. But we can allow ourselves the luxury of speculation here. After all, our ignorance about the workings of the universe is still considerable. So let's try to put aside our many preconceptions about scientific knowledge generally and psychic stuff in particular. Perhaps we should approach the matter from a different direction. If in fact we can exert pervasive and large-scale psychic influence on events, we might need to tell another sort of story altogether. It might be that we need to adopt what I've elsewhere called the *magic-wand hypothesis*.[36] This is the idea that psychically influencing events isn't a step-by-step process, like riding a bike or driving a car. In those cases we monitor events and make necessary adjustments on the basis of constant feedback from our ongoing activities. By contrast, this view proposes that we influence events to turn out a certain way just by wishing or wanting that outcome—so long as the wish takes place under favorable conditions. In that respect, psychically influencing events would be like waving a magic wand. There's no piecemeal, careful, and vigilant choreographing of actions behind the scenes. So in my blind driver case, we wouldn't need to posit ongoing and detailed psychic scanning, or an ongoing psychic nudging (or puppeteering) of the various actors on the stage, just to make sure the right people are in the right place at the right time. On the magic-wand scenario, if conditions are right when we have our wish, then *poof!* the desired result occurs.

Naturally, many people quickly dismiss this notion, and unfortunately they often do so by caricaturing it—for example, by claiming that it requires us to be psychically omnipotent. But the magic-wand hypothesis concerns only the structure or analysis of a certain causal process, not its extensiveness or limits. It proposes a direct psychokinetic link between the intention (or wish) and the effect, unmediated by a series or collection of subprocesses. Claiming that psychokinetic causation works directly in this way is by no means the same thing as claiming that our psychic efforts are always successful, or that we can do anything we want by PK. In fact, every child knows that. Even in legends, bearers of magic wands don't have unlimited power: the wands only work under the right conditions. Sometimes magic wands sputter or fail, and sometimes their effects are neutralized by the effects of other individuals' magic wands. It's actually a very complex and interesting matter whether the magic-wand hypothesis has any merit. Among other things, it concerns some very knotty issues about the nature of causality generally. In any case, the topic is too complex to address here. For now, it's enough to note that various bodies of evidence point to the existence of at least *occasional* large-scale PK,[37] and that a magic wand-type explanation of synchronicities seems, therefore, to be a genuine option in logical space.

Nevertheless, I suspect that my blind driver case wasn't caused by psychic manipulations behind the scenes (whether direct or byzantine). I believe it was simply a very strange and real coincidence that just happened to be unusually appropriate to my life. Still, if ESP and PK play any kind of under-the-surface role in life, we'd expect many of those operations to result in situations that strike us as both coincidental and meaningful. So I don't want to rule out psi-mediated coincidences entirely. But I think we need to be extremely cautious about supposing that we or others are psychically engineering them.

And of course, it will be exceedingly difficult to figure out, in any given case, what the underlying story really was. Determining why an apparent synchronicity occurred will be no easier than figuring out why a given psi experiment succeeded or failed. In that respect, understanding synchronicities will be as complex and daunting as unraveling the causal picture in Katie's case, or in the case of Dennis Lee. And no doubt it's why apparent psychic events, both in the lab and in real life, will continue to be hotly debated.

Postscript: Some Thoughts on Astrology

1. Theoretical Background

Opponents of astrology, like some skeptics about parapsychology, routinely—though I believe disingenuously—overestimate the importance of theoretical knowledge. They often argue that if we can't scientifically explain how astrology might work and lead to detailed, accurate predictions, we're not entitled to conclude that there are genuine astrological facts to which astrologers have gained (or can gain) access. They might say, for example, "I can't accept that the arrangement at birth of celestial bodies (especially extremely distant ones) makes a difference to a person's character, or that there's a connection now between the placement of those objects and present or future events. Nothing we know scientifically about the world suggests a mechanism for these alleged connections." As far as parapsychology is concerned, some would say, "I can't accept that a table levitated (or that someone received information directly from a remote location, or influenced a random number generator by thought alone). It simply makes no sense (or is overwhelmingly improbable) in terms of our scientific knowledge."[1] Surprisingly, even some parapsychologists make claims of this sort. For example, I've often been told that psychokinetic influence on random number generators is more probable than larger-scale phenomena (such as table levitations or materializations) because in the former case we have some idea how to integrate the phenomena into current scientific theory.

Now don't misunderstand me: I believe we should respect the achievements and the explanatory power of science. But to me it's astonishing that anyone would say these things. The authority of science is not absolute. In fact, science periodically undergoes radical transformations, and positions that at one time seemed absurd later attain the status of received knowledge.[2] Besides (and even more to the point), it's completely obvious that we can know *that* something is the case without knowing *why* it's the case.

Science started with, and has always been driven by, the desire to explain what we've already and undeniably observed to occur. In fact, it's easy to rattle off long lists of phenomena we've ascertained to be genuine before we had—or before we at least settled on—a theory as to why or how they occurred. Think, for example, of lightning, thunder, heat, rain, earthquakes, sunrise and sunset, lunar cycles, tides, magnetism, organic growth and development, aging, tooth decay, inherited characteristics, memory, pain, and hair loss (some of these we still don't know how to explain).

Of course, our labels for (and interpretations of) some of these phenomena have changed in the process of trying to make sense of them. Over time we've usually found new ways of systematizing observed regularities and drawing links between them and other things we observe or believe about the world. We knew that objects burned in combustion, whether we explained it (say) with respect to phlogiston or oxygen. Various symptoms of disease and ill health have been recognized for millennia, whether those conditions were explained in terms of imbalance of bodily humors, demonic influence, or microorganisms. Even very unusual phenomena, such as instances of exceptional ("photographic") memory and the appearance of musical or mathematical prodigies and savants, occurred indisputably, even though we've struggled with various attempted explanations of them. But no matter how we characterized and organized these occurrences and tried to connect them with other items in experience, we knew for sure that the events we were trying to explain really happened. Clearly, we didn't need to have *any* explanation at hand to know that they were real.

Many critics, then, seem to have it backwards. Theoretical speculation requires, from the beginning, careful and systematic observation. Without the initial accumulation and systematization of observed facts, scientists won't even begin to know what they're theorizing about. Moreover, as the history of science demonstrates, we often think we know how to explain observed facts until better explanations come along. So obviously, our currently preferred explanations never provided much (if anything) in the way of additional assurance that the phenomena were real. On the contrary, no matter what science eventually takes the phenomena to be, their reality was our starting point, the source of our puzzlement and our urge to find an explanation.

Actually, the extent of our pretheoretical or prescientific knowledge is much wider than the above examples suggest. We build the most mundane but vital aspects of our lives on countless observed facts without knowing how to explain them. Long before we have so much as a clue as to what an explanation of the facts would even look like (e.g., when we're children), we learn that fire produces heat, that by eating we can make hunger disappear, that some objects float on water while others don't, that we have certain regular urges (e.g., to urinate and sleep), that various interesting sounds emanate from certain of our orifices, that consuming specific beverages leads to certain (often pleasant) altered states, that certain behaviors (e.g., crying) elicit certain reactions in others, and that we can produce extremely pleasant sensations by various kinds of self-stimulation.

It's also well known that a person's physical or mental states can be affected (and sometimes permanently conditioned) by features of that person's environment. Astrology rests on the claim that these environmental relationships extend to our connections with celestial states of affairs. Some may doubt whether these alleged relationships are genuine, and it's perfectly legitimate to raise those doubts. But there's nothing inherently wrong with suggesting that the relationships are real. And in fact, we can have good grounds for claiming they *are* real without knowing why that is. We need only to spot the regularities and determine whether they're persistent and robust.

So if there's a scientifically credible and causal story to tell about alleged astrological connections, we'll obviously have some serious work ahead of us. But in the meantime, we can continue to refine and extend our observations and see whether we can generate successful predictions from the correlations we observe. In short, we can try to get a handle on the phenomena pragmatically so that we have at least a working knowledge of the domain. The analytic knowledge of it can always come later, if it ever comes at all. And it needn't come at all, especially if the regularities in question turn out to be as fundamental as natural regularities get. But in any case, without the practitioners (those with a working knowledge) to guide them, theoreticians often wouldn't even know where to look. For example, acupuncture theorists (Eastern or Western) first needed the groundwork laid for them by those who figured out how to use needles to heal. In principle at least, and as far as we know, astrologers might be in the same boat.

2. Personal Background

Since I took my first careful look at the parapsychological evidence in the mid-1970s, I've had to confront—and often dispel—a number of personal intellectual prejudices. Most of these I acquired in the process of cultivating the intellectual snottiness essential for membership in the academic mainstream. But even after shedding many of my unreflective biases and cheap pretensions, some remained. One of these was the belief that astrology is nonsense and a refuge for the credulous. Of course, considering the vagueness of so many published astrological forecasts, that bias wasn't totally without merit. But I also knew that I couldn't reject a field of inquiry simply because it appealed to naive or foolish adherents. After all, I knew it was appropriate to study ESP, PK, and the evidence suggesting life after death, even though parapsychology attracted many uncritical believers (some of whom, for no reason other than their interest in the subject, declared they were parapsychologists). I simply believed, without really looking into the matter, that astrology wasn't worth the time.

However, there was at least one chink in my armor. Although I hadn't read any ostensibly careful studies on the merits of astrology, I knew that Michel Gauquelin had found some surprising similarities in the horoscopes of athletes.[3] And I knew that an attempt to debunk Gauquelin's results, conducted by the Committee for the Scientific Investigation of Claims of the Paranormal (CSICOP), led instead to an embarrassing replication of them, something its leaders shamefully tried to cover up.[4] So I had some reason to think that astrology might deserve a closer look, but I admit I wasn't eager to pursue it. I knew I'd have to risk making more deep changes in my worldview and possibly confront yet another blast of scorn and ridicule from the many (even more ignorant or cowardly) members of the academy with whom I still associated.

Fortunately, my life conspired to frustrate my laziness. I married a remarkable woman who, in addition to being exceptionally well educated and intelligent, with impeccable credentials in both clinical and experimental psychology as well as psychometric research, was also an apparently gifted astrologer, capable of making reliable, detailed, and accurate predictions. I needed to understand what was going on, and I needed to probe her claim that she was doing something quite different from what the vast majority of so-called astrologers were doing.

I'm still at only the most preliminary stage of coming to grips with all this. But I think there's some value in presenting a progress report of sorts, indicating what's shaken my complacent and dismissive attitude toward astrology. So I present this portion of the book as a postscript, a collection of intriguing personal anecdotes. I don't think they help dispel the mystery of astrological proficiency, but I believe they suggest strongly that many have prematurely closed the door on astrology.

3. Gina's background

My wife Djurdjina (Gina) is originally from the former Republic of Yugoslavia. She taught psychology for eighteen years at the University of Novi Sad and enjoyed a legitimate, respected, and perfectly mainstream career, during which she accumulated a long list of publications (one book and nearly one hundred articles) and professional presentations in clinical, experimental, and social psychology. During her country's devastating and protracted civil war, faculty salaries plummeted dramatically, and at one point Gina's university was paying her only about $2 a month. Not surprisingly, then, Gina began looking for additional sources of income. It turned out that she found a lucrative market in professional sports for the astrological skill she'd been perfecting over the years.

For reasons that should be clear enough, I prefer not to mention the identities of those for whom Gina worked. It's enough to note that for six years she served as psychologist/astrologer for several European soccer teams and another soccer team in China. Drawing on her expertise and experience in psychology as well as her acquaintance with team personnel, and armed with birth dates and times for as many players, coaches, and officials as possible (including players and coaches on the opposing teams), Gina was able to make specific and accurate predictions about forthcoming games. And because (according to Gina) much of astrological forecasting—like weather forecasting—concerns tendencies and trends, not strictly deterministic causal chains, Gina could determine which potential outcomes are capable of being influenced and altered. That, in turn, allowed her to suggest corresponding strategies to coaches and thereby enhance their teams' chances of winning. Most of Gina's astrological work was for two teams, and in both cases it seems her combination of psychological and astrological guidance enabled those teams to rise to the top of their respective leagues or divisions (from previous positions of overall mediocrity).

In a moment I'll mention some details concerning this work; but I should probably also note that Gina found an additional demand for her astrological services within the Serbian mafia, primarily doing economic forecasting for their black market business (not their drug business). I can't go into specifics about this (I value my knees), but I believe it indicates something about Gina's success to note that this employment provided her with nearly ten years of protection from the ravages of the civil war. While others suffered, Gina thrived. The mafia made certain she wanted for nothing. (In fact, Gina could have had her own Ferrari, but she realized there would be no point in doing so. There was no place to park the car where it wouldn't be stolen or vandalized by her desperate neighbors, or destroyed by the bombs falling nearby.) In any case, I suspect that if the mafia hadn't found Gina's guidance helpful, they wouldn't have continued to rely on her, especially for such a long period.[5]

Granted, many willingly pay for services without any decent evidence that their service providers are actually competent. Accordingly, it proves nothing about Gina's abilities to note merely that she enjoyed continued employment as an astrologer. But the mafia members who supported Gina are neither stupid, naive, nor blindly loyal when it comes to matters of business. And considering how often they consulted Gina for her forecasts, they had ample opportunity to determine whether she was reliable. Moreover, I find it hard to believe that, especially during the desperate period of civil war, her mafia employers would have hesitated to cut Gina loose, or at least stop seeking her astrological advice, if they weren't profiting from her recommendations.

There *was* a price Gina paid for having her astrological forecasting so highly valued within this organization: mafia members would call her at all times of the night requesting horoscopes. Moreover, there were frequent awkward moments when they would call for Gina at her university office, wearing (apparently obligatory) dark glasses and parking their big cars in front of her building. Understandably, Gina preferred not to advertise this particular affiliation. Later, when she saw the movie *Analyze This* (about a psychologist counseling a mob boss), she was astonished at how closely certain events in the movie paralleled her own life.

Gina had become interested in astrology many years earlier, after being unimpressed with the horoscopes provided by some local practitioners. In fact, Gina had been angered by the exorbitant fees local astrologers were charging for what she considered to be worthless astrological readings. But because she's naturally inquisitive and open-minded, she couldn't help but wonder whether there was anything *at all* to astrology, and so she began to study it on her own. She collected and read dozens of books, but concluded they were as stupid and useless as the readings she had received earlier.

Around this time, Gina met a Swiss astrologer, Jakob Eugster, who encouraged her to ignore the received varieties of astrological theories, which he had also found to be worthless. Instead, he encouraged Gina to try an empirical approach to the subject: to calculate horoscopes and then to *observe*. During this period of her life, Gina was working primarily in clinical psychology, and she would routinely calculate charts of her patients, as well as of friends and acquaintances, and she also studied the published charts of many hundreds of other people. What she found was that by applying her understanding of clinical and general psychology to the reading of horoscopes, patterns simply began to pop out. Before long, Gina was noticing a variety of regularities between features of charts and such things as occupation, talents, psychopathologies, and various personality traits. Over the years, Gina continued to refine her ability to read charts, partly through continued practice and partly through time spent with Jakob at his school in Switzerland.

Before going further with this saga, let me pause for a few introductory remarks about astrology. This is not the place for a detailed examination of astrological theory, and in any case I'm not the person to provide it. But for those readers who know even less about astrology than I do, perhaps the following will be helpful.

In calculating a horoscope, Western astrologers typically produce what's known as a *chart*. It's a graphical representation of the sun, moon, and planets, surrounded by the twelve star constellations of the Zodiac, from the standpoint of a certain location on earth at a particular time. Like many others, Gina typically uses a circular figure, or *chart wheel*, to represent a horoscope. The chart wheel is the usual tool of Western solar astrology, and underlying its use is the assumption that celestial objects and their locations in the sky can influence human life and events on earth. So charts are, as it were, maps of the heavens, usually for the moment of birth, for a person, event, or even (say) for an idea or nation.

Unlike some astrologers who take a strongly deterministic view of the influence of the planets, etc., on human behavior, Gina believes that celestial influence comes in varying degrees. She therefore tries to detect which events or behaviors are free from celestial influence, and to what extent and under what circumstances they're free. Ostensibly, that's why Gina is able to suggest courses of action that could prove useful in sports and in other enterprises.

It's clear that whatever Gina is doing when she reads a horoscope, the process is anything but mechanical. However, calculating the charts themselves is relatively straightforward, and when it's possible Gina happily relies on several computer programs to save her the labor. But reading the charts, like (I suppose) practicing medicine—or clinical psychology—is both an art and a skill, and to some extent it probably can't be taught. But even if teaching astrology is limited in its efficacy, to the extent astrological competence relies on instinct and talent, teaching may also be indispensable, at least while the underlying talent or skill is emerging. Analogously, one can accomplish only so much in teaching people without musical gifts how to play an instrument. But to someone naturally talented musically, instruction can constructively channel and develop those gifts to an exquisite degree. I suspect something like that happened with Gina in her relationship with Jakob. She had, on her own, begun to figure out how to apply her intelligence and skills to the reading of horoscopes, and I believe Jakob helped her to become a virtuoso.

4, Sports Forecasting

So what has Gina done with her combination of psychological and astrological expertise? Although she has plenty of anecdotes from the period before we met, I'll limit myself primarily to achievements for which I was present.

When Gina first came to the US to live with me, she was still working for a team in China. Several times each week the team's coach would phone us for Gina's suggestions about how to play his game. Prior to these phone calls, Gina would spend several hours with the charts of players, coaches, etc., to see who would have a good day or bad day, who was likely to score or screw up *at quite precise moments in the game*, which opposing players were likely to be dangerous at certain points, when the judges were likely to make good or bad calls, etc. So Gina would advise the coach, in great detail, what the course of the game would be and how the psychologies of the team personnel and judges, on the day of the game, would match the character of that particular game. For example, Gina would tell the coach on one occasion that it's best to begin the game by emphasizing defense, and on another occasion to play very aggressively within the first ten minutes. She would say, for example, that opposing player number 23 would be very dangerous at 35:30 of the game, or that the coach (or specific players) would be particularly able to deal with (or likely to be flustered by) something happening at a certain point in the game. In fact, she would tell the coach when the opposing teams (and which players) were most likely to score a goal, and then she would recommend the best strategy for preventing it (i.e., the best way to use the players, given their psychology at that moment).

It was clear that Gina was on to something, and the coach obviously found her forecasts indispensable. (That had been true as well with the European teams she had advised before this.) Gina was working without a formal contract with this team; she was getting paid under the table. Moreover, it was the coach's decision alone to rely on Gina's guidance, and he made that decision independently (and I believe without the knowledge) of the team owners. So nobody was forcing him to phone Gina from China every few days to get her detailed recommendations. In fact, he was clearly upset when Gina's activities in the US interfered with her ability to produce timely reports for him. Once again, I'm not claiming that Gina's abilities are genuine just because somebody was willing to pay for them—but as with Gina's mafia employers, her soccer coach had several opportunities each week to test and confirm the reliability of Gina's forecasts. In fact, although his team had never come close to a championship prior to Gina's assistance, they were now regularly beating better-funded and ostensibly more talent-heavy teams within their Asian league.

One incident in particular stood out for me. At one point, Gina's preparatory work indicated that it would be better if the coach played the reserve goalkeeper rather than the regular goalkeeper. Now in professional soccer, that's something that's almost never done. Usually, reserve goalkeepers see action only if the regular goalkeeper is disabled. Not surprisingly, then, the coach initially refused to accept Gina's recommendation, and the team lost that game very badly. But Gina saw that the same situation would obtain for the next two games: the regular goalkeeper would not have a good day, while the reserve goalkeeper would have a tremendously lucky day. This time, Gina persuaded the coach to heed her advice, and her team won those two games by shutouts, beating much better-funded teams from Shanghai and Beijing.

Now what interested me most about this was the fact that Gina had never predicted that the reserve goalkeeper would play well. She had seen only that he would have a good day. And in fact, while this player was in goal, *his skill was never actually tested*. Despite the fact that the Shanghai and Beijing teams were formidable opponents, on those game days they couldn't make a shot on goal. Every attempt went either high or wide, and it seemed as if the teams were squandering a golden opportunity to capitalize on their opponent's unprecedented vulnerability. Obviously, the reserve goalkeeper, a young man of relatively modest ability and very limited experience, was having an exceptionally good day.

I should mention that although Gina's position with her various teams was kept as quiet as possible (and thus never formalized beyond a verbal agreement), other teams eventually learned of her involvement. This is hardly surprising. After all, Gina had requested precise birth records for the players, coaches, etc., which goes well beyond the information usually required, and which must have made at least some people curious. And besides, movement of players between teams, as well as ordinary interaction between members of different teams, would have made it virtually impossible to keep Gina's activity a complete secret. So eventually, opposing teams began posting false birth information about their players, and Gina's team began to do this as well, just in case other teams likewise starting seeking astrological guidance. At any rate, Gina reports that her teams had ways of securing accurate birth information about opposing teams' personnel; so their attempted misinformation campaigns were ineffective.

Incidentally, Gina doesn't know whether any other astrologers were working in professional soccer, but she's confident that they probably were no better than the average newspaper astrologer and were unable to make any but the most general (if not totally vacuous) predictions. In fact, Gina suspects that with the possible exception of Jakob, no one could match her skill at astrological sports forecasting, and that eventually she was better at this than even Jakob, who simply lacked her interest and experience in that domain. And this was not an arrogant boast; it merely reflects Gina's view that her success resulted first from her ability to apply her knowledge of psychology to the reading of horoscopes, and second from her accumulated experience in working within professional sports. Besides, by Gina's estimate, in six years she provided inaccurate information only three times. So if that's correct, her self-assessment is completely reasonable.

Gina eventually severed her ties to European and Asian soccer, but she began to learn about American football and baseball. Because she's an avid sports fan (and in fact very athletic herself), she very much enjoyed the process. To date, Gina hasn't been able to find work with any major US sports franchise; she simply lacks the connections in this country that would get her in the front door. Nevertheless, she found an outlet for her skills. During the 2005 National Football League Playoffs, Gina thought she might as well take advantage of the fact that I have family living in Las Vegas by placing bets on some of the games. I watched this process closely, especially since it was my money we were betting, and frankly also because (despite my having been born in Vegas) I'm appallingly spineless when it comes to gambling.

Gina got this idea after seeing how well she could predict the course and the outcome of some games early in the playoffs. She hadn't been certain she'd succeed at this, because she didn't understand the games as deeply as she knew soccer, and also because she was working with less information about the participants than she preferred and was accustomed to having in soccer. From the Internet Gina was able to learn what she at least assumed were the correct birth dates of the players and coaches, but she had no way of finding out the crucial times of their birth. Nevertheless, she found that she was able to make some rather accurate and precise forecasts. At the very least, she could tell which team was likely to win, how probable that victory would be, and whether the game was likely to be high scoring or low scoring. Moreover, she also had some idea when in the game the different teams would have their best opportunities to score, when the momentum was likely to shift from one team to the other, and how the players and coaches would be able to handle the challenges posed by the specific character of the game. On that latter issue, for example, Gina said she could see how the personalities of the Pittsburgh Steeler players matched that of the head coach, and how they would be psychologically better suited than their opponents for dealing with the challenges of the games. Gina didn't come up with these ideas based on information in the newspapers, on TV, or on the Web. The only time she ever consulted anything other than a horoscope was searching the Web for birth dates.

I'm sorry now that I didn't keep detailed records of what Gina did during the playoffs; I had no idea at the time I'd eventually write about her exploits. So I merely observed her as she spread dozens of chart wheels around her, and I listened to her as she showed me charts for particular games and indicated how they represented the probable course of action for those games. For example, in the first-round playoff game between the Cincinnati Bengals and the Steelers, Gina saw that the home team (Cincinnati) would suffer something quite ugly and outcome-determining early in the game. And in fact, the Bengals' quarterback sustained a possibly career-ending injury on his first pass attempt. The Steelers won the game handily, as Gina had predicted.

We started placing bets when Gina determined that the oddsmakers' underdogs were very likely to win. So we bet on the Steelers to beat the Indianapolis Colts (the heavy favorites) and the Denver Broncos to beat the New England Patriots. Let's just say we did very well. We also bet on Gina's subsequent picks of Pittsburgh over Denver, and finally (in the Super Bowl) over Seattle. Only on that last game were we betting for the team favored to win. So we did very nicely overall (in fact, our winnings supported a large chunk of a summer vacation).

As pleasant as it was to win, it was even more fascinating to see how Gina's fairly detailed predictions were confirmed during the course of the games. For example, when the Steelers played the Colts, Gina predicted that late in the fourth quarter, the officials would do something unusually momentous. It also looked to her as though Steeler defensive player Troy Polamalu would play a vital role during this time. Gina showed me the portion of both the overall game's chart wheel and Polumalu's chart wheel corresponding to that final segment of the game, and she explained to me how the positions of the planets led her to that prediction. Now although many would have predicted that Polumalu would be one of the keys to Pittsburgh's defensive game (he's a great player), Polumalu's chart indicated to Gina that he would be especially influential at certain times rather than others, one of which was late in the fourth quarter. And in fact, with about five minutes left in the game, referee Pete Morelli reversed what looked to most observers like a clear pass interception by Polamalu. With the interception, the Steelers seemed to have a victory clearly within reach; at that point they enjoyed a 21–10 lead over the Colts. But Morelli's reversal gave the Colts a crucial opportunity to regain the lead, and they very quickly closed the gap to 21–18. The Steelers eventually won (in one of the zaniest conclusions in playoff history), and it's notable that the referee's action was not just another ordinary reversal of a call. Later, the NFL made an unprecedented announcement that Morelli had made the wrong decision when he overturned the interception.

For all the games on which we placed bets, Gina told me beforehand what the general flow of those games would be—for example, in which parts of the games the teams would have momentum, or when they would have scoring opportunities. She accurately predicted which games would be easy victories and which would be struggles. She also mentioned that specific players were likely to score in specific quarters (and sometimes at even more specific points in the games). Again, I regret not having taken careful notes of these predictions. I knew Gina was working with less data than she had for the soccer teams she advised, and I was too busy fretting about losing money. Also, I'm not sure it would have been wise to make the situation more test-like and probably more pressure-filled than it was already (thanks to my anxiety) by systematically and carefully having Gina record specific predictions ahead of time. But for what it's worth, I can report that Gina's specific predictions about game flow and players scoring were generally accurate.

5. Further Astonishments

This was not the only situation in which Gina tried using astrology for betting or gambling. During her tenure with the Serbian mafia, she would provide advice to the organization's professional gamblers, and apparently they found it as helpful as her advice on matters of illegitimate business. They relied on it for years and kept returning for more. Although Gina doesn't pretend to understand very well how astrology might work in these situations, apparently professional gamblers knew what to make of the information she provided.

So on one of our trips to Las Vegas, we thought we'd see whether Gina could figure out optimal times for playing slot machines. As far as Gina could tell, the time we had chosen for our trip wasn't particularly favorable financially. But she found what appeared to be a forty-minute window of opportunity beginning one day at 2:30 a.m. Admittedly, we weren't sure what to do with that information. We figured it didn't mean that we'd win on just *any* machine we tried. Since many slot machines are actually amusing audio-visual experiences, or at least experiences we enjoy, we thought it more likely that we'd have good fortune on machines that entertained us, or with which we felt some kind of connection at the time. We also weren't sure whether Gina's charts indicated that we'd continue to have good fortune playing machines on which we'd already won, or whether we should move on to another machine after a significant win. We decided on the latter course.

For the purpose of comparison, we played slot machines at no less than a dozen nonoptimal times throughout our visit and adopted that same strategy. On some of those occasions, we didn't enjoy even temporary, modest success with any machine (although we found many slots whose animation we enjoyed). On other occasions, we sometimes won a little bit by advancing through one of the machine's bonus rounds, but we had no continued success on that machine or any other. We wanted to carry on with these trial rounds—purely in the interest of science, of course—but we had only limited funds for this investigation, despite playing only one- and five-cent machines.

We were naturally curious, then, to see what would happen during Gina's predicted window of opportunity. We dragged ourselves out of bed and to the casino around 2 a.m. Fortified with a little bit of coffee, we started playing the machines around 2:15, placing maximum bets on the penny or nickel slots. At around 2:30, but not before, we started doing well. We'd invest no more than several dollars in a machine and very quickly win anywhere from $15 to just over $65. After a "big" win (considering our low-stakes betting), we'd move on to another machine that looked inviting, and the scenario would be repeated. We'd invest a few dollars, win back twenty or thirty dollars or more, move on, and win again. The forty minutes passed very quickly, and Gina, flushed with success, decided she could keep going. But nothing she tried after 3:10 a.m. succeeded. After about fifteen minutes of losing, she eventually gave up, and we still came out nicely ahead.

I realize there are many ways to interpret our spasm of success, including appealing to player-PK; so I report this experience as no more than a suggestive episode. Nevertheless, it's certainly interesting that despite many hours of time logged with slot machines during our several days in Vegas, the only time we had any continued success and came out ahead was during the forty-minute period Gina had previously identified as our time to win.

A different sort of anecdote is also worth sharing, illustrating the precision of some of Gina's astrological inferences. Gina generally prefers not to do individual horoscopes, at least professionally. She will do them for friends and relatives, but only infrequently for clients. On one occasion a friend asked Gina to do her horoscope. This friend knew her own birth date, but because she couldn't locate her birth certificate she didn't know her time of birth. Now when Gina does a personal horoscope, she actually does a *group* horoscope. She usually wants to know the birth dates and times of significant people in the client's life, and also the dates and times of death of significant others. She also likes to have information about major events in the client's life, such as a marriage or divorce, major illness, purchasing a first house, or the start of a new job. In Gina's view, the dates of these various events should all line up in the correct horoscope. That is, in a person's chart there will be a time of birth for which those events appear at the dates and times on which they actually occurred. But then Gina can work backward from the calendar information about the events and (as it were) triangulate the correct time of birth. She did this for my friend, who soon thereafter located her birth certificate. It turned out that Gina had nailed her birth time to the minute.

I imagine that some readers are sympathetic (or at least open) to paranormal explanations, but that they remain contemptuous or strongly suspicious of all things astrological. Moreover, some of these readers might think that what Gina is doing is really not astrology at all, and that in fact it's independent of her astrological calculations. They might propose that Gina is precognitively gifted, and that she uses horoscopes the way others might use a crystal ball or tea leaves—that is, as a kind of focusing device, a Gina-friendly means of tapping into psychically acquired information.

Gina's response to this would be that of course to some extent she's using *psychological* knowledge and skills—as she believes any good astrologer must in order to understand a person's horoscope. Even more generally, Gina maintains that one still needs a good "nose" to interpret a horoscope—that is, a sense for recognizing what's relevant and important. In her own case, she would say she developed this instinct after much practice in the empirical approach recommended by Jakob. Gina also concedes that one *could*, at least in principle, use psychic abilities as a substitute for astrological expertise. However, she notes that this requires a deeper level of personal engagement than letting calculations do much of the work.

So Gina would say that, as long as one is really doing astrology and not simply using horoscopes as a psychic focusing device, the calculations are critically important—arguably, the most important part of an astrological chart. In fact, Gina contends that most astrologers seldom (if ever) accurately figure a person's time of birth, and that the resulting errors can be momentous. However, it's difficult to explain what, exactly, the problem is without revealing more of Gina's distinctive approach than she'd like. I hope the following remarks will be enough to clarify, if only slightly, what Gina does differently.

All astrologers represent periods of calendar time by means of intervals along a chart wheel, and those intervals are specified by the number of degrees along the 360-degree circumference of the circle. But Gina's method of using those intervals *for the purposes of prediction and checking a person's time of birth* is radically different from that adopted by most astrologers. And the difference has to do with the way time is measured.

Most people are familiar only with *solar* time, for which a day is twenty-four hours long, and which is measured roughly with respect to the time it takes the earth to rotate once on its axis and for the sun to appear at its previous location in the local sky. However, the earth moves slightly along its orbit during the course of one rotation. So it turns out that the earth must actually rotate approximately 361 degrees before the sun is again at its previous position in the sky. Therefore, a more accurate way to measure the earth's 360-degree rotation is with respect to the position in the sky of a distant star rather than the sun. Using this measurement, we can define a *sidereal* day, and this day is almost four minutes shorter than a solar day.

Now in astrology, it's presumably important to be accurate about the position of heavenly bodies at specific times. Not surprisingly, then, astrologers transform periods of calendar time into this more precise sidereal time when calculating their charts, and there are standard conversion tables and formulas for converting from ordinary solar, or calendar, time to sidereal time.

Up to a point, Gina adheres to this practice. However, for the purposes of prediction and checking birth times, she uses *astronomical* time, measured with respect to the apparent circular path the sun takes along its ecliptic. During the earth's orbit around the sun, the sun appears to us to stand in front of different stars, and eventually the sun and solar system seem to travel in a circular path around the twelve constellations of the Zodiac. That entire apparent trip is called an astronomical day, and it's roughly equivalent to one solar or sidereal *year*. Moreover, an astronomical day is represented by only one degree on a chart wheel, and when that's converted or translated into sidereal time, it has a value of about four minutes. So in Gina's preferred system of measurement when making predictions, one calendar year of a person's life is represented by only four minutes (or one degree) on the chart wheel.

Without going into more detail than Gina wants, what this means is that a four-minute mistake in specifying a person's birth time will lead to a one-year mistake in making predictions based on the horoscope. For example, suppose we predict that a person born at 2:40 a.m. on January 12, 1980, will marry this year. However, if we mistakenly take that person's birth time to be 2:44 (or 2:48), then according to Gina's approach we'd infer that the person would marry next year (or in two years). Clearly, if the mistake in birth time is larger still, predictions will be off by an even greater degree in terms of years. So if an astrologer gets the time of birth wrong, say by thirty minutes, predictions from a horoscope based on that time will be massively incorrect, especially if the predictions extend reasonably far into the future. Thus, one of the secrets of Gina's success in predictions has to do with her ability to check precisely a person's time of birth.

That's why, when Gina works on a person's horoscope, she incorporates as many vital events as possible into that person's chart. She argues that hospitals are frequently cavalier about recording precise birth times, and so she uses these other life events to help her pinpoint the actual—not simply the officially recorded—time of birth. In the case mentioned above, the two results happened to be the same, as they sometimes are. But Gina suggests that the reason many people are so dissatisfied with astrological readings is that their astrologers (a) are working only with the officially recorded birth time, and (b) don't know how to *correct* the time of birth and find the time that accurately mirrors the person's life. Similarly, if no birth time was specified from the start, presumably they also don't know how to work backward and calculate the person's actual time of birth.

Not surprisingly, Gina says that preparing horoscopes for a sports team makes different demands on calculations than producing horoscopes for a single person. That's because in sports, what usually matters is the outcome for the next game—that is, for a period in the immediate future. But when doing an individual's horoscope, Gina is typically more concerned with looking into the person's longer-term future. That's why she reverts to astronomical time in her calculations. As Gina describes it, it's as if she expands her vision and views a person's life from a very high altitude. But in sports, she needs to be precise about events happening within smaller units of time (the duration of a game, or various periods in a game). Gina describes that process as more like viewing life from a microscope than from an airplane. And for this specific kind of work, Gina taught herself—with considerable trial and error—how to make the appropriate calculations. As far as she knows, nobody else knows how to do this.

Again, to protect her apparently preeminent position in this area, Gina prefers not to reveal details about the exact calculations she uses. Suffice to say that when Gina learns the accurate starting time of the game, she then knows how to determine the placement of the main players at various times during the game. For example, in soccer Gina can determine who has opportunities to score and at what points in the game those opportunities arise. Next she can look at the game's chart wheel and see when goals are likely to occur. Then she can see which players are likely to score at the times when goals are likely to be scored. Moreover, when those goals are for the opposing team, Gina can then assess the probability of preventing the goals from occurring, and she can suggest specific strategies for defending against them. Her recommendations will hinge on information obtained from her knowledge of the players' personalities and abilities, and some of that knowledge concerns astrologically guided information about the players' state of mind, good fortune, etc., at precise times in the game.

I should also add that this fine-grained approach, focusing on individual scores, will work more easily in some sports than in others. In particular, it works best in games where scoring is relatively infrequent (e.g., soccer and American football), rather than in a sport such as basketball, which is saturated with scoring, where individual scoring opportunities are accordingly less momentous, and where other kinds of events become more individually significant (e.g., a player's fouling out, or a team's breaking out of a period of poor shooting). Gina has only recently begun to apply her astrological knowledge to basketball, and so she's still figuring out how to interpret the information at her disposal. Nevertheless, Gina believes that with practice, she'll be able reliably to identify, say, momentum shifts and when notable periods or flurries of scoring are likely to occur.

But let's return to more personal, domestic applications of Gina's astrological skills. As you might expect, Gina has worked extensively both on her own horoscope and on mine, and she has often used those results to pinpoint the optimal time for various projects or activities (not just gambling). For example, Gina selected a day and time to get married, and also a time to buy and build a house. I can report that these matters have all gone extremely well—and in the case of our marriage, arguably contrary to what one would have predicted on the basis of my previous matrimonial adventures.

I've been particularly interested in the way we've used Gina's astrological forecasting to determine (when possible) the best times to leave home for both domestic and international travel. For example, during my recent year-long sabbatical, we had many opportunities to use this kind of advice. Gina would examine our various departure options to see what the resulting charts indicated for the period of our trip. And if the charts looked problematical, Gina would tell me what sorts of problems they predicted (e.g., emotional difficulties, health issues, or simply troubles with the process of traveling). On one occasion, however, Gina withheld the full information from me, because she didn't want me to be worried over what looked to her like a disastrous chart. This was a case when she felt we had no reasonable or good option for leaving home. And that trip was, indeed, extremely difficult. The weather was awful; Gina got sick; she had a very painful visit with her seriously ill sister; and I got robbed of all my money, credit cards, and photo IDs.

But in most cases, we've been able to select among various departure options, some of which Gina determined were decidedly better than others. And when Gina finds one she really likes, in every case, those trips have been a breeze. In fact, in those cases it often happens that things go smoothly to an unprecedented degree. Of course, it's difficult to quantify the accuracy of Gina's predictions in these cases, and so I submit my various anecdotes as nothing more than suggestive.

Nevertheless, consider this. On one trip during the summer we planned to drive from Maryland to New England. We were going to take a route I've driven at least thirty times before, often at the same time of year, and without exception that drive has been irritating at certain specific points along the way, especially on weekdays. Morning rush hour around the Baltimore Beltway is always a pain, with very heavy and slow traffic and often long periods of starting and stopping. The same has been true around Wilkes-Barre and Scranton, PA, usually as the result of road construction (which in that area seems never to end). And from the New York/Connecticut border through Hartford, the traffic has likewise always been extremely heavy, especially during the mid-to-late afternoon (which is when I invariably reached that point in my journey).

Now when I've made this trip in the past, I've routinely left home between 8:30 and 9:00 a.m. That's not because I'm inductively challenged. Rather, it's because I always aimed to arrive at my destination at a certain time in the late afternoon, and on the basis of my experience departures during this period have consistently led to hassle-prone driving, especially at the usual problem areas. On this occasion we were traveling on a weekday, and Gina determined that we needed to leave at 8:50 a.m. I told Gina I was surprised by her prediction, and I explained to her what my previous experiences had been. In fact, even though Gina prefers to sleep late, I urged her to leave very early in the morning, so that we could beat the rush hours in Baltimore and Connecticut. However, Gina insisted that if we left at 8:50, the drive—and in fact, the trip itself—would be smooth sailing. I seem to recall arrogantly scoffing at this forecast, although Gina kindly claims that my behavior was more amusing than annoying. Nevertheless, I'm sure I played the role of condescending, experienced traveler, assuring Gina that we could anticipate the same traffic problems I'd confronted many times before.

But Gina was right. In the thirty years I've made this trip, not once have I encountered so few delays and obstacles. In fact, Gina and I breezed through every one of the usual problem areas, and we experienced no delays at other points along the way. The heavy traffic around Baltimore moved briskly. Moreover, although we found the usual road construction at several locations in Pennsylvania, it didn't slow us down. And finally, although we reached Connecticut around 3:30 in the afternoon, and although traffic was heavy, it moved smoothly, without the customary bumper-to-bumper annoyances. We returned home also on a weekday and again encountered no delays, either in Connecticut, Pennsylvania, or when we reached the Baltimore Beltway around rush hour.[6]

Of course, I realize that every time I've made this drive between Maryland and New England, *some* departure times were likely to be more favorable than others, even during the thirty-minute period in which I usually

left home. Presumably, traffic snarls and construction delays vary in severity, even at the usual trouble spots, and even during the approximate times
I've reached those areas. So, some might think that the odds were fairly
good that, sooner or later, I'd hit periods of smooth traffic in otherwise difficult stretches of highway.

Still, the only time in thirty years I've experienced no difficulties whatever during the drive is the one time Gina decided when to depart. Were it
not for her accuracy and success using astrology in other contexts, it would
be easy to minimize its relevance in connection with this incident. But under the circumstances, I feel I have to give some weight to an astrological
interpretation of the events.

I must emphasize that while this case strikes me as unusually impressive,
it's not isolated. Here's another typical example. On the basis of our departure
time, Gina predicted that our return to the US from a recent trip to Europe
would be especially easy. And in fact, when we arrived at Washington Dulles
airport, we made it through baggage claim, immigration, and customs in
record time. Our bags were first off the plane, whereas usually we wait a very
long time, and too often our bags don't appear until days later. Then we had
no delay at immigration control or customs, despite the fact that we've invariably been slowed down in the past, either by long lines or by Gina's Yugo-
slavian passport. And then to top it off, our shuttle home was waiting for
us—something that has never before happened at Dulles airport.[7] In fact, it
was especially surprising considering how quickly we retrieved our luggage
and got through immigration. Typically, international travelers aren't ready
to be picked up within the first thirty minutes after their plane lands, and
shuttle drivers usually take that into account. In seven or eight previous trips
back to Dulles, we've had to wait at least ninety minutes before we could get
through these various procedures and board the shuttle home. This time, we
were headed home in less than fifteen minutes.

As interesting and suggestive as these cases may be, I realize that I'm
working with a very small sample. Fortunately, I expect our travels to continue for a while, so there should be ample opportunity to gather more data.
And from now on, I'll keep more systematic records.

6. Summing Up: Astrology

I know from my own struggles with the data of parapsychology that personal
intellectual prejudices don't disappear overnight, or without an active effort
to combat them. I brought some very well-entrenched biases against astrology into my relationship with Gina, and they are by no means banished,

although it should be clear by now that they're considerably bruised. Gina's accuracy in astrological forecasting seems conspicuously tied to quite specific features of the chart wheels she calculates, and it's something I've now seen on many occasions.

However, despite these recurring correlations, I suspect there has to be more to the story—in particular, a psychic element, whether it's Gina's extrasensory and wide-ranging scanning for relevant information, her psychokinetic nudging of events, or her telepathic influence. Gina even contends that after she determines what the relevant astrological tendencies are, she knows how to psychically influence those tendencies either positively or negatively. And she admits that she often tries to do this, both with personal and sports horoscopes. But if she can really do these things consciously, presumably she can also do them unconsciously and thereby create the impression (to herself and others) that the horoscopes give accurate forecasts on their own. Nevertheless, Gina insists that properly calculated horoscopes provide crucial information all by themselves. She would argue that the horoscopes either simplify the process of adding her own psi to the mix or else render her own psychic influence superfluous.

Without question, Gina's worldview is psi-friendly. She has no doubts about its reality, and she regards herself and others as potentially powerful psychic agents. She also believes strongly that psi abilities can be used for good and for harm. So unlike many other intellectually sophisticated Westerners, she's not constrained by biases against the reality of psychic functioning, including the intrusive use of psi to affect everyday events. In that respect, Gina is less inhibited about having psychic powers than the great spiritualist mediums and their "superstar" successors. In fact, like people in some less industrialized cultures, she's both comfortable with those powers and also wary of the ways others might use similar powers for their own, possibly unsavory, ends. To put it in terms few Westerners like, she accepts the reality of both "white" and "black" magic.

So, am I living my own version of the TV show *Bewitched*? Or more to the point: is there anything in all this that can help us construct a picture of reality in which Gina's activities and those of Katie, Serios, Home, and others makes sense? As far as astrology is concerned, I still feel we need to be cautious. Although it's clear, to me at least, that Gina's predictions are reliable enough to conclude that she's on to something, it's not clear what that something is. Gina understands and interprets her calculations within the context of one sort of astrological theory and (perhaps most important) on the basis of a very distinctive approach to making calculations. However, she also realizes that false theories can generate true predictions. So although she's quite sympathetic to astrology as an explanatory and predictive framework, she recognizes that her success at forecasting doesn't mean that her underlying astrological assumptions are true, or even probable.

As I see it, Gina has the same kind of pragmatic command of a domain that we find among good acupuncturists, whose theoretical underpinnings are also up for grabs. Some acupuncturists are particularly good and reliable at treating various kinds of ailments, but they often disagree among themselves over the theory that best explains their success—for example, whether a traditional acupuncture theory (positing the existence and movement of chi energy) is needed at all, and if so whether one should adhere (say) to an eight-element or five-element theory. In fact, even physicists disagree (sometimes sharply) over the theoretical foundations of their discipline, despite the fact that the equations of modern physics have proven to be exceptionally useful and reliable. As the history of science (and in particular, scientific revolutions) has made clear, it's always a good idea to remain somewhat tentative and humble about one's theoretical commitments.

Of course, there's an important difference between the current status of physics and that of astrology. We accept theories in physics because physicists successfully apply those theories over and over. So, for example, the theory of relativity was strongly supported because it allowed others besides Einstein to make accurate predictions. But we don't have an analogous situation in Gina's case. Obviously, Gina's underlying astrological assumptions would be better supported if other astrologers could match her predictive success. But (at least as far as I know) that hasn't happened. Of course, in the case of relativity Einstein wasn't the only person who *tried* to apply the theory. By contrast, Gina says that apart from Jakob (who died a few years ago), only a handful of others follow her general approach, and no one else she knows uses that approach in the way she does. As I explained earlier, the many astrologers who fail to generate predictions as reliably as Gina apply a different method of calculating horoscopes. So although Gina and other astrologers might share some general beliefs about the relevance of astronomical and geographical facts to a person's history, they're not all doing the same thing.

For now at least, I think we must look at Gina as a single case study. Arguably, it's analogous to what we would have confronted had no one but Einstein tried to test the predictions of relativity. It's not analogous (as some might think) to the hypothetical situation in which others besides Einstein tried but failed. Granted, no other body of scientific theory currently coheres with astrological claims about the relevance to our lives of the positions of celestial bodies. But the fact remains that Gina's forecasts are based on astronomical and geographical data and calculations, and I find it increasingly difficult to believe that this information is only fortuitously relevant to her ability to generate reliable predictions. So if evidence of Gina's forecasting accuracy continues to mount, the question remains: what sort of theory, other than astrological, explains the relevance of that data to Gina's success?

Nevertheless, at this stage I'd recommend the appropriately cautious conclusion that we have evidence of *Gina's* success, not the success of her theory. So while there may not yet be strong support for interpreting her success along astrological lines, I'd say we have reason enough to justify further investigation and to at least keep an open mind about Gina's theoretical point of view. In the meantime, whatever the best underlying explanation turns out to be, I'm quite comfortable seeking Gina's advice on travel and other domestic and professional matters, and I'm ready to put more money on sporting events.

7. Summing Up: Parapsychology

As far as the psychic side of things is concerned, we can bring both this chapter and the book to a close by returning to several issues considered briefly in previous chapters, especially in chapter 2. I noted there how the great spiritualist mediums were probably aided psychologically by the belief that they only mediated—rather than directly produced—their phenomena. I observed how the physical phenomena of mediumship dwindled considerably in scale as psychics came to entertain or accept full responsibility for the phenomena's occurrence. I also noted that people in some parts of the world consider psychic functioning to be an everyday fact of life, and they accept both the positive and the negative aspects of psi as a matter of course. So in those cultures, the fear of one's own psi is not the potent inhibitory force it seemed to be for many European and American mediums and psychics.

The heyday of spiritualism saw the clash of two distinct worldviews or explanatory frameworks for psychic functioning. That of the spiritualists (or simply spiritists) took personal consciousness after bodily death to be the primary source of séance-related phenomena. From this survivalist point of view, mediums were merely channels or facilitators, not psychic "engines" themselves. The more ontologically modest, or scientific, picture that eventually and largely displaced this view attributed the phenomena exclusively to still-living, embodied agents: the mediums or their sitters. And to many it seemed that one or the other of these pictures—but not both—had to be correct. But in fact, these two views about the source of psi aren't mutually exclusive. If we're willing to grant the reality both of postmortem survival and of ESP and PK, they can live happily side by side. In fact, apart from the spiritistic addition of discarnate agents to the inventory of things in nature, they seem to have exactly the same picture of psychic functioning. That's because the survivalist picture actually *presupposes* the exercise of psychic abilities, the same ones the anti-spiritualist or anti-survivalist picture attributes to living, embodied agents.[8]

This is easy to see, and to keep things simple, we'll focus initially just on ESP. Recall, first, that ESP comes in two basic flavors: telepathy and clairvoyance. Very roughly, telepathy is a direct mind-to-mind interaction, and clairvoyance is a direct nonsensory awareness of (or response to) physical events. So for example, it would be telepathy if one person's thought about Bugs Bunny caused a remote person to think about Bugs Bunny or something closely related to that thought (e.g., the Easter Bunny or Elmer Fudd). It would be clairvoyance if a burning house directly caused someone at a remote location to think about a house on fire, or simply fire.

Now suppose a medium says to you the following about your deceased Uncle Harry: "Uncle Harry knows you're eager to quit your job." And suppose that claim about you is true. In that case, how does the medium know what deceased Uncle Harry is thinking? If (as spiritists would maintain), the medium can really have such knowledge, it could only happen by telepathy—that is, by direct mind-to-mind interaction between the medium and your deceased uncle. Furthermore, if deceased Uncle Harry's personal consciousness really continues somehow to exist in the absence of his physical body, and if you've never told anyone how you feel about your job or otherwise behaved in some way that betrays those feelings, the only way Uncle Harry could know about them would be by telepathy—direct mind-to-mind interaction, either with you and your thoughts, or with the medium (who gained that information telepathically from you).

Suppose, next, that the medium says to you: "Uncle Harry is glad you're wearing the necklace he gave you." Now how would deceased Uncle Harry know *that*? It's a physical state of affairs, not one of your mental states. Nevertheless, it could be by means of telepathy, if Uncle Harry gets the information directly from the medium's or your thoughts about the necklace. But let's suppose the scenario is not telepathic. In that case, since deceased Uncle Harry no longer has physical sensory organs, the only way he could know what you're wearing would be by means of clairvoyance, a nonsensory awareness of that physical state of affairs.

Obviously, a similar observation applies to PK. If deceased Uncle Harry can directly modify a medium's body and through her levitate a séance table, that would presumably be the same kind of direct mental influence on a physical state of affairs we'd attribute to the medium if she levitated the table by thought alone. So these mediumistic scenarios seem to require precisely the psychic capacities that psi-friendly anti-survivalists ascribe only to the living.

Of course, if we allow postmortem agents into the causal network, that only exacerbates the "source of psi" problem noted in earlier chapters. It's often difficult enough to tease out which living persons are responsible for apparent psychic effects, or how much various potential agents contribute to the final result. But if we also open the door to after-death influence, the inventory of potential culprits becomes even more unmanageable. No doubt that's enough for some to reject the survivalist picture right from the start. But it's clearly unacceptable to rule that picture out just because it's messier than we'd like. There's no reason to think Nature decorates her house according to our aesthetic preferences.

But no matter what position we ultimately take on the issue of postmortem survival, I believe we're left with the reality of at least some of the phenomena reported throughout the history of parapsychology. In fact, at our current and still rudimentary level of understanding, it doesn't matter which explanatory framework we're currently drawn to. It doesn't matter, for example, whether Katie's foil, Home's accordion phenomena, or Ted Serios's photos were produced wholly by those individuals, or in concert psychically with others, or whether these people mediated actions of agents outside our familiar physical reality; or something else altogether. We're left, in any case, with events for which our current and standard stock of scientific explanatory options seems conspicuously inadequate. Although I realize many see that as cause for suspicion and alarm, to me it's exciting. It's another humbling reminder how much we still don't understand about the world.[9]

Table A1. Summary of Katie foil analysis

Samples		Mn†	Ni	As	Ag	Cd	Sn	Pb	Bi
10/2/86	nose	5.19	57.66	5.78	30.66	23.35	32.31	16.39	0.12
12/15/86	?	1.95	51.14	6.77	34.05	29.60	31.25	19.16	0.24
2/5/87	tongue, lips	2.24	36.66	4.76	25.08	20.57	23.31	29.69	0.11
3/29/87	?	6.39	40.73	6.87	36.73	29.47	37.13	23.00	0.16
4/5/87	body	4.12	41.56	7.20	34.60	28.21	29.49	27.57	0.29
5/7/87	abdomen, back	3.83	60.29	6.85	33.92	27.18	36.59	22.88	0.23
3/17/88	face	3.61	62.16	7.21	35.59	27.77	34.03	99.79	0.12
4/12/88	abdomen	6.70	41.87	6.90	39.21	30.54	33.59	17.54	1.77
6/23/88	abdomen	5.68	42.52	8.52	37.57	28.04	33.27	30.15	0.18
Controls									
34670.00		19.32	106.00	18.00	70.57	1.51	33.83	51.26	1.88
35684.00		25.64	104.33	16.20	69.70	1.19	49.12	56.18	2.08
35690.00		21.47	132.71	14.78	70.29	0.23	47.99	47.17	1.88

† units of metals are given in concentrated ppm (parts per million).

This table shows the concentration of various elements in different samples of the Katie foil. The control measurements were made on three samples of a commercially purchased foil to give an idea of the reproducibility of the measurement technique. There is no question that the Katie foil was the same throughout all samples, based on the similarity of all the element concentrations.

APPENDIX 2: REVIEW OF PREVIOUS
ANALYTICAL EFFORTS

A thorough review of the past efforts to chemically analyze the metal samples concluded that the experiments were done in a scientifically valid manner.

Additional analysis of the foil is not necessary at this time. Upon identification of the proper control, comparison assays will be done.

Table A2. Composition analysis of foils

Metal (%)	Katie Foil	Control Foil
Na	0.008506	0.004836
Mg	0.000677	0.000395
K	0.011932	0.002329
Mn	0.000147	0.001967
Ni	0.004434	0.011004
Zn	17.440033	16.162433
As	0.000563	0.001700
Se	−0.000796	0.006661
Rh	0.000909	0.000978
Ag	0.003822	0.007465
Cd	0.003498	0.000141
Sn	0.002580	0.003666
Sb	0.001141	0.000960
Pb	0.002299	0.005111
Bi	0.000012	0.000209
Sum (%)	17.48	16.21
Cu (%)	82.52	83.79
Total	100.00	100.00

Table A3. Compositional analysis of foils

Metal (%)	K/C	C/K
Na	1.76	0.57
Mg	1.71	0.58
K	5.12	0.20
Mn	0.07	13.41
Ni	0.40	2.48
Zn	1.08	0.93
As	0.33	3.02
Se	−0.12	−8.37
Rh	0.93	1.08
Ag	0.51	1.95
Cd	24.75	0.04
Sn	0.70	1.42
Sb	1.19	0.84
Pb	0.45	2.22
Bi	0.06	16.95
Sum (%)	1.08	0.93
Cu (%)	0.98	1.02

Metal Fingerprinting

- The major metal constituents are consistent with "composition leaf" of a #3 variety. Composition leaf is also known as Dutch gold. This imitation leaf is yellow in color with a standard composition of Cu/Zn, 82/18%. The control sample is more consistent with composition leaf #2 ½. [Obtain composition leaf of this type.]
- Minor constituents are added to composition metals to produce specific effects. Significant levels of tin (1%), lead (1.5 to 4.5%), iron (0.5%), aluminum (0.5 to 1.0%), manganese (0.5 to 2.5%), nickel (1 to 2%), and arsenic (0.03 to 0.25%). No obvious markers are present.
- The minor components do offer the opportunity to fingerprint the source of composition leaf. Consultation with a forensic chemist (not to be identified). The total impurities for the Katie Foil and the control are 0.040% and 0.047%, respectively.
- The minor impurities that show significance differences between the control and the Katie foil are potassium, manganese, cadmium, and bismuth. Until the proper controls are obtained, no meaning can be derived from this data.
- I am sending letters to foil/leaf sourcing companies to determine if a match can be made. [Obtain permission.]

Alternate Assays

- Physical measurements of the foils are being made. Thickness of the foil is important to its sourcing.
- The foils will be submitted for visual microscopy.
- The enhanced levels of potassium and sodium ions do suggest the presence of inorganic salts. This may be derived from natural processes (e.g., handling, body sweat, etc.).
- The confirmation of inorganic salts may be accomplished with ion chromatographic analysis of the surface wash solutions. This work has been submitted for analysis, and the results are expected within the next two weeks.
- The patches of organic(?) material on the surface is being investigated. Solutions derived from solvent washing of the foils have been submitted for mass spectral analysis. This approach will allow us to identify and oils and/or organic compounds.

GLOSSARY

apportation (or teleportation). The paranormal movement of an object (the apport) from one location to another.

clairvoyance. Direct nonsensory awareness of (or response to) physical events.

ESP. Extrasensory perception; roughly, the nonsensory awareness of (or response to) mental and physical states of affairs. *See also* clairvoyance *and* telepathy

macro-PK. PK on observable objects. Allegedly distinguishable from *micro-PK* on very small-scale unobservable processes, though this distinction is far from clear (see Braude 1997b for a discussion).

materialization. The creation of an object *de novo*, out of nothing.

mediumship. Often now called "channeling"; the process of receiving, transmitting, or otherwise mediating interactions between the familiar physical world and a realm of postmortem surviving spirits. *Physical* mediums channel the production of physical phenomena (e.g., object movements, materializations), and *mental* mediums channel thoughts or communications.

PF. Parapsychology Foundation, in New York

PK. Psychokinesis (or mind over matter); physical events produced simply by an individual's intention, bypassing the usual sorts of physical interventions needed to produce similar physical occurrences. *See also* macro-PK

poltergeist. Paranormal physical phenomena (e.g., sounds, object movements) seemingly caused by an invisible agent, but centered usually around the presence of a particular living individual (the *poltergeist agent*). As opposed to *haunting* phenomena, which tend to center around a place rather than a person.

psi. Shorthand for the adjectives "psychic" or "paranormal" and the nouns "psychic phenomena" and "paranormal phenomena." Allegedly more theoretically neutral (or less controversial) than the terms it replaces.

source of psi problem. Because psi (assuming it exists) can presumably be triggered unconsciously, and because we have nothing like a meter to determine

183

where psi influence is coming from, the difficulty of determining which person (or persons) is responsible for a given apparent psi effect.

spiritism. The belief that the spirits of individuals can survive bodily death and continue to interact with and act through still-living humans (mediums).

spiritualism. A religion founded on the belief that living humans can mediate the actions and communications of surviving spirits of deceased individuals.

SPR. The (British) Society for Psychical Research

survivalist. Someone who believes in the persistence of (at least part of) a person's mind or personality after bodily death.

synchronicity. Acausal meaningful coincidence; associated with a theory formulated by C. G. Jung.

telepathy. Direct mind-to-mind interaction, bypassing known sensory channels.

thoughtography. The production of images on photographic media by thought alone.

vibuti. Holy ash allegedly produced paranormally by Sai Baba (and some others).

NOTES

Preface

1. These issues turned out to be major themes of my book, *The Limits of Influence* (Braude 1997b).

2. Eventually, after immersing myself in much more parapsychological data, and also after doing detailed research on hypnosis, dissociation, psychopathology generally and multiple personality in particular, I felt more or less up to the task. The results of my inquiry were published in *Immortal Remains* (Braude 2003).

3. For an account of this, see Braude 2003.

4. Braude 1991; Braude 1995.

5. Braude 1986. The 1997 edition adds another chapter and makes substantial revisions and editions to the original text.

Chapter 1

1. I've explored the issues, data, and reasons for resistance to the phenomena in my book, *The Limits of Influence* (Braude 1997b).

2. Haraldsson 1987.

3. This is a position I advocated, at least tentatively, in Braude 1997b.

4. For example, in the case of D. D. Home, there are many reports of materialized hands, usually ending at the wrist, carrying objects around the room. The objects were warm and flesh-like, observers could shake hands with them or poke holes in them with their fingers (the holes would afterward close up), and eventually the hands would dissolve in the observers' grasp. For a description and discussion of these and other cases, see Braude 1997b.

5. See, e.g., Randall 2003.

6. For a further discussion of how the prevailing belief system affected the evolution of macro-PK during the Spiritualist movement, see Braude 1997b, chapter 2. And for a shorter version, see chapter 2 here.

7. This used to be known exclusively as hysterical paralysis, and is now classified as a form of conversion disorder.

8. Schwarz 1987, 1988a, 1988b, 1997a, 1998b, 1998c, 1999.

9. In that respect, Katie's case differs from the case of Mirna Nazzour, a Syrian woman who, inspired by a picture of the Virgin Mary that seems to exude olive oil, goes into a religious ecstasy and while entranced produces unusual quantities of olive oil on her skin. Here, however, it's reasonable to think that the oil was already a significant part of her diet. See Resch 1997.

10. McMoneagle 2000, 2002.

11. Kurtz is the editor of *Skeptical Inquirer* Magazine and a founding member of the Committee for the Scientific Investigation of Claims of the Paranormal (CSICOP), an organization ostensibly dedicated to combating various forms of irrationalism, and indirectly committed to promoting Kurtz's version of religion: secular humanism. In my view, CSICOP is mostly an ill-disguised organ for distributing its own brand of dishonest and sloppy thinking.

12. For an example of Kurtz's superficially authoritative scholarship, see Kurtz 1985. To see why it's shameful to cite Trevor Hall as an authority on the case of D. D. Home, see Braude 1985. And see Braude 1997b as a remedy to Kurtz's inadequate evaluation of the Palladino case.

13. This generalizing from the unrepresentative cases is called the "straw man" fallacy. To see how this strategy has been used in other parapsychological cases, see Braude 1997b.

14. Eisenbud 1967, 1989.

15. *Nature* 300, Nov. 11, 1982, p. 119.

Chapter 2

1. Especially Braude 1997b.

2. Arguably, the Brazilian medium Carlos Mirabelli was even more spectacular. For a brief introduction to this case, see Braude 1997b.

3. For more details, see Braude 1997b.

4. Braude 1997b; Inglis 1977.

5. For an interesting discussion of this view, see Eisenbud 1992.

6. See chapter 6 for a discussion of this issue in a different context.

7. See, e.g., Honorton 1993; Keil, Hermelin, et al. 1976; Pratt 1977; Varvoglis 2003.

8. Those wishing to pursue the matter further can look at my more detailed examination of the issues in Braude 1997b.

9. See, e.g., Gauld and Cornell 1979.

10. Braude 1997b, chapter 1.

11. For more examples, see Braude 1997b, chapter 1.

12. Loftus 1979, 27.

13. Loftus 1979, 24–25.

14. Braude 1997b, chapter 1.

15. See, e.g., Brandon 1983; Hall 1962, 1984.

16. For more detail, see my review of Hall's book on Home, Braude 1985. And see Inglis 1983 for a review of Brandon's book.

17. See Podmore 1902 and 1910.

18. These individual differences have proven to be quite stable. See, e.g., Hilgard 1965; Perry 1977.

19. Many examples are provided in Braude 1997b.

20. Home 1863, 1888.

21. Initially, you might think that effects of this sort could be produced by Home surreptitiously exerting an effort of his own. But since Home suffered from tuberculosis throughout his adult life, it's highly unlikely that he had enough physical strength to produce the effects by normal means.

22. Crookes 1874; Medhurst, Goldney, et al. 1972.

23. Crookes 1874, 12; Medhurst, Goldney, et al. 1972, 25.

24. Crookes 1874, 13; Medhurst, Goldney, et al. 1972, 26.

25. Crookes 1874, 14; Medhurst, Goldney, et al. 1972, 27.

26. Lamont 2005.

27. E.g., that Crookes went to Home's apartment and watched him change clothes.

28. E.g., the material out of which Crookes's cage was constructed. Lamont also claims that Home removed the accordion from the cage, when in fact it was his hand that he removed. And nine witnesses were present for the test, not four, as Lamont claims. Equally disappointing, when Lamont suggests various (frequently highly implausible) ways in which Home might have faked the materialization of warm, mobile, fleshy spirit hands that ended at the wrist, he conveniently ignores aspects of the accounts that are likely to be most problematical for the debunker. These include reports that although the spirit hands had been solid enough for sitters to shake hands with them, they then melted or dissolved in their grasp.

29. For more on that topic, see Eisenbud 1992.

30. For another example, see Hall 1984 and my review of this book, Braude 1985.

31. Of course, I strongly recommend my survey in Braude 1997b.

32. Feilding 1963; Feilding, Baggally, et al. 1909.

33. Gauld 1968, 224.

34. Dingwall 1962, 190.

35. Carrington 1907.

36. Inglis 1977, 426.

37. Dingwall 1962; Inglis 1977.

38. Feilding 1963, 217–19; Feilding, Baggally, et al. 1909, 507–9.

39. Feilding 1963, 276; Feilding, Baggally, et al. 1909, 566.

40. Or at least read the more extensive summary in Braude 1997b.

41. Feilding 1963, 107; Feilding, Baggally, et al. 1909, 397.

Chapter 3

1. See http://www.mindshiftinstitute.org/Article_New_Nobel.htm.

2. For an account of the dramatic episode that eventually led me to parapsychology, see the preface to Braude 2003.

3. Braude 1997b.

4. For a detailed summary of the best cases, see Braude 1997b.

5. Schwarz 1985, 3. Further information on Nuzum's activities in the world of magic can be found at http://beyond-magick.tripod.com/id4.html. According to that site, "Joey Nuzum continually works with some of the top magicians and magic manufacturers in the world as both a consultant and advisor as well as inventing magic feats and stunts for them." That's actually a more extreme claim than I've seen anywhere else, and I'm not sure about its accuracy. If it were true, Joey would presumably be more affluent. In any case, there's no doubt that Joey is a professional magician, and there's also no doubt that many of his apparent PK feats look suspiciously like standard magic tricks.

For example, George Hansen noted, "Schwarz's [Schwarz 1985] descriptions of macro-PK phenomena produced by Joe Nuzum read like descriptions from the conjuring literature. The reader may wish to compare the pictures of the match under the glass on page 21 of Schwarz's article with that of page 45 in *Tannen's Catalog of Magic No. 15* (Louis Tannen, Inc., 1985). One might also compare the third feat of Affidavit A (p. 17) with the effect called 'Rupert's Pearls' (sometimes known as 'Devil's Tears') advertised on page 17 of the June 1986 issue of *Linking Ring*. Many other equally striking comparisons could be made. To Schwarz's credit, he did consult with several other magicians; however, those he spoke to seemed unaware of a number of standard magic tricks" (Hansen 1990, 44).

6. Schwarz 1994, 99.

7. Personal communication, June 21, 1994.

8. Personal communication, Nov. 14, 1994.

9. Mikki, a creative and meticulous investigator of ostensible haunting sites, took detailed notes on the occasion, and also for the next evening's session. My memory and I are greatly indebted to the accounts she prepared thereafter and circulated privately.

10. Braude 1997b.

11. Information Unlimited, 1994. As of this writing, the device is still available and advertised on the website of Information Unlimited. See http://www.amazing1.com/hyp.htm.

12. Imich 1997, 336.

13. See Braude 1997b for details about this case.

14. Imich 1996.

15. Braude 1997b.

16. Imich 1996, 1997.

17. Bert Schwarz, who—more than anyone else in parapsychology—knows Joey well, describes him as "athletically built" and notes that he's five feet eleven inches tall and weighs 180 pounds. Schwarz 1998a, 32.

18. Personal communication, July 2, 2005.

19. Schwarz 1997b, 1998a, 2005.

20. Nevertheless, I still think Bert should mention that Joey is a performing magician. He noted this in his first report on Joey, but has not mentioned it since.

Chapter 4

1. Nineteenth-century investigators of physical mediums sometimes observed and photographed projections or pseudopods of various lengths and thicknesses which apparently left the medium's body and moved objects in the vicinity (see, e.g., Braude 1997b; Crawford 1918, 1919, 1921). But many good cases of macro-PK lack these features.

2. But it's not unprecedented in the history of macro-PK. Some of the great spiritualist mediums were also unusually cooperative. For example, Eva C. submitted to full cavity searches, and she even agreed to ingest an emetic, knowing that by vomiting she could show that she wasn't simply regurgitating the substances that emerged from her mouth. For details, see Braude 1997b.

3. Personal communication, June 14, 2005.

Chapter 5

1. See, for example, Broad and Wade 1982; Koestler 1971.

2. I defend this view at length in Braude 1997b.

3. For a more detailed discussion of these issues, see Braude 1997b, chapter 1.

4. For those readers who are keeping track, this would be wife number two, not to be confused with the subject of chapter 8.

Chapter 6

1. Fukurai 1931.

2. Eisenbud 1967, 1989. These two editions differ substantially and are both worth reading. The later edition omits some material from the first edition and replaces it with new material, including responses to critics.

3. See Eisenbud 1967, 182, and Eisenbud 1989, 127.

4. Eisenbud 1977, 419.

5. "The Cruel, Cruel World of Ted Serios."

6. Gardner 1981.

7. *Nature* 300, Nov. 11, 1982.

8. Eisenbud 1967, 235, and Eisenbud 1989, 171.

9. The images are reproduced in Eisenbud 1989, 150.

10. See Eisenbud 1967, 167–69, and Eisenbud 1989, 145–48.

11. This wasn't the first gallery exhibition of Ted's photos. For two weeks in December 1990, Ted had an exhibit all to himself at the Marta Cervera Gallery in New York City.

12. Braude 2004, 2005.

13. See Braude 1997b, for examples taken from the study of macro-PK.

Chapter 7

1. For a more detailed discussion of ways to normalize coincidences, see Diaconis and Mosteller 1989; Watt 1990.

2. Jung 1973.

3. Braude 2002; Price 1953.

4. H. H. Price also noted this similarity between Jung's discussion of causality and the quaint perspective on causal relations adopted by seventeenth-century Rationalists. See Price 1953.

5. This was my opinion when I first addressed the topic of synchronicity in *ESP and Psychokinesis*, and I still believe it's correct. For a recent example of how dreadful the more recent literature on synchronicity can be, see (at your own risk) the incoherent paper by Storm (Storm 1999).

6. Braude 1979.

7. Several Web sites carried or mentioned a June 15, 2004, case from Peachtree City, Georgia. See, for example, http://www.nfbnet.org/pipermail/4alabama/2004 -June/001228.html (accessed November 21, 2005).

PEACHTREE CITY, Ga. (AP)—A blind man drove a golf cart for two miles through the winding streets of Peachtree City, accompanied by his guide dog—and an inebriated friend giving instructions—before running into a parked car, police said.

Nobody was hurt, but Samuel McClain, 35, of Stockbridge and Michael Johnston, 47, of Peachtree City were charged with reckless conduct "due to the blatant disregard for public safety," a police report said.

The report said McClain was driving the cart Saturday while Johnston gave directions after having six or seven beers and "admittedly under the influence of alcoholic beverage." Also on the cart was McClain's golden retriever guide dog.

The city of 34,000 about 25 miles south of Atlanta has about 80 miles of paved cart paths and 9,000 registered carts that residents use for daily tasks like going to the grocery or taking children to school.

The most recent case I've found is of an Iraqi-born man, blinded by a bomb blast (also partially deaf and suffering from leg tremors), who was arrested in April 2006 for driving his friend's Peugeot in Oldbury, England. But the friend was not drunk, apparently he was simply stupid. See http://news.bbc.co.uk/2/hi/uk_news/

england/west_midlands/5313370.stm, and also http://blog.washingtonpost.com/offbeat/2006/09/blind_driver_pleads_not_guilty.html (accessed November 21, 2006).

8. The story (from www.crystalair.com, accessed February 13, 2005) reads:

24-year old Alin Popescu is blind. The Romanian man doesn't let it slow him down, but ended up in an argument with friends who told him he was useless because he couldn't see. Alin wanted to prove to them that he could do anything if he set his mind to it.

So Alin did what any man would do trying to prove a point: he stole a car. Alin managed to break into the car without any help, and then used a screwdriver to start the ignition. He even then proceeded to drive down the street. That's where things went a little wrong, and police found him unconscious behind the wheel after he crashed into a tree.

"I only crashed because I was not sure of the way home," said Alin after his arrest. Yes, that and the fact that you couldn't see where you were going.

9. See http://www.ananova.com/news/story/sm_137531.html (accessed February 27, 2006). The story reads:

Police officers in Germany who stopped a car driver after he was reported weaving slowly down a street found he was not only drunk but he was also blind.

The man told officers he had always wanted to try it and had borrowed his friend's car after having a few drinks and setting off at night through the town of Mainz.

The 33-year-old man was arrested but he insisted he was being extremely careful and assured them that he was taking it in stages, driving a couple of feet before stopping, getting out and walking around the car with his arms outstretched to check for obstacles.

A police spokesman says the car had been lent to the man but that he did not have a driving licence [sic] because of his blindness—and he should not have been in charge of a vehicle because of his drunkenness.

The man had managed to get the car out of a school car park and nearly 50 ft up the road before locals called police.

An alcohol test found he was three times over the limit.

10. See http://openweb.tvnews.vanderbilt.edu/1985-5/1985-05-17-NBC-15.html (accessed February 27, 2006).

11. See http://www.nzherald.co.nz/topic/story.cfm?c_id=142&ObjectID=103 51988 (accessed February 27, 2006).

12. See http://news.bbc.co.uk/2/hi/africa/4229468.stm and http://news.bbc.co.uk/2/hi/uk_news/england/oxfordshire/3638934.stm (accessed February 27, 2006).

13. I also found some mention on the Web of blind motor sports or other organized events in which the blind get to handle vehicles while accompanied and

guided by sighted companions. One event in Fonda, NY, took place on a race track, and in Pittsburgh "25 men and women . . . spent a Sunday afternoon tooling around Bud Kunkel's 100-acre farm just off the Butler County Airport" (www.wpabold .org/boldarticle1993.html, accessed February 11, 2005). Obviously, these recreational events are significantly different from the Mississippi and Maine cases.

And for the record, I also found a report of a blind speedboat driver pulling a blind water-skier. See http://www.waf.uk.com/blind.html (accessed February 27, 2006).

14. Jung 1973, 15n26.

15. Jung 1963, 152.

16. Jung 1973, para. 916, emphasis added.

17. Jung 1973, para. 942.

18. It's tempting to say "arranges" here, rather than "operates on." And perhaps that shows how covertly causal the principle of synchronicity really is. Of course, Jung would not have recognized anything causal here.

19. Jung 1973, 86n71.

20. *Ibid.*

21. Indeed, I'd say that much (if not all) of what is now called "cognitive science" rests on this mistake. I can't elaborate the point here, but I can refer the interested reader to Goldberg 1999; Heil 1981; McDonough 2001.

22. As I note in more detail below, synchronistic explanations are always situation-specific. For example, a principle of synchronicity won't connect (say) exploding sounds to arguments *generally*. Presumably, what's meaningful is the connection between a particular argument and a particular sound. To put the point in a more philosopher-friendly way, a natural synchronicity principle would operate on property *tokens* rather than property *types* (or universals).

23. See, e.g., Jung 1973, para. 846.

24. Morris 1992, 150.

25. Please note that I'm not attacking the concept of an archetype, which at least in its original form in Jung's writings seems to have some explanatory value (though not in the present context). Many of Jung's followers, however, have expanded the inventory of archetypes far beyond what Jung envisioned, and in the process have perverted and undermined Jung's original conjecture.

26. See, e.g., Jung 1973, para. 944–45.

27. Notice, too, that we have considerable flexibility as to which events we take to be causes of other events. We could say that Jones's upset stomach was caused by his eating a spicy meal. But we could also trace his upset stomach to his having a delicate digestive system, or to the events in Jones's past that led him to develop a delicate digestive system, or to Jones's failure to take his ulcer medications, or to the history of ethnic cooking which led to the use of certain spices, or to the distraction of the chef who used more chile than usual when preparing the dish, and so on. For further comments on the significance of this and related examples, see Braude 1997b.

28. Just to be clear, I'm certainly not proposing that we take B.'s belief seriously. In fact, many questions about it need to be addressed immediately—for example, in what language does the universe prefer to make puns?

29. See Grattan-Guinness 1978.

30. *Ibid.*, 953.

31. Braude 1997a, 1997b.

32. For surveys of the hypnosis literature, see Gauld 1992 and Braude 1995. And see Braude 1995 for a survey of the relevant issues regarding Dissociative Identity Disorder.

33. The latter would be a real-life and large-scale version of so-called psi-missing. See Braude 2002 for a discussion of psi-missing.

34. I'd suggest, as well, that the possibility of negative psychic influence hasn't been taken seriously enough by those who conduct studies in psychic healing—or so-called therapeutic touch. Assuming the sought-for effects can occur, I see no way to guard against unwittingly harming subjects in either the test or control groups.

35. See, e.g., Braude 1992, 1997a, 1997b, 2003.

36. Braude 1997b, 2003. See also Eisenbud 1970, 1992, for further examples of how psi might work like a magic wand and on a large scale.

37. See my discussions of the so-called super-psi hypothesis in Braude 1997b, 2003.

Chapter 8

1. For the record, I should add that it's highly questionable whether psychic phenomena are improbable relative to current scientific knowledge. That view may rest on a suspicious assumption that the domain of the psychological reduces to that of the physical. For more on this, see Braude 1997b.

2. This is an issue commonly associated now with Kuhn 1970. But for a more subtle treatment, see van Fraassen 2002.

3. In particular, he found that "sports champions tend to be born when the planet Mars is either rising or culminating in the sky much more often than it does for ordinary people" (http://www.encosm.net/mars_effect.htm). For a chronology of the controversy this engendered, see http://www.planetos.info/marchron.html.

4. Kammann 1982, and Rawlins 1981. For more on the original results and the literature they spawned, see Ertel 1988, 1996, 1997; Gauquelin 1955, 1983, 1988; Kurtz 1997.

5. I suppose I should mention briefly how Gina hooked up with the mafia in the first place. Originally, she was contacted by a woman (we'll call her M.) whom she knew slightly from her hometown and who was connected with the mafia. M. was facing prosecution for a murder she had allegedly committed, and she thought Gina might have connections that would help her. Gina never learned the precise details of the alleged crime; M. was evasive and never gave anyone, including her own lawyers, the same story twice. Anyway, Gina reasoned that the poor victim

was already dead, and so there was nothing she could do to help him. Maybe she could still help M., in various ways.

So first, Gina pulled some strings and helped M. avoid prosecution (I gather this is still appallingly easy to do in Serbia), and then she set about working on M.'s character. But the mafia was so grateful for Gina's behind-the-scenes legal assistance that they took Gina under their protective umbrella. Soon thereafter, they learned about her astrological activities, and Gina's reliable advice endeared her to them even more.

In the meantime, Gina counseled the alleged (and, frankly, probable) murderess, gradually weaned her from the mafia and helped her battle her alcoholism. Eventually, M. resumed her education, got a legitimate job as a schoolteacher, and as of this writing has just received her degree in engineering, with a final research project on digital photography. I attended the party celebrating the event, and I can report that the others in attendance were only university colleagues and family (not "family"). A genuine Serbian success story.

6. For that matter, the rest of the trip was a joy. We had fabulous weather (although it rained as soon as we left), great food, excellent company, and killer shopping.

7. The reason may be that in good traffic, Dulles is seventy-five minutes from our home and from the home base of our shuttle service, and traffic is seldom good. That day it was typically heavy.

8. Braude 2003.

9. I'm quite aware that this chapter, probably more than my others, has the potential to rub readers the wrong way. So I'm very grateful to several friends for their helpful comments on earlier versions. Whatever flaws remain I blame entirely on them. I'd particularly like to thank James Spottiswoode, Jerry Barnes, Bruce Aune, Dan Pearlman, and Rob Rifkin.

REFERENCES

Brandon, R. 1983. *The Spiritualists*. New York: Alfred A. Knopf.

Braude, S. E. 1979. *ESP and Psychokinesis: A Philosophical Examination*. Philadelphia: Temple University Press.

———. 1985. "Review of Trevor H. Hall, *The Enigma of Daniel Home*." *Journal of the Society for Psychical Research* 53: 40–46.

———. 1986. *The Limits of Influence: Psychokinesis and the Philosophy of Science*. New York and London: Routledge & Kegan Paul.

———. 1991. *First Person Plural: Multiple Personality and the Philosophy of Mind*. New York and London: Routledge.

———. 1992. "Psi and the Nature of Abilities." *Journal of Parapsychology* 56: 205–28.

———. 1995. *First Person Plural: Multiple Personality and the Philosophy of Mind*. Lanham, MD: Rowman & Littlefield.

———. 1997a. "Some Thoughts on Parapsychology and Religion." In C. T. Tart, ed., *Body Mind Spirit: Exploring the Parapsychology of Spirituality*. Charlottesville: Hampton Roads: 118–27.

———. 1997b. *The Limits of Influence: Psychokinesis and the Philosophy of Science*. Lanham, MD: University Press of America.

———. 2002. *ESP and Psychokinesis: A Philosophical Examination*, Revised Edition. Parkland, FL: Brown Walker Press.

———. 2003. *Immortal Remains: The Evidence for Life After Death*. Lanham, MD: Rowman & Littlefield.

———. 2004. "Les Psychographies De Ted Serios." In C. Chéroux and A. Fischer, eds., *Le Troisième Oeil: La Photographie et L'occulte*.Gallimard: 155–57.

———. 2005. "The Thoughtography of Ted Serios." In C. Chéroux and A. Fischer, eds., *The Perfect Medium: Photography and the Occult*. New Haven: Yale University Press: 155–57.

Broad, W. and N. Wade. 1982. *Betrayers of the Truth: Fraud and Deceit in the Halls of Science*. New York: Simon & Schuster.

Carrington, H. 1907. *The Physical Phenomena of Spiritualism.* Boston: H. B. Turner & Co.

Crawford, W. J. 1918. *The Reality of Psychic Phenomena.* New York: E. P. Dutton & Co. Reprinted, Mokelumne Hill, CA: Health Research, 1970.

———. 1919. *Experiments in Psychical Science.* London: Watkins.

———. 1921. *The Psychic Structures at the Goligher Circle.* New York: E. P. Dutton & Co.

Crookes, W. 1874. *Researches in the Phenomena of Spiritualism.* London: J. Burns.

Diaconis, P. and F. Mosteller. 1989. "Methods for Studying Coincidences." *Journal of the American Statistical Association* 84: 853–61.

Dingwall, E. J. 1962. *Very Peculiar People.* New Hyde Park, NY: University Books.

Eisenbud, J. 1967. *The World of Ted Serios.* New York: William Morrow & Co.

———. 1970. *Psi and Psychoanalysis.* New York: Grune & Stratton.

———. 1977. "Paranormal Photography." In B. Wolman, ed., *Handbook of Parapsychology.* New York: Van Nostrand Reinhold: 414–32.

———. 1989. *The World of Ted Serios,* 2nd Edition. Jefferson, NC: McFarland & Co.

———. 1992. *Parapsychology and the Unconscious.* Berkeley, CA: North Atlantic Books.

Ertel, S. 1988. "Raising the Hurdle for the Athletes' Mars Effect: Association Co-Varies With Eminence." *Journal of Scientific Exploration* 2: 53–82.

Ertel, S. and K. Irving. 1996. *The Tenacious Mars Effect.* Somerset: Urania Trust.

———. 1997. "Biased Data Selection in Mars Effect Research." *Journal of Scientific Exploration* 11: 1–18.

Feilding, E. 1963. *Sittings With Eusapia Palladino and Other Studies.* New Hyde Park, NY: University Books.

Feilding, E., W. W. Baggally, and H. Carrington. 1909. "Report on a Series of Sittings With Eusapia Palladino." *Proceedings of the Society for Psychical Research* 23: 309–569.

Fukurai, T. 1931. *Clairvoyance and Thoughtography.* London: Rider & Co.

Gardner, M. 1981. *Science, Good, Bad and Bogus.* Buffalo: Prometheus Books.

Gauld, A. 1968. *The Founders of Psychical Research.* London: Routledge & Kegan Paul.

———. 1992. *A History of Hypnotism.* Cambridge: Cambridge University Press.

Gauld, A. and A. D. Cornell. 1979. *Poltergeists.* Boston, London, and Henley: Routledge & Kegan Paul.

Gauquelin, M. 1955. *L'Influence Des Astres, Etude Critique Et Experimentale.* Paris: Le Dauphin.

———. 1983. *The Truth About Astrology.* Oxford: Blackwell.

———. 1988. "Is There a Mars Effect?" *Journal of Scientific Exploration* 2: 29–51.

———. 2005. "Is There Really a Mars Effect?" http://www.encosm.net/mars_effect.htm.

Goldberg, B. 1999. "Are Human Beings Mechanisms?" *Idealistic Studies* 29: 139–52.

Grattan-Guinness, I. 1978. "What Are Coincidences?" *Journal of the Society for Psychical Research* 49: 949–55.

Hall, T. H. 1962. *The Spiritualists*. London: Duckworth & Co.

———. 1984. *The Enigma of Daniel Home* . Buffalo: Prometheus.

Hansen, G. P. 1990. "Deception by Subjects in Psi Research." *Journal of the American Society for Psychical Research* 84: 25–80.

Haraldsson, E. 1987. *Miracles Are My Visiting Cards: An Investigative Report on the Psychic Phenomena Associated With Sathya Sai Baba*. London: Century.

Heil, J. 1981. "Does Cognitive Psychology Rest on a Mistake?" *Mind* 90: 321–42.

Hilgard, E. R. 1965. *Hypnotic Susceptibility*. New York: Harcourt, Brace & World.

Home, D. D. 1888, 1976. *D. D. Home, His Life and Mission*. London: Trübner & Co.

———. 1863, 1972. *Incidents in My Life*. Secaucus, NJ: University Books.

Honorton, C. 1993. "A Moving Experience." *Journal of the American Society for Psychical Research* 87: 329–40.

Imich, A. 1996. "Informal Work With Joe Nuzum." *Network* No. 62, December: 36–37.

———. 1997. "Joe A. Nuzum, A Little-Known Psychic." *Journal of the Society for Psychical Research* 61: 336–37.

Information Unlimited. 1994. *Amazing and Fascinating Devices*. Summer, no. 28A. Amherst, NH.

Inglis, B. 1977. *Natural and Supernatural*. London: Hodder & Stoughton.

———. 1983. "Review of R. Brandon, *The Spiritualists*." *Journal of the Society for Psychical Research* 52: 209–12.

Jung, C. G. 1963. *Memories, Dreams, Reflections*. A. Jaffé, ed. London: Routledge.

———. 1973. *Synchronicity: An Acausal Connecting Principle*. Princeton: Princeton University Press.

Kammann, R. 1982. "The True Disbelievers: Mars Effect Drives Skeptics to Irrationality." *Zetetic Scholar* 10: 50–65.

Keil, H. H. J., B. Hermelin, M. Ullman, and J. G. Pratt. 1976. "Directly Observable Voluntary PK Effects: A Survey and Tentative Interpretation of Findings From Nina Kulagina and Other Known Related Cases of Recent Date." *Proceedings of the Society for Psychical Research* 56: 197–235.

Koestler, A. 1971. *The Case of the Midwife Toad*. New York: Random House.

Kuhn, T. 1970. *The Structure of Scientific Revolutions*, 2nd Edition. Chicago: University of Chicago Press.

Kurtz, P. 1985. "Spiritualists, Mediums, and Psychics: Some Evidence of Fraud." In P. Kurtz, ed., *A Skeptic's Handbook of Parapsychology*. Buffalo, NY: Prometheus Books, 177–223.

Kurtz, P., J. W. Nienhuys, and R. Sandhu. 1997. "Is the 'Mars Effect' Genuine?" *Journal of Scientific Exploration* 11: 19–39.

Lamont, P. 2005. *The First Psychic: The Peculiar Mystery of a Notorious Victorian Wizard*. London: Little, Brown.

Loftus, E. 1979. *Eyewitness Testimony*. Cambridge, MA: Harvard University Press.

McDonough, R. 2001. "Why the Computational Theory of Mind Doesn't Compute." *Metascience* 10: 442–47.

McMoneagle, J. 2000. *Remote Viewing Secrets: A Handbook*. Charlottesville, VA: Hampton Roads.

———. 2002. *The Stargate Chronicles: Memoirs of a Psychic Spy*. Charlottesville, VA: Hampton Roads.

Medhurst, R. G., K. M. Goldney, and M. R. Barrington, eds. 1972. *Crookes and the Spirit World*. New York: Taplinger.

Morris, R. 1992. "Spontaneous Synchronistic Events As Seen Through a Simple Communication Model." In B. Shapin and L. Coly, eds., *Spontaneous Psi, Depth Psychology and Parapsychology*. New York: Parapsychology Foundation, Inc.: 137–62.

Perry, C. 1977. "Is Hypnotizability Modifiable?" *International Journal of Clinical and Experimental Hypnosis* 25: 125–46.

Podmore, F. 1902, 1963. *Mediums of the Nineteenth Century, 2 Vols*. New Hyde Park, NY: University Books.

———. 1910, 1975. *The Newer Spiritualism*. New York: Arno Press.

Pratt, J. G. 1977. "Soviet Research in Parapsychology." In B. Wolman, ed., *Handbook of Parapsychology*. New York: Van Nostrand: 883–903.

Price, H. H. 1953. "Review of C. G. Jung and W. Pauli, *Naturerlärung Und Psyche*." *Journal of the Society for Psychical Research* 37 (673): 26–35.

Randall, J. L. 2003. "Francis Ward Monck and the Problems of Physical Mediumship." *Journal of the Society for Psychical Research* 67: 243–59.

Rawlins, D. 1981. "Starbaby." *FATE Magazine* 34, October.

Resch, A. 1997. *Paranormologie Und Religion*. Innsbruck: Resch Verlag.

Schwarz, B. E. 1985. "K: A Presumed Case of Telekinesis." *International Journal of Psychosomatics* 32 (1): 3–21.

———. 1987. "Apparent Materialization of Copper Foil, Case Report: Katie." *Pursuit* 20 (4): 154–58.

———. 1988a. "Katie: Nostradamus Automatic Writing, Possible Direct Writing and Psychic Nexus of an Illiterate (Part 1)." *Pursuit* 21 (2): 50–61.

———. 1988b. "Katie: Nostradamus Automatic Writing, Possible Direct Writing and Psychic Nexus of an Illiterate (Part 2)." *Pursuit* 21 (3): 116–27.

———. 1994. "Presumed Paranormal Linkage of Rings." *International Journal of Psychosomatics* (41): 95–103.

———. 1997a. "Presumed Materializations—Joe Nuzum." *Alternate Perceptions* Issue 38 (Spring): 38–46.

———. 1997b. "Cascade of Possible Materialization Effects Case Report: Katie and Arlene's Christmas Encounter." *Alternate Perceptions* Issue 40 (Fall): 43–52.

———. 1998a. "Joe A. Nuzum's Possible Levitations." *Alternate Perceptions* Issue 41 (Winter): 32–49.

———. 1998b. "Katie and the Golden Butterfly: Possible Materialization—Part 1."
Alternate Perceptions Issue 42 (Spring): 44–45.

———. 1998c. "Katie and the Golden Butterfly: Possible Materialization—Part 2."
Alternate Perceptions Issue 43 (Summer): 30–39.

———. 1999. "Psychic Nexus and Recurrent Possible Apportations, Case Report:
Katie and Waldo." *Alternate Perceptions* Issue 45 (Winter): 53–55.

———. 2005. "Joe Nuzum's Mustard Powder Explosion." www.mysterious-america
.net/joeynuzum.html.

Storm, L. 1999. "Synchronicity, Causality, and Acausality." *Journal of Parapsychology* 63 (3): 247–69.

van Fraassen, B. C. 2002. *The Empirical Stance.* New Haven: Yale University Press.

Varvoglis, M. P. 2003. "Scientists, Shamans, and Sages: Gazing Through Six Hats."
Journal of Parapsychology 67 (Spring): 3–16.

Watt, C. 1990. "Parapsychology and Coincidences." *European Journal of Parapsychology* 8: 66–84.

INDEX